RELIGION AND SPIRITUALITY

RELIGION: BELIEFS, THEORIES AND SOCIETAL EFFECTS

RELIGION AND SPIRITUALITY

Additional books in this series can be found on Nova's website
under the Series tab.

Additional E-books in this series can be found on Nova's website
under the E-book tab.

RELIGION AND SPIRITUALITY

RELIGION: BELIEFS, THEORIES AND SOCIETAL EFFECTS

PIERRE BELLAMY
AND
GUARIN MONTPETIT
EDITORS

Nova Science Publishers, Inc.
New York

Copyright © 2012 by Nova Science Publishers, Inc.

All rights reserved. No part of this book may be reproduced, stored in a retrieval system or transmitted in any form or by any means: electronic, electrostatic, magnetic, tape, mechanical photocopying, recording or otherwise without the written permission of the Publisher.

For permission to use material from this book please contact us:
Telephone 631-231-7269; Fax 631-231-8175
Web Site: http://www.novapublishers.com

NOTICE TO THE READER

The Publisher has taken reasonable care in the preparation of this book, but makes no expressed or implied warranty of any kind and assumes no responsibility for any errors or omissions. No liability is assumed for incidental or consequential damages in connection with or arising out of information contained in this book. The Publisher shall not be liable for any special, consequential, or exemplary damages resulting, in whole or in part, from the readers' use of, or reliance upon, this material. Any parts of this book based on government reports are so indicated and copyright is claimed for those parts to the extent applicable to compilations of such works.

Independent verification should be sought for any data, advice or recommendations contained in this book. In addition, no responsibility is assumed by the publisher for any injury and/or damage to persons or property arising from any methods, products, instructions, ideas or otherwise contained in this publication.

This publication is designed to provide accurate and authoritative information with regard to the subject matter covered herein. It is sold with the clear understanding that the Publisher is not engaged in rendering legal or any other professional services. If legal or any other expert assistance is required, the services of a competent person should be sought. FROM A DECLARATION OF PARTICIPANTS JOINTLY ADOPTED BY A COMMITTEE OF THE AMERICAN BAR ASSOCIATION AND A COMMITTEE OF PUBLISHERS.

Additional color graphics may be available in the e-book version of this book.

Library of Congress Cataloging-in-Publication Data

Religion : beliefs, theories, and societal effects / editors, Pierre Bellamy and Guarin Montpetit.
    p. cm.
Includes bibliographical references and index.
ISBN 978-1-61470-382-2 (hardcover : alk. paper) 1. Religion. I. Bellamy, Pierre. II. Montpetit, Guarin.
BL50.R426367 2011
200--dc23

2011022222

Published by Nova Science Publishers, Inc. † New York

CONTENTS

Preface		vii
Chapter 1	Infant Mortality and Religious Culture: A Comparative Approach of Two Swiss States (1860-1930) *Anne-Françoise Praz*	1
Chapter 2	Free Will Perceptions and Religion in Patients with Schizophrenia and Their Caregivers *Amy Weisman de Mamani, Michael Mejia,* *Kayla Gurak, and Stephen Sapp*	33
Chapter 3	"Do Beliefs Really Have Societal Effects? Implications for Theories of Religion" *Craig T. Palmer, Ryan O. Begley,* *Kathryn Coe, Ryan M. Ellsworth* *and Lyle B. Steadman*	55
Chapter 4	Spirituality, Secularity, and Well-Being *Karen Hwang*	73
Chapter 5	Maimonides' Views *Leonard Angel*	91
Chapter 6	The Architecture of Nonconformist Christian Religion and National Identity *Stephen Roy Hughes*	103

Chapter 7	A Possible Neuroscience Approach to Some Health Benefits Related to Religion	**143**
	Angelica Rosat Consiglio	
Chapter 8	Does Religion Cause Violence?	**161**
	Joseph Chuman	
Index		**183**

PREFACE

This book presents topical research in the study of the beliefs, theories and societal effects of religion. Topics discussed from authors across the globe include the resurgent interest in the philosophical thinking of Ibn Rushd of Cordoba for modernizing the Islamic world; infant mortality and religious culture; religious beliefs and psychological functioning in patients with schizophrenia; the societal effects of religion; the association between religion, spirituality and medical outcomes; nonconformist religious worship and the question of religion and violence.

Chapter 1- At the end of nineteenth century, infant mortality in the Catholic canton of Fribourg was one of the highest in Switzerland; in the neighbouring Protestant canton of Vaud, it was well below the national average. To what extent can these differences be attributed to religious culture? After an overview of some hypotheses that have been used to explain religious differentials in infant mortality, this chapter presents a new mechanism implicating the state institutions and policies.

Chapter 2- This chapter explores how free will perceptions relate to religious beliefs and values and psychological functioning in patients with schizophrenia and their family members. The paper begins with a discussion of what free will means and where laypeople stand on the question of its existence (from the literature, it appears that the overwhelming majority of the general public do subscribe to a free will perspective). Next the authors review psychological research on free will. Studies suggest that belief in free will has benefits to both the individual (e.g., greater self-esteem) and to society (e.g., lower rates of aggression and crime). Next the authors discuss components of free will and their premise that free will subsumes the following constructs: locus of control, self-efficacy, motivation, and meaning-making coping. They then turn to an overview of how free will and religion interact. The authors contend that a free will perspective is compatible with most Western religious views because most of these religions are founded on the premise that free will exists. The second section of the paper addresses how free will relates to functioning in patients with schizophrenia and their caregivers. Two case examples are presented. Drawing from the literature, their own empirical studies, and the numerous patients and caregivers the authors have treated as part of their Schizophrenia Family Project, they propose the following hypotheses: For both patients and their relatives, those who endorse greater free will beliefs (toward self) will experience greater psychological well-being and greater quality of life. For patients, the authors also propose that the severity of their psychiatric symptoms will be less severe. Finally, this chapter will examine how free will perceptions may relate to religious beliefs and values to impact mental health in schizophrenia patients and their relatives. Implications from this review suggest that mental health practitioners in contact with individuals with schizophrenia and their caregivers may better serve them by fostering the notion that, despite the illness, they are still free to assume an active, autonomous role in the course of their lives. More empirical research in this area is clearly needed.

Chapter 3- It is typically assumed that religious beliefs have important societal effects, and that these effects include the promotion of cooperative behavior among people who hold the same religious beliefs. This chapter will argue that although there is indeed abundant evidence for an association between religion and cooperative behavior, the assumption that this societal effect is the result of religious *beliefs* is unwarranted. The chapter will first describe the problematic nature of assuming that the societal effects of religion are the result of shared religious beliefs. It will then argue that this assumption can, and should, be replaced by a focus on certain behavior, specifically talk; that is, communicating acceptance of supernatural claims. It will then describe how such talk, as a form of communication, may produce the societal effect of increased cooperation that so often is attributed to shared religious beliefs. It will then respond to criticisms of this shift from studying the societal effects of religious beliefs to the study of the societal effects of religious talk. Finally, to demonstrate the strength of this proposition, and its importance in current debates regarding religion, it will apply the theoretical issues raised in the paper to the example of asserting that the deadly societal effect of suicide bombings are caused by religious beliefs.

Chapter 4- The last few years have seen a great deal of research on the association between religion, spirituality and medical outcomes. This research has not been without controversy however, in terms of methodological and analytical issues. One particular under-researched area concerns the increasingly visible sub-population of individuals who identify themselves as "nonreligious," a group that includes atheists, agnostics and individuals who believe in god(s) but do not identify with one particular religion. As a result, relatively little is known about the health and quality of life within this particular group, not only in comparison to religious individuals, but also within nonreligious populations as well. The proposed chapter plans to cover three major issues: 1) a brief summary of the controversies concerning religion-health research; 2) reasons for the neglect of nonreligious individuals to date and reasons for increasing attention to them; and 3) what the current research does indicate about the nonreligious, particularly about affirmative atheists (as opposed to simply "nonreligious").

Chapter 5- Maimonides (1135 – 1204) is generally regarded as a great philosopher. But most of the twenty-five propositions that he listed and regarded as indubitable are rejected or doubted by almost all philosophers today. The way most philosophers reject or doubt these supposedly indubitable propositions is reviewed in the following pages. Contemporary theologians may want to be clearer than they have been about whether they agree or disagree with the propositions that Maimonides thought to be indubitable. There are enough issues, often buried issues, in the shift from Maimonides' time to our time so that attention to the gap between what seemed indubitable in Maimonides' time, and what seems incorrect or dubitable now may provoke a useful conversation at a general theological level.

Chapter 6- It has often been simplistically asserted that the elaboration or simplicity of a Christian religious building depends on the type of Christian worship practised there. That a Catholic Church exhibits a very elaborate edifice, an Anglican or Episcopalian Church a very traditional and impressive structure and that nonconformist chapels are simple prayer-halls reflecting Puritan worship practices inspired by Calvin and others. Others see dense areas of nonconformist worship as nothing more than an expression of newly found and expressed worker independence lacking the expression of any particular minority or cultural grouping. The following article seeks to show that rather different causal factors determined the degree of elaboration of a religious structure and that the overall density of a type of non-state religion was equally determined by resurgent ideas of cultural and national identity within small nations. These trends are largely, but not exclusively, explored using the details available from a long-term large-scale study of religious buildings of Wales and also of the religious buildings of the global Welsh diaspora (Royal Commission; Coflein).

Chapter 7- The 1990s were considered the Decade of the Brain; currently, importance is being given to translational research, in a mutual feedback between basic and applied health sciences. Another tendency, sometimes controversial, is the neuroscience approach of spirituality and religion, mainly triggered by some recognized benefits they bring to mental health. Isolated efforts are being made to identify the biological basis that might help explain these benefits.

Chapter 8- Among the most dramatic and unpredicted phenomena of the past thirty years has been the resurgence of religion on the world scene. Defying secularization theorists who predicted that religion would increasingly retreat to the margins of society in the wake of industrialization, modernization and scientific development, religion has returned with energy born of four centuries of relative privatization and rejection from the political sphere. Not only has religion challenged the presumptions of the liberal secular state, it has forced itself on the world with paroxysms of violence which have dashed the hopes that the close of humankind's bloodiest century would usher in a new epoch of peace.

In: Religion
Editors: P. Bellamy and G. Montpetit

ISBN 978-1-61470-382-2
©2012 Nova Science Publishers, Inc.

Chapter 1

INFANT MORTALITY AND RELIGIOUS CULTURE: A COMPARATIVE APPROACH OF TWO SWISS STATES (1860-1930)

Anne-Françoise Praz
University of Fribourg, Switzerland[*]

ABSTRACT

At the end of nineteenth century, infant mortality in the Catholic canton of Fribourg was one of the highest in Switzerland; in the neighbouring Protestant canton of Vaud, it was well below the national average. To what extent can these differences be attributed to religious culture? After an overview of some hypotheses that have been used to explain religious differentials in infant mortality, this chapter presents a new mechanism implicating the state institutions and policies.

We first examine the impact of religious norms. Protestant and Catholic doctrine did not consider the loss of infant in the same way. These teachings might influence the parental behaviour in respect to the survival of their children. However, a causal pathway that leads from dogmatic discourse to the relevant individual behaviour is difficult to substantiate and to test.

---

[*] This text is a revised version of a paper presented in November 2008 at Cambridge University (UK), in the PhD seminar of Professor Simon Szreter. The author wishes to thank the participants and Prof. Simon Szreter, for their helpful remarks.

Religious norms are likely to play a critical role in shaping behaviour only when religious authorities diffused them regularly and have at their disposal a menu of rewards and sanctions encouraging the faithful to conform. In the period under study, such an impact is difficult to attest, as church institutions were loosing influence.

At the turn of the 20th century, religion gains an impact on demographic processes above all through mechanisms implicating the state institutions and policies. In examining carefully the health and population policies and the discourse put forward by cantonal elites to legitimate them, we then show the influence of religious culture on political, legislative and administrative priorities.

Using standard demographic measures and Cox regression analysis of the determinants of infant mortality, we test our hypotheses on a comparative sample of four villages that differed systematically in the main explaining variables for the period of the so called fertility transition (1860-1930). The prevalence of gastroenteritis in the Catholic canton, even in the years 1900-1930 when overall infant mortality is declining, attests to the absence of adequate health measures.

INTRODUCTION

The relationship between religious affiliation and demographic trends has been established in many studies. The study of the influence of religion has generated an abundant literature in historical demography, mainly focused on the relationship between religion and fertility, especially during the period known as the first fertility transition (1860-1930), namely the generalisation of marital fertility control in Europe. In this context, the late fertility decline of Catholic populations has been largely attributed to the strict prohibition of contraception in the Catholic doctrine, opposed to Protestant tolerance and even a certain moral justification of contraceptive practices (Noonan, 1969, 531-535; Perrenoud, 1974). Recent research poses new methodological requirements. Studies using individual-level data are strongly recommended, as they permit to disentangle the complex skein of causality determining demographic processes; it is individual parents that make the decisions; the bigger an aggregate, the less it is homogeneous in respect to the main determining factors. When individual data are not available, aggregate statistics can provide new insights when analysed at the regional levels, in order to detect spatial variations in demographic patterns. But whatever the type of data, correlation between demographic indicators and religious appurtenance is not sufficient evidence of the impact of religion; researchers cannot but go a step further and specify through what mechanism this impact of religion works (Derosas and van Poppel 2006).

Compared to the extensive research on religion and fertility, the issue of infant mortality has received less attention. However, recent studies highlight the interest of the questioning, as the explanation of infant mortality in the European past might shed light on similar problems in many contemporary countries. Moreover, the complexity of the mechanisms involved represents a real challenge. The following chapter commences with on overview of some hypotheses that were used to explain religious differentials in infant mortality and some preliminary theoretical considerations before we present our main argument. We then try to demonstrate that, during the first fertility transition, religion had a strong impact on demographic processes, above all through causal mechanisms implicating state institutions and policies. In the second part, after having presented our sample and our research design, we elaborate this argument for the Swiss case, focusing on the causal impact of religion on infant mortality, with a short overview of the relation of religion and fertility, which is the broader issue. The statistical to test our hypotheses is subsequently laid out; we use standard demographic measures and Cox regression analysis of the determinants of infant mortality, applied on individual data collected in a comparative sample of four Swiss villages that differed systematically in the main explaining variables for the period 1860-1930.

RELIGION AND INFANT MORTALITY: A CONTROVERSIAL RELATIONSHIP

Scholars dealing with the impact of religion on demography emphasise the importance of controlling for the "characteristics hypothesis", which posits that – more than religion itself – it is the socio-economic and demographic variables associated with religious communities that explain differences in demographic trends. For example, Catholics are more likely than Protestant to live in rural environment, where the type of dwelling could have an impact on infant survival; the socioeconomic structure as well as the level of income could differ strongly. Demographic behaviour like early marriage, as often usual among Muslim women, might increase the risk of difficult delivery and neo-natal infant mortality. Religion can also coincide with ethnicity or isolated groups, genetic factors being thus susceptible to play a role. An additional mechanism explaining differentials in infant mortality among religious communities with non religious factors, namely a variation of this characteristics hypothesis, has been put forward by a recent study on infant and child mortality in Holland. The authors suggest that the social isolation of small religious groups lowered their exposure to certain kinds of infectious disease, and they demonstrate the pertinence of such a hypothesis in accounting for the lower mortality of Jewish children in the city of The Hague (van Poppel and al. 2002). Once these socio-economic and demographic variables are taken into account, religious differentials should disappear. A few studies have tested this characteristics hypothesis with individual data in the field of infant mortality, but they all agree in attesting that differences between religious groups persist, after controlling for socio-economic status and demographic characteristics, and that genetic factors are unlikely to account for much of the variation in mortality (Reid 1997, Derosas 2000).

A second set of explanations refers to the so called "particularised ideology hypothesis" that emphasizes the role of religious doctrine. Religion, as a particular system of belief and values, generates a corresponding set of norms that frame and limit the individual decision making and the practices of everyday life. Regarding fertility, the prohibition of contraception in Catholic doctrine is a well know example. In the area of overall mortality, certain religious teachings are likely to influence behavioural patterns and attitudes regarding health. So, the lower mortality rate of Adventists is attributed to religious regulations that promote abstaining from tobacco and alcoholic beverages and refraining from meat consumption. Jews are thought to be more ready to attend to their health and that of their families and to make better use of medical care, as a consequence of rabbinic teachings. Specific prescriptions such as the obligation of carefully examining food and table for the presence of worms and insects that are not allowed to be consumed, contribute to more hygienic feeding (van Poppel 1992).

In identifying the religious teachings able to influence individual behaviour, Calvin Goldscheider insists that historians should consider not only the elements influencing demographic behaviour directly, but also those that do so indirectly. He points to norms about the value of children and education, and those concerning sexuality and gender roles (Goldscheider 2006). As every religion expresses concerns about parental conduct, attitudes relevant for procreation and infant mortality could well fit into such a particular normative framing.

After having specified the religious teachings likely to influence demographic trends, it remains to demonstrate through what mechanism this influence changes individual behaviour. Certain studies use a sociological model, stating that individual adherence to religious norms explains behaviour: the reasons inciting parents to care more about children's health should relate to their endorsement of religious teachings. Thus, they evaluate to what extent people subscribe to religious norms, a procedure relying on indicators of religiosity. Such indicators are not only difficult to produce they often contradict each other – a problem we also encountered in our research. To give an example: a classical measure of religiosity is the proportion of parishioners attending important church services, and such statistics were available for my sample in a series of parochial reports. However, I noticed that the more religious village in my Catholic sub-sample, according to this indicator, had a lower fertility and a lower infant mortality, so going against the correlation expected. Another indicator, proposed by Ron Lestheaghe (Lestheaghe 1991), is the proportion of marriages during Lent and Advent, periods in which marriage should not be celebrated following the Catholic rules. This indicator is more interesting, as it can be collected at the individual level. Again, it is in the more religious village of my sample, according to the indicator of church attendance, that marriages during these prohibited periods occurred more often. So, in historical research, except when we can make use of oral history methods – a research strategy only available for recent periods – it is very difficult to produce reliable information about individual religious beliefs. Actually, this difficulty conceals a problem of methodology: the mechanism linking religiosity with a given demographic behaviour is not specified. We don't trace the pathway that leads from religious beliefs to the proximate determinants of infant mortality or fertility.

Research based on the "particularised ideology hypothesis" is more convincing when they turn to religious institutions, their shaping of the social environment, their role in diffusing teachings and in enforcing norms related directly or indirectly to demographic behaviour. Kevin McQuillan states that religious values are likely to play a critical role in shaping demographic behaviour only when religious authorities have at their disposal a menu of rewards and sanctions encouraging the faithful to conform (McQuillan 2004). In this model, conformity to religious norms does not need to presuppose that individuals believe in the doctrine. Church institutions translate norms and values into costs and benefits, and individuals conform in order to avoid the costs of transgression. These costs are not only the moral costs associated with religious believes – for example the fear of God's punishment –, but also social costs like stigmatisation in the religious community, access denied to welfare services provided by the churches, or exclusion from important social positions.

This mechanism emphasizing the role of religious institutions comes across new difficulties for the period of the first demographic transition, namely the end of the nineteenth century and the beginning of twentieth, when changes in fertility and infant mortality are more pronounced and therefore more in need of explanation. Actually, this period coincides with a process of secularisation and of waning influence of religious institutions. These lost their ability to reward or sanction conformity to their norms as they were marginalized or became very cautious and avoided insistence on controversial issues. A striking example is the attitude of the Catholic Church, attested by studies in Belgium, France and Switzerland, who refrained from reminding the faithful of the prohibition of contraception; in order to prevent conflicts that might have accelerated the process of secularisation already under way (Sevegrand 1995, Servais 2001, Praz 2006). Scholars are therefore compelled to explain the higher fertility of Catholic families otherwise than by moral costs associated with transgression of the doctrine, and have to answer a new research question: If church institutions were not able or unwilling to enforce compliance with religious norms, through what mechanism did these norms have an impact?

In this research perspective, we suggest a third kind of hypothesis linking religion and demographic behaviour, by turning to the role of state institutions. During the first demographic transition, state institutions were gaining social influence at the cost of church institutions. The state took over many social functions, traditionally fulfilled by the churches, such as health and education, that strongly influence demographic processes,. State institutions were indeed more efficient, as they were able to enforce policies that constrained all families, and not only those who felt a sense of attachment to a religious community. But we suggest that state institutions acted as a mediator between religious norms and the corresponding demographic behaviour. The political elites had an interest in supporting religious values. On the one hand, and this is more the case for conservative elites, religious values could help them to maintain their political influence over the population. On the other hand, progressive elites that strived to implement changes took advantage of a language and an argumentation pertaining to a religious culture familiar to most citizens.

This "state policies hypothesis" is in line with David Kertzer's argument, stating that the cultural factors shaping demographic behaviour should not be considered separately from the political ones (Kertzer 1995). Political forces select some aspects of the cultural sphere and give them an institutional substance, transforming cultural norms into laws and rights that can be enforced on a general level, thus creating new constraints for individual behaviour. Historical research must point out what values and norms were selected in this way and how they were translated into concrete state policies. We will develop this argumentation below for the Swiss case.

SAMPLE, DATA AND COMPARATIVE RESEARCH DESIGN

Switzerland figures as "a miniature laboratory" to study the impact of religion on demography and the role of state institutions. Four languages, two religions, a lack of communication between linguistic groups and a long historical antagonism opposing Catholics and Protestants that have both limited the contacts between the different areas and thus in the period under study upheld heterogeneity. The political organisation, based on strong federalism supplied by a real fiscal autonomy gives to the 25 provinces (named cantons) important competences in many domains of legislative and administrative governance, as key areas like population and health policy.

We used a comparative approach, contrasting two Swiss cantons, situated in the French-speaking part of the country, that were religiously homogeneous during the period studied. The canton of Fribourg was Catholic, led during all the period by a conservative party that collaborated closely with the Catholic Church. This collaboration was motivated first by convergence of interests – the conservative elites were suspicious of modernisation and strived to maintain the rural character of the canton – and second by strategic purposes; to secure the conservative vote within a population mostly dispersed in the countryside and still not very much affected by the rise of the written press, it was crucial to use the network of parishes and religious associations. The political opposition was not well organized and fragmented. The Protestant canton of Vaud was led by a progressive government, the result of a democratic revolution. As Protestant ministers were associated with the conservative groups, the new government put them under state control and weakened their influence in civil institutions like schools, welfare services, or local administration. Perceived as hostile to democracy, the ministers lost their prestige among the popular classes, thereby hastening a decline of religiosity.

8 Anne-Françoise Praz

However, religious ideology did not vanish and I will show how Protestant values pervaded the political discourse. Moreover, these political struggles resulted in the emergence of a dissident Protestant church, whose members pertained predominantly to professional classes, and consequently many physicians were among them.

To isolate the impact of these cultural and political variables, I selected two pairs of villages, each pair sharing very similar economic conditions. The first pair (Chavornay/VD and Broc/FR) had experienced the same transformation in agriculture before 1900, namely the shift from cereal crop to intensive dairy farming, a shift that occurred slightly later in the Protestant village; from 1900 on, they experienced industrialisation, with the same industry, which happened to be a chocolate factory. The second pair consists in two neighbouring communities (Chevroux/VD and Portalban-Delley/FR) that maintained an economic structure based on agriculture and fishing. We collected individual data in these four villages. Demographic data – a family reconstitution covering marriages celebrated between 1860 and 1930 – is based on the parochial and civil registers, supplemented by local population registers and censuses. As we used event history analysis, which has more flexible rules in data selection, we could keep 86 per cent of the data collected, namely 5381 legitimate births for 1848 married and fecund women under observation.

The sample permits to eliminate the "characteristics hypothesis", as our set of data has been chosen so as to control severely the effects of socio-economic variables at the macro and the micro level, and to isolate the influence of institutional factors on fertility (Smith, 1989, 178). The "social isolation hypothesis", stating that small religious groups living apart are less exposed to contamination, is obviously not the case for our villages that are religiously homogenous and pertain to the dominant political and religious ideology in their respective cantons.

EXPLAINING RELIGIOUS DIFFERENTIALS IN FERTILITY: A FIRST APPLICATION OF OUR MODEL

In spite of these very similar economic conditions, demographic behavior differed greatly between Catholic and Protestant villages. Regarding fertility, the decline took place clearly later in the Catholic villages.

Table 1: Cox regression of the determinants of fertility by periods (all villages)

Variables	1860-1878		1879-1898		1899-1914		1915-1930	
	N. of obs: 1804 *Prob > chi2 = 0*		*N. of obs: 1848* *Prob > chi2 = 0*		*N. of obs: 2354* *Prob > chi2 = 0*		*N. of obs: 2415* *Prob > chi2 = 0*	
	Relative risk	P>|z|	Relative risk	P>|z|	Relative risk	P>|z|	Relative risk	P>|z|
Mother's age **at child birth**								
(reference: 25-29 years)	1.00	ref.	1.00	ref.	1.00	ref.	1.00	ref.
15-19 years	1.16	0.54	1.18	0.36	1.14	0.55	1.11	0.57
20-24 years	1.09	0.37	1.05	0.63	**1.28**	0.00	1.13	0.16
30-34 years	**0.80**	0.01	**0.72**	0.00	**0.82**	0.01	**0.72**	0.00
35-39 years	**0.76**	0.01	**0.55**	0.00	**0.59**	0.00	**0.57**	0.00
40 years and more	**0.21**	0.00	**0.17**	0.00	**0.16**	0.00	**0.13**	0.00
age unknown	1.01	0.93	**0.73**	0.02	1.24	0.03	1.32	0.02
Religion Catholic	**1.25**	**0.00**	**1.29**	**0.00**	**1.25**	**0.00**	**1.14**	**0.06**
(ref.: Protestant)	1.00	ref.	1.00	ref.	1.00	ref.	1.00	ref.
Father's occupation								
(ref. farmer, land owner)	1.00	ref.	1.00	ref.	1.00	ref.	1.00	ref.
labourer, unskilled worker	0.92	0.38	0.89	0.21	0.90	0.20	0.95	0.60
factory worker	1.56	0.19	0.77	0.31	**0.77**	0.00	**0.71**	0.00
trade-craftsman, civil servant	**1.17**	0.08	**0.76**	0.00	**0.86**	0.06	**0.76**	0.00
highly qualified occupation	1.02	0.95	0.87	0.58	**0.73**	0.08	**0.75**	0.07
occupation unknown	0.74	0.00	0.35	0.04	*deleted* *		*deleted*	
Birth place **of the mother**								
(ref: the same village)	1.00	ref.	1.00	ref.	1.00	ref.	1.00	ref.
the same canton	1.02	0.79	1.03	0.71	1.04	0.56	**1.16**	0.06
an other canton	1.13	0.41	**1.20**	0.09	1.11	0.33	1.05	0.66
Abroad	**1.69**	0.01	0.86	0.73	0.99	0.95	0.74	0.13

Note: bold printed rates are significant at minimum 90%.
*Because of very few occurrences.

Table 1 presents the results of a Cox regression model of the determinants of fertility by periods. This analysis aims to measure the impact of religious affiliation on fertility, controlling at the same time the influence of other variables: the *women's age*, known as the major biological determinant of fertility, the *husband's occupation*, an indicator for socioeconomic status, the *birth place of the mother*, as mothers born in the village are likely to be more sensitive to the weight of social norms and the influence of the parochial priest. The variable *Catholic religion* observes the impact on fertility of the mother's affiliation to Catholicism, compared to affiliation to Protestant religion (the reference category, assigned the value 1). As the results of this variable attest to, the Catholic mothers, compared to the Protestant ones, always have a higher relative risk of giving birth. The most important difference appears in the second period (1879-1898), when the likelihood of another birth for Catholic mothers is 29% higher than those of Protestant mothers. Yet, research in the Episcopal archives on pastoral literature and correspondence demonstrate that a clear reminding of the prohibition of contraception by the Catholic Church was missing at that time and taken up only in the last period (1915-1930).

The "state policies hypothesis" permits to explain this seeming contradiction. We turned to school policies, following John Calwell's thesis, which argues that mass education is a primary determinant of fertility decline, since it increases the costs of children, both monetary and opportunity costs (Caldwell 1980). In both cantons studied mass education was implemented during this second period (1879-1898), marked by a significant difference in Catholic and Protestant fertility. Now, the school policies differed greatly, according to religious culture. Content analysis of qualitative material such as political discourse, educational periodicals and school manuals demonstrates that Catholic and Protestant culture did not consider in the same way the importance of education, and especially in the case of girls. These respective discourses and ideologies shaped school policies. The Protestant canton implemented compulsory schooling more efficiently as school attendance was regularly controlled and absenteeism severely repressed. In the Catholic canton, the control and repression of school absenteeism was relatively haphazard, and the school system permitted many exceptions in school attendance for teenagers, especially for girls, whose parents often took them out of school before the legal age.

To evaluate the impact of these discourses and policies on the chances of children to get education, and therefore on the costs of children for their parents, we constituted a data base of the school career of the children of our villages, based on our demographic data and on information from administrative sources on the cantonal and local level (pupil listings, school attendance statistics and correspondence of the school authorities). For the

5042 legitimate children who survived until age 15, we managed to reconstitute the school career of 2353 of them (1333 boys and 1020 girls). We could demonstrate that in the Protestant villages, parents incurred important costs for the education of their children, both girls and boys. In the Catholic canton, due to gender discrimination justified in religious culture and permitted by school policies, Catholic parents avoided an important part of the growing costs of children. Consequently, fertility control was less imperative (Praz, 2005, 2006 and 2007).

EXPLAINING RELIGIOUS DIFFERENTIALS IN INFANT MORTALITY: A NEW CHALLENGE

We now turn to the issue of infant mortality, i.e. the deaths in the first year of life per 1000 recorded live births, which is more decisive for life expectancies than child mortality (defined as mortality between 1 and 5 years); in fact, work on child mortality is still to be done, and the relationship between infant and child mortality remains understudied. Regarding infant mortality, recent research has amply showed that for most European countries a significant decline began at the end of the nineteenth century and continued till the outbreak of the Great War. For countries for which long term data is available at the national level, researchers are able to demonstrate that this decline was preceded by a first one that occurred more or less a century before. For Switzerland however, this cannot be confirmed as regular and standardized data is only available from the end of the nineteenth century.

Table 2: Infant mortality rates (0-1 year) by cantons
(per thousand - stillbirths not included)

	1871-1880	1881-1890	1891-1900	1901-1910	1911-1920	1921-1930
Fribourg	252,0	223,4	198,2	172,4	134,0	83,5
Vaud	178,1	161,3	155,6	128,7	85,8	52,3
Suisse	205,7	173,3	154,1	126,2	90,7	59,2

Source: Francine van de Walle, One Hundred Years of Decline - The History of Swiss Fertility from 1860 to 1960, vol 2, table 4.2 (manuscript, University of Neuchâtel, 1977).

Around 1870, according to this official data, Switzerland was one of the countries with a relatively high infant mortality. However, the levels varied markedly from one canton to another, and the example of our two cantons is paradigmatic. In the Catholic canton of Fribourg, 1 in 4 babies died during their first year between 1871 and 1880, many more than the national average, while the Protestant canton of Vaud was well below this average (cf. table 2).

In spite of these striking differences in levels, infant mortality is attributed in both cantons to the same dominant causes. Contemporary testimonies, namely official reports of sanitary officers, medical and philanthropic publications, as well as the causes of death noted in the civil registers we consulted, confirm what has been attested to by many studies on other countries. If the babies survived the first month of life although marked by the threat of the so called endogenous mortality (genetic defect, weak constitution, bad conditions of delivery), they then mostly died of gastroenteritis and other digestive diseases, due to inadequate food or contaminated milk and water. Respiratory diseases seem to play a less important role; other indications given in registers or in some testimonies are difficult to interpret; for example, the term "convulsions" constitutes an ill-defined category and may have included different causes of death.

According to this prevalence of digestive diseases, the most important prevention was prolonged breastfeeding because of its many virtues: it is sterile, it meets al the infant's nutritional requirements and permit avoiding inadequate infant feeding, and moreover has immunological properties that provide protection against many kinds of infections. When breastfeeding is not possible, special attention to infant feeding and care is requested. In this context, information on adequate infant feeding and improvement of food control and hygienic facilities (water supply, plumbing, sewage systems and rubbish disposal) becomes of paramount importance to reduce the risk of contamination. And all the more so, as many testimonies indicate that breastfeeding was declining during this period, in both cantons and especially in the villages of my study, as a consequence of women working in factories, or their more intensive work in agriculture, and sometimes because of mother's bad health conditions.

Catholic and Protestant Attitudes towards Infant Mortality

Can we attribute the striking cantonal differences in infant mortality to religious culture? This question is in line with some conclusions of recent research, asserting that "in the long run, cultural factors were essential to the breakthrough in the fight against high mortality" (Schofield, Reher and Bideau

Infant Mortality and Religious Culture 13

1991, 16-17). An initial step towards an explanation of religious differentials in infant mortality consists in identifying the religious teachings likely to influence behavioural patterns and attitudes regarding health and the religious norms concerning parental care.

Protestant and Catholic doctrine did not consider the loss of infants in the same way. As highlighted by Alfred Perrenoud for French-speaking Switzerland, the Protestant teachings stressed the parental responsibility for children (Perrenoud 1974). Parents were considered as collaborators in God's creation through their activity in caring and educating children. This increased investment in human capital encouraged them to have less children in order to fulfil this responsibility. Consequently, lower fertility of Protestant families can contribute to reduced infant mortality, because when children are less numerous each receives more parental attention[1].

Contrasting with this responsibility for the quality of children, Catholic teachings promoted a moral of procreation essentially quantitative and fatalistic. In the canton of Fribourg, Catholic parents were invited "to accept with pleasure and gratitude all the children that God might well give them"; they also were invited to trust in Providence for providing the necessary means to bring them up[2]. The faithful were taught to accept humbly the physical pain and sickness that God allows and the death of a child had to be accepted as God's will. The gravity of the loss of infants was mitigated: in Catholic teachings and rituals, this death is even transformed into a positive event, as a dead child can intercede in heaven for its family. While an infant death was considered as a parental failure in the Protestant doctrine, the same event did not call into question the purpose of marriage as defined in Catholic pastoral literature: "to give saints to the Church and elected to Heaven". [3]

Another factor that is of relevance is the attitude towards innovation. Catholic populations were more susceptible to popular believes in "religious" treatments of illness, instead of taking recourse to modern medicine. In the second half of the nineteenth century, the Catholic Church launches in many European countries a wide campaign of revival of popular piety, in order to regain control of the faithful and to fight against modernism. The cult of the Virgin Mary, apparitions, pilgrimages and miraculous healings experienced a

---

[1] Actually, relationship between fertility and infant mortality is not unidirectional: a significant decrease in child mortality also accelerates the adoption of birth control, a high number of surviving children weighing heavily on the family budget (van de Walle, 1992, Reher 1999).

[2] Mgr Bovet André, Instruction pastorale sur la vie familiale, Fribourg, 1914.

[3] Abbé E. Descloux, Préparation au Mariage. Conseils à la jeunesse, Fribourg, 1907.

renewed popularity, and this was especially the case in the canton of Fribourg. Priests instilled suspicion against modernity, warned about newspapers and books, an attitude that did not favour openness to information on medical, hygienic or scientific issues.

Protestant culture considers more positively scientific advancement and knowledge. Both men and women are encouraged to develop the intellectual capacities God has given them for their own spiritual enlightenment and for individual autonomy, thus permitting them to work in God's honour. Protestant ethics emphasize the importance of vocations, and this contributed to the high esteem in which professionals like physicians were held. As co-creators, human beings have to use their intelligence to understand nature and to improve it. Therefore, it may be assumed that Protestant populations – more familiar with written media and more attentive to scientific medical discourse – developed an earlier awareness of the benefit and significance of hygienic measures. This information began to be popularized during the period under study, namely at the end of the nineteenth century, along with the Pastorian revolution.

We might suppose that these religious teachings and traditions influence the parental concern for the survival of children. However, a pathway that leads from religious discourse to relevant behaviour is difficult to substantiate and to test. Anyway, whatever the parental concern, it must be translated into concrete behaviour, namely more or less adequate care, in order to have an impact on infant survival. The question is whether the means are available do permit this care: the access to valuable information, the availability and cost of hygiene, health services, etc. and the role of institutions is crucial in this regard. For my period and sample, state institutions became the most adequate structure to provide this information and these services[4]. A careful comparative analysis of the implementation of health policies and of the discourse put forward by cantonal elites to legitimate them will help us to trace the impact of religious culture on political, legislative and administrative priorities. We will show that influence for two crucial measures that lead to lower infant mortality: the statistical apparatus and data, necessary to get a clear view of the problem and to conceive adequate measures, and the fight against gastroenteritis, the most important cause of infant mortality.

---

[4] In the Protestant canton of Vaud, health and welfare services were totally taken over by the cantonal government. In the Catholic canton of Fribourg, although public health also became legally a state attribution, the concrete realisations were delayed; traditional religious and charity networks played a role in welfare services, but they were concerned with orphans and illegitimate children only.

The Statistical Data and Apparatus

In Switzerland the federalist system slowed the standardization of statistics and the production of data. The first national census was performed only in 1850. A Federal statistics office was set up in 1860 and conducted from this date on a national census every ten years. In 1876, a Federal Act obliged all cantons to secularise the registry office and impose the same procedures for the vital registration by civil officers; with this data, the Federal office was able to produce unified statistics of the number of births, marriages and deaths. In the reports that cantonal governments published every year to inform Parliament and the public about their activities, the cantons had the obligation to publish annual tables of the number of births, marriages and deaths. This obligation did not include other data and syntheses produced by the Federal office, as infant mortality rates by cantons and districts, which were available since the middle of the 1870's in federal publications. The statistical data published by the cantons varied greatly, before and after the federal unification, as cantons made a selection of the federal data at their disposal and as some of them even produced their own supplementary data and calculations.

NAISSANCES.

DISTRICTS.	LÉGITIMES.		ILLÉGITIMES.		TOTAL.
	Garçons.	Filles.	Garçons.	Filles.	
Sarine . . .	351	312	43	25	731
Singine . . .	174	173	33	34	414
Gruyère . . .	298	250	19	17	584
Lac . . .	194	229	11	17	451
Glâne . . .	196	187	10	11	404
Broye . . .	174	178	24	27	403
Veveyse . . .	126	110	7	7	250
Sommaire	1513	1439	147	138	3237

Le nombre total des naissances étant de 3257 , dont 285 illégitimes, il en résulte que , sur 11 naissances , il en est une d'illégitime.

Figure 1: The births in the canton of Fribourg (as given in the 1861 cantonal report).

As the data published by the canton of Fribourg demonstrates, population trends and infant mortality in particular were of no concern to the government. In the cantonal reports, demographic data was very scarce, limited to the federal tables of the number of births, marriages, and deaths. Demographic trends were considered more as indicators of good morality than of public health. For example, the stable number of inhabitants was considered as a reassuring sign that the population was not yet attracted by the "mirages" of the big cities, outside the canton. The increasing number of births was praised, as showing that married people were as yet untouched by "immoral practices"; the fact that this high fertility was correlated with high infant mortality remained hidden.

Figure 1 presents a table of births given in the 1861 report, before the federal unification. The categories used in this table are relevant of the dominant concern of the cantonal government. The first classification does not use a demographic criterion, but a legal and moral one: legitimate versus illegitimate children. This category will later disappear in the tables produced by the Federal office, replaced by a biological and medical criterion: stillbirths versus live births. The text under the table gives the only calculation regarding population trends that was made in these reports between 1860 and 1883: the rate of illegitimate births (*une naissance illégitime pour 11 naissances – one in eleven*). Yet, a birth rate could have been calculated, as the necessary data were already on hand. But obviously, the cantonal government was not interested in publishing, and perhaps even in knowing this rate. Until the end of the century, these reports persisted in making use of demographic indicators to highlight moral issues. Since 1883, they give the suicide rate, since 1884 the divorce rate by districts, indeed extremely low and of marginal interest with respect to demography. But suicide is a grave sin in Catholic doctrine; divorce also was not tolerated and Fribourg opposed strongly the Federal marriage legislation that introduced legal divorce in 1875.

By contrast, the issue of infant mortality remained invisible in cantonal reports, where the first infant mortality rate was published in 1899 only. When in 1870 the Federal statistics office asked the cantons to provide data about infant deaths during the first year, month by month, the government of Fribourg protested officially against this obligation, qualified as "a luxury of information". Another revealing indicator is the place of demographic data in the cantonal reports. They were put under the chapter "registry office", in the section "police department", and not in the section "economy department" and even not in the chapter "population health". Until the end of the century, there was no link between demography and health in these reports. When complaints about infant mortality were regularly voiced in the chapter about public health, it was without any reference to statistical data. A change only occurred around 1900, with the creation of the cantonal statistics office,

Infant Mortality and Religious Culture

directed by a statistician, and with the nomination of another scientist, professor of medicine and bacteriology, as secretary of the cantonal health council. From this date on, the cantonal reports made systematic links between health and demographic statistics, and published detailed data on general and infant mortality. A more scientific approach of the problem became perceptible, albeit enquiries on the causes of infant mortality were only planned, but not conducted.

The contrast with the canton of Vaud is striking. The vital registration was secularised in 1835 already and became a state concern well before the federal law (1876). Significantly, this section of vital registration was supervised by the cantonal health council. A cantonal statistics office was instituted in 1860 already, the second of the 25 cantons of Switzerland. In the cantonal reports, population data pertained from the beginning to the chapter "public health". The first calculation given in 1860 was the excess of births over deaths, in order to predict the overall number of inhabitants for the next year. After the federal unification, the canton carried on publishing its own data that stressed the scale of population growth and the concern for mortality. The number of stillbirths was reported, qualified as a scandalous waste, and attributed to the incomplete training of midwives. The importance of having more accurate statistics on mortality led in 1886 to the creation of a cantonal health office, endowed with its own statistics department. From then on, many pages in the reports were dedicated to infant mortality, with elaborate data: for example, the prevalence of mortality due to gastroenteritis was analysed by districts with the results presented in tables and maps. During the years 1880, the cantonal heath office set up two enquiries on the prevalence and causes of puerperal fever and gastroenteritis. Relations between gastroenteritis and infant feeding were examined, and the questionnaire asked detailed questions on breastfeeding or artificial feeding, on the use of spoon, of baby-bottle, with tube or without tube. Obviously, the investigators were well aware of the latest development of medical science, as many physicians had warned against tube feeding bottles, which were very convenient for busy mothers, but impossible to clean correctly.

This importance given to population statistics and to scientific inquiries, as well as the focus put on certain topics reveal the influence of religious culture. For the Protestant elite, population was a wealth, a human capital, not to be wasted. As co-creators, human beings were held responsible for the conservation of life; they have to use their intelligence to understand nature and to improve it. This ideology can be traced in the political discourse, in phrases speaking of the "conservation des enfants" (safe-keeping of children) not only an individual responsibility, but also a state concern. This religious culture combined with politics, as the party in power presented itself as the champion of progress, a commitment to the obligation to be pro-active in many domains.

The Catholic elite by contrast were influenced by a culture of fatality, in which demographic trends pertained to God's plans; they had not be understood or changed. For the conservative party, which had other public priorities than health policies, this ideology also legitimated its inactivity in this domain. To be sure, this view did not remain unchallenged, and the sources attest to civil servants or physicians who asked for more accurate data and measures against infant mortality. However, they met with little success in modifying political priorities.

The Fight against Gastroenteritis

To improve notably child survival, health policy measures have to be conceived and implemented in order to reach the neediest (Lee, Vögele, 2001, 65-96). According to this requirement, cantonal differences are again striking. In Fribourg, the first measures were taken in the 1890's. They are typical of the way the cantonal government proceeded, namely half-heartedly under external pressure. A publication of the Federal office, taken up by the newspapers, focused on the high infant mortality in Fribourg and gave the canton a bad press[5]. A host of measures were then proposed, as public conferences, teaching of childcare in schools, health centres, distribution of sterilized milk, etc., but only two were finally implemented, whose effectiveness moreover was rather limited.

Imitating other cantons, Fribourg printed a brochure about infant care that was to be diffused among parents by the civil officers. However, its diffusion proved problematic for many reasons. The civil officers had first to give the brochure to "each father who asked for it", later to each father who declared a first birth and finally at every birth. A new edition was not immediately ordered when the stock ran out, and the civil officers remained without material for years. The minutes of the health council indicate that the distribution of these brochures stopped altogether after 1910. Moreover, the same source indicates that most of the parents did not read the brochures

---

[5] Crevoisier, Louis (1889), « Enquête statistique sur la mortalité infantile en Suisse pendant les dix années 1876 à 1885 », Journal de statistique suisse, (1889), 108-143.

Infant Mortality and Religious Culture

(Bosson 2002). This is explained by the very sparse diffusion of popular literature and written media in general during this period in Fribourg; the population was literate, but the habit of reading was not widespread. This attitude was enhanced as the Catholic culture traditionally considered reading with suspicion and as the Catholic Church in Fribourg realized only at the end of the nineteenth century that popular press could be a useful means in order to maintain its influence.

The brochure rightly warned of the danger of feeding babies too early with cereals and promoted breastfeeding. At the beginning of 20th century, insistence on breastfeeding is also perceptible in religious discourse. According to new directives given by the Catholic bishop for the pastoral care of marriage, the duty to breastfeed was reminded to each bride by the parish priest. Breastfeeding was presented as a Godly institution and mothers who neglected this natural duty were stigmatized as egoistic. In line with this religious discourse, cantonal authorities also strived to promote breastfeeding. In 1916 they implemented a prize rewarding the midwives who could attest to a minimum of ten mothers, among their patients, who had breastfed for at least eight months. In the following years, although the prize was financially attractive, the number of midwives registered for it remained under 20 per cent of the total of authorized midwives. This should be a reliable indicator that for many women it was impossible to breastfeed for so long and it attests that breastfeeding was not a question of religiosity. The recourse to midwives instead of the diffusion of written information would have been effective, as they were ideal mediators between authorities and population and could have popularized medical knowledge among mothers, especially concerning adequate infant feeding, the need for boiling the water, of thorough cleaning of the bottles, etc. Unfortunately, the mere insistence on breastfeeding without the recognition of the social realities that made its practice very difficult, risked making matters worse. In addition, a recurrent problem in Fribourg at the time was the shortage of midwives and their lack of medical education.

The careful medical training and the severe control of midwives was the most important measure taken by the canton of Vaud in order to fight infant and maternal mortality. From 1882 on, all midwives had to attend a complete course at a modern maternity hospital for one year. In 1886, a Sanitary Act reinforced their obligations: each midwife received a delivery register, in which she had to write down indications on the situation of the mothers and their babies. Every year, midwives were asked district by district to attend a conference, to show their registers to physicians who asked them medical questions. In the case of insufficient knowledge or of high mortality among her mothers and babies, a midwife had to attend a complementary course; she was reprimanded or even lost her licence. Brochures on infant feeding were also diffused, but first to the midwives, to encourage teaching hygienic principles to mothers and families. The canton also introduced the teaching of hygiene in primary schools, with childcare lessons for older girls. In 1886, a new Sanitary Act introduced measures that indirectly reduced the prevalence of gastroenteritis, given the decline of breastfeeding. In case of an epidemic, the cantonal government could compel the communes to make an enquiry about sanitary conditions and to improve the water supply and the sewage system if necessary. A regular bacteriological control of the public fountains was instituted in 1890. At the turn of the century another Act imposed sanitary rules in buildings. The communes were compelled, but at the same time incited by cantonal subventions, to improve sanitary conditions. This act also reduced the risk of respiratory diseases, as each commune was compelled to organise an isolation place for the sick, who could not be isolated properly at home, and to provide free disinfection of houses and clothes for poor families. This kind of measures was taken up in Fribourg only in the late twenties.

STATE POLICIES AND INFANT MORTALITY: A STATISTICAL ANALYSIS

The comparative sample of the four villages we used in our study is particularly appropriate for testing the impact of these very different health policies on the levels of infant mortality. As indicated, these villages have been chosen so as to control severely the effects of socio-economic and to isolate the influence of institutional factors. Moreover, this choice of villages is interesting regarding environmental conditions that could influence infant mortality. In the first pair of villages (Chavornay/VD and Broc /FR), these conditions were relatively favourable, with a rather dry and sunny climate. The contrast with the second pair of villages (Chevroux/VD and Portalban-Delley/FR) was striking as they were situated on the shores of the same lake; the winter was particularly humid. We have collected aggregate data for each village, as well as individual data which will permit a more sophisticated statistical analysis.

Descriptive Statistics at the Village Level

To give a first picture of infant mortality trends, we turn to descriptive statistics at the village level. These aggregate data must be considered with caution. Moreover, they are difficult to interpret: between 0 and 1 year many mortality risks are conflated. It gives an approximation that permits formulating problems and hypotheses that we be tested later on individual data.

The periodisation refers to relevant events related to infant mortality trends at the cantonal level. For example, the first period ends with the implementation of the 1886 Sanitary Act in the canton of Vaud. A similar benchmark is not available for the canton of Fribourg, as a new Sanitary act was only implemented in the late twenties; so I use the date of 1908, which marks the beginning of the fertility decline in the canton.

During the first period (1860-1885), in the absence of sustained sanitary measures, it is very likely that differences in infant mortality were mostly due to climatic conditions and breastfeeding practices. This hypothesis can account for the higher rates in the lake villages. On the one hand, the humid climate favoured respiratory diseases. On the other hand, mortality due to gastroenteritis should also have been high, as the mothers in the fishermen's families had to wean children early, because they had to work along with their husband on the fishing boat. However, only individual data permits to test the correlation between mortality and the father's occupation. The higher rates in the Protestant village or Chevroux are intriguing.

Table 3: Infant mortality (0-1) rates (per thousand) by villages and periods (total of live births)

	1860-1885	1886-1907	1908-1930
Broc/FR *industrialized around 1900*	137.4 *(371)*	131.0 *(519)*	64.8 *(1187)*
Chavornay/VD *industrialized around 1900*	131.0 *(664)*	90.7 *(573)*	79.4 *(680)*
Delley-Portalban/FR *non industrialized*	154.7 *(407)*	188.5 *(366)*	92.8 *(266)*
Chevroux/VD *non industrialized*	171.4 *(441)*	167.0 *(425)*	59.5 *(235)*

Source: Parochial and civil registers of Broc, Portalban-Delley, Chavornay and Chevroux (Stillbirths are not included).

22 Anne-Françoise Praz

We can point to the fact that this village was more exposed to both risks: all the houses were situated near the lake, and the proportion of fishermen's families was higher than in the neighbouring Catholic village. For this first period preceding the establishment of official vital registration, an under-estimation of deaths in Catholic villages is also plausible. Lorenzetti and Perrenoud have estimated that the real number of infant deaths might be higher by 23% (Lorenzzetti and Perrenoud, 1999).

Infant mortality is clearly declining in the Protestant village of Chavornay during the second period (1886-1907), and this could attest to the impact of the Sanitary Act. To disentangle the different mortality risks (gastroenteritis, respiratory diseases or endogenous mortality due to conditions of delivery) it is pertinent to rely on a statistical analysis on individual data. This decline remains slight for Chevroux. Contemporary testimonies confirm that this area was affected during this period by recurrent epidemics of diphtheria, scarlet fever and measles. The higher rate in Delley-Portalban, the Catholic lake village, also indicates this problem. We might suppose that the rate would have been still higher in Chevroux in the absence of the Sanitary Act.

The level of infant mortality decreases significantly during the last period (1908-1930) which corresponds to the beginning of the fertility decline in Fribourg and with industrialisation in two of the villages. The rate of the village of Broc is clearly lower than the total rate of the canton of Fribourg for the corresponding period, and this result suggests a new hypothesis we will later test on individual data. It could be assumed that industrialisation increased the income of many families, thus permitting higher expenditure for such items as better food, accommodation and clothing, all helping to strengthen resistance against infectious diseases. The increased resort to powdered milk is also attested to in the region, as nearby two factories were set up and running intense advertising.

Event History Analysis of the Determinants of Infant Mortality

For this analysis, we rely on our data file of 1848 legitimate children, born in the four villages between 1860 and 1930; each record of a child consists of a set of values for independent variable that are supposed likely to influence infant mortality (cf. table 4). The dependant variable is the risk of death in a given period.

Infant Mortality and Religious Culture 23

A first set includes biological variables that play an important role during the fist months. *Child's sex* refers to the higher likelihood of endogenous mortality for male babies, a well-known phenomenon. It is also important to control for *mother's age,* as babies have a higher mortality risk when the mother is older and therefore less resistant (the risk of very young women becoming mothers is of no relevance in our sample as the age of marriage was homogeneously high). This mortality risk is also important, when the interval with the previous birth is short and the previous child still alive, implicating a heavy burden on mother's care and a risk of infant neglect. A second set includes socio-economic and demographic variables. The variable *father's occupation* is an indicator of socio-economic status and income, whereas the *mother's employment in factory* tells us whether the mother was able or not to breastfeed for a longer period; the number of *siblings* according to sex shows the level of pressure on family budget. Finally, the environmental variables permit to test the impact of the climate of the *lake villages* and to evaluate the risk associated with various diseases; the variable *seasonality* is particularly aimed at disentangling the risk of respiratory diseases that peaks in winter and, when the babies are weaned, the risk of digestive diseases highest in summer. This variable has been constructed as a categorial variable, dividing the year in four seasons. Summer months is the reference category; if the mortality is significantly lower during the winter months compared to the reference, this indicates an important prevalence of gastroenteritis.

We relied on the model developed by Brecchi, Derosas and Oris (Brecchi and al. 2003). Since mortality risks change very rapidly at the beginning of life, these authors propose a segmentation of infant life in four stages: the first month (to capture the risks associated with endogeneous mortality), from one to six months, from six months to the first birthday (a critical period because of weaning), and from 1 to 4 years. We consequently constituted four files, each for the corresponding stage of survival; from the first file to the fourth, the number of children reduced progressively.

Using a Cox regression, we assess the impact of each variable on the relative risk of dying, during the relevant period. The same statistical test, using the aforementioned variables, has been applied for each segmented sub-file, comparatively on the Catholic and Protestant villages, and this for two periods: before and after 1898, which is the date of the setting up of the factories[6].

---

[6] A finer periodisation, taking into account the implementation of the Sanitary act for example, is not possible, as the number of deaths would have been too low in relation to the number of independent variables.

Table 4: Cox regression of the risk of infant mortality between 1 and 6 months

	Fribourg 1860-1898 Number of obs. = 1039 Prob > chi2 = 0.3595		Vaud 1860-1898 Number of obs. = 1520 Prob > chi2 = 0		Fribourg 1899-1930 Number of obs. = 1962 Prob > chi2 = 0.0026		Vaud 1899-1930 Number of obs. = 1308 Prob > chi2 = 0.1181	
Biological variables	*Relative risk*	*P>|z|*	*Relative risk*	*P>|z|*	*Relative risk*	*P>|z|*	*Relative risk*	*P>|z|*
Child's sex male	1.03	0.89	1.07	0.76	0.72	0.16	1.14	0.69
(reference: female)	*1.00*	*ref.*	*1.00*	*ref.*	*1.00*	*ref.*	*1.00*	*ref.*
Mother's age at child birth *(reference: 25-29 years)*	*1.00*	*ref.*	*1.00*	*ref.*	*1.00*	*ref.*	*1.00*	*ref.*
15-19 years	1.42	0.74	0.87	0.89	0.92	0.94	0.00	1.00
20-24 years	1.26	0.62	1.69	0.16	1.38	0.41	1.87	0.27
30-34 years	2.31	0.02	0.88	0.73	1.33	0.40	1.41	0.55
35-39 years	1.41	0.47	1.57	0.24	0.65	0.38	2.45	0.16
40 years and more	**2.68**	0.07	1.34	0.56	0.49	0.35	1.03	0.98
age unknown	1.85	0.22	2.11	0.06	1.67	0.26	4.44	0.01
Previous birth interval and child survival *(ref.: more than two years and alive)*	*1.00*	*ref.*	*1.00*	*ref.*	*1.00*	*ref.*	*1.00*	*ref.*
1st born	1.61	0.25	1.16	0.68	1.20	0.65	0.62	0.39
less than two years and alive	1.31	0.37	**1.93**	0.02	1.37	0.29	1.47	0.33
less than two years and dead	2.43	0.41	0.00	1.00	0.00	1.00	0.00	1.00
more than two years and dead		*deleted*	0.00	1.00		*deleted*		*deleted*
Socio-economic and family variables								
Father's occupation *(reference: farmer - land owner)*	*1.00*	*ref.*	*1.00*	*ref.*	*1.00*	*ref.*	*1.00*	*ref.*
day-labourer, fishermen, unskilled worker	0.57	0.12	**2.18**	**0.01**	0.89	0.73	0.55	0.35
factory worker		*no factory*		*no factory*	**0.45**	0.04	1.29	0.56
trade-craftsman, civil servant	0.67	0.35	1.22	0.48	0.63	0.24	0.56	0.26
highly qualified occupation	1.39	0.66	1.78	0.44	0.27	0.20	1.67	0.51

Infant Mortality and Religious Culture

	Fribourg 1860-1898 Number of obs.= 1039 Prob > chi2 = 0.3595		Vaud 1860-1898 Number of obs.= 1520 Prob > chi2 = 0		Fribourg 1899-1930 Number of obs.= 1962 Prob > chi2 = 0.0026		Vaud 1899-1930 Number of obs.= 1308 Prob > chi2 = 0.1181	
occupation unknown	1.33	0.52	1.56	0.30	*deleted*		*deleted*	
Mother factory worker	*no factory*		*no factory*		**1.81**	0.08	**2.80**	0.07
Siblings number of elder brothers	0.99	0.96	0.99	0.87	1.35	0.00	0.97	0.80
number of elder sisters	**1.18**	0.04	**1.33**	0.00	1.01	0.93	1.20	0.09
Environmental variables								
Village / lake village non-industrialized	0.85	0.49	**1.86**	0.01	1.31	0.36	0.97	0.95
(reference: industrialized village)	*1.00*	*ref.*	*1.00*	*ref.*	*1.00*	*ref.*	*1.00*	*ref.*
Seasonality *(reference: July-August-September)*	*1.00*	*ref.*	*1.00*	*ref.*	*1.00*	*ref.*	*1.00*	*ref.*
January-February-March	1.19	0.59	**0.59**	0.07	**0.54**	0.07	0.95	0.92
April-May June	1.17	0.62	0.76	0.31	0.79	0.45	1.46	0.41
October-November-December	0.70	0.31	**0.55**	0.05	**0.53**	0.06	1.55	0.34

Note: bold printed rates are significant at minimum 90%.

Table 4 presents the more interesting results obtained, namely the analysis of the determinants of infant mortality between 1 and 6 months, and especially the values of the variable seasonality. For the fist period (1860-1898) in Fribourg, the mortality risk was not significantly associated with a season, as no period obtained significant results. We know, through aggregate measures, that infant mortality was high in the nineteenth century. These results mean that in Catholic villages, babies died as frequently in winter as in summer. Gastroenteritis was surely an important risk, but it was not higher than the risk of the winter diseases. In the canton of Vaud, the values and significance obtained for the winter months indicate that mortality was clearly lower during winter. We can conclude that gastroenteritis was a real problem, while respiratory diseases presented a relatively lower risk.

To test the hypothesis that the risk of gastroenteritis concerned especially the children in fishermen's families, we can look, for the same period, at the result of the variable *father's occupation*. In the Protestant villages, the risk of dying between 1 and 6 months is double for the babies of day-labourers, fishermen and unskilled workers, compared to the children of farmers, the reference category. For the lake village, this category was homogenous; it was mostly made up of fishermen; moreover, fishermen had periodically to work as day-labourers or unskilled workers, when the fish became scarce. The environmental variable *lake village* is also associated with a higher mortality risk in this sample.

The results of the second period (1899-1930) are also instructive. In the canton of Vaud, seasonality is no longer significant. As contemporary sources attest to the decline of breastfeeding, this result should be attributed to better information on infant feeding, to higher quality of water and to the sanitary control of milk. In the canton of Fribourg, infant mortality remains very sensitive to seasonality as it is significantly higher in summer, attesting to the persistence of gastroenteritis. Thus the hypothesis of a positive effect of the diffusion of powdered milk is falsified. Even if mothers used it, they probably did not prepare it properly, thus indicating that information was still lacking. We know from mortality rates that infant mortality was declining in the Catholic villages during this period. This analysis permits to conclude that this decline was not due to a decrease of gastroenteritis and should be attributed to other causes. The better standard of living associated with industrialisation can explain it. Better clothing and housing reduced the mortality due to respiratory diseases. This fact is supported by the result of the variable *father's occupation*, which indicates a significant lesser risk for babies of factory workers in the Catholic sample, compared to babies of farmers. We know that the director of the chocolate factory in Broc built houses for the workers, with separate rooms, a lot of light, running water and a small garden. Here, as with the fishermen, the variable *factory workers* is not only a proxy for income but also for certain environmental conditions. This finding is in line with a contribution made by Alice Reid, who was able to take advantage of a set of individual data of the 1911 British census. She demonstrates that location appears to be more important than class. "To a fairly large degree, infant mortality differentials by social class are observed because environment is not controlled for." (Reid 1997, 138)

Anyway, children of workers lost this advantage when the mother too was working in the factory. The result of the variable *mother factory worker* is

Infant Mortality and Religious Culture

27

clear. Children born to these mothers had a higher mortality risk than children born to female non factory workers. We know that in both factories, maternal leave did not exceed one month, thus obliging mothers to terminate breastfeeding very early. The higher value obtained by the same variable on the Protestant side is intriguing. We must keep in mind that the result of the variable mother factory worker on the Protestant side should not be compared directly with the result on the Catholic side, but with the result of the reference category, that is the children of non working mothers, on the same side. Consequently, this result does not mean that the children of the Protestant working mothers were worse off than those of the Catholic mothers, but that the difference between children of working and non working mothers was more important for the Protestant sample.

What about the variable *siblings*? We introduced this numeric variable to test the impact of parity, more exactly of the number of children already born and surviving. Some studies show that first-born children have a higher mortality risk and this is attributed to a conscious or unconscious neglect. Other researches show that we find more often the situation where siblings of all birth orders were exposed to rather similar risks of infant mortality. However, we can ask to what extent the mortality risk was influenced by family composition, distinguishing between brothers and sisters. If we look at the first period, we can see that the number of elder brothers has no influence on the mortality risk; the number of elder sister increases this risk. What does it mean? My answer is that the higher the number of elder female siblings, the higher the probability that the oldest will be of an age to take care of the infant instead of the mother, which could also mean early weaning. However, we have no convincing explanation for explaining why the number of elder brothers becomes significant for the second period in Fribourg...

This table presenting the results for the mortality risk between one and six months does no show the existence of neglect practices differentiated by sex. However, the sex variable becomes significant when we observe the mortality risk for the first month (table not given). In the Catholic villages of Fribourg, for the period prior to 1900, the mortality risk is significantly higher for male babies during the first month. Male babies have 62% more risk of dying during the first month than female babies. We know that male babies have generally a weaker constitution. The high level of this biological risk is amplified by bad sanitary conditions or bad medical training of midwives and this result confirms the deficiency of health policies.

CONCLUSION

With this comparative analysis of infant mortality in Switzerland we have come closer to answering the question of the ways in which religion influence health and mortality. The most important finding is that, for the period 1860-1930, in which both fertility and infant mortality trends changed markedly, state institutions were the most efficient force able to modify the set of constraints and opportunities shaping the relevant individual behaviour for the survival of children. During this period, a new means of reducing significantly infant mortality was at hand thanks to the discoveries of Pasteur, which permit taking effective measures to combat the prevalence of digestive diseases during the first year. As religious institutions lost their prerogatives in health care and assistance, the role of state institutions was crucial for the diffusion of pastorian techniques and for taking up the challenge of conceiving and implementing adequate measures able to reach the neediest. This process also explains the findings highlighted in other research, that Catholicism exerted a negative influence on health espescially after the 1880s (van Poppel 1992).

The influence of religious culture on the attitudes of political elites proved decisive to accelerate or delay the implementation of adequate health policies. Protestant and Catholic culture differ strongly in in their consideration of the loss of children, in the importance of investment in human capital for terrestrial life, not just for the hereafter, and moreover in their suspiscious or positive attitude towards science. Consequently, regions of Protestant culture are better able to grasp the importance of the second economic revolution taking place in Switerland as well as throughout the Western world at the turn of the century. The revolution is conceptualized by Douglas North as 'a fundamental change in the productive potential of society as a consequence of a basic change in the stock of knowledge and a consequent, equally basic, change in organisation to realise this productive potential' (North, 1981, 171). Human capital became more important, and thus the quality of childcare and mass education, resulting in a trade-off between quality and quantity of children. The different approaches of the two cantonal governments in the use of scientific knowledge (statistics, medicine) to inform policy, and in the concern for human capital as a political priority are paradigmatic, and affected the actual policies they implemented. The results obtained in our analysis of the determinants of infant mortality demonstrate that effective health policies were able to reduce the most important risk of infant mortality (digestive diseases) in the Protestant sample, while this risk remained clearly higher in the Catholic canton.

Infant Mortality and Religious Culture   29

The pathways through which religion influence the behaviour of individuals and shape institutional structures are manifold. It is of paramount importance to demonstrate a causal mechanism that can be tested on individual data, instead of correlations between aggregate. But a word of caution is appropriate. In the long run perspective, religion might well appear less and less a cause of evolution but turns into an effect of deeper structures. In historical research this turning point might easily escape attention.

REFERENCES

Bosson, Alain (2002), "La lutte contre la mortalité des nourrissons en Suisse: enjeux et mesures de prévention (1876-1930)", *Cahiers d'histoire – Lyon*, 47 (1/2), 93-125.

Breschi Marco, Derosas Renzo and Oris Michel (2003), "About the Determinants of Infant and Child Mortality. The Fatal Years in Comparative Perspective", in Bengtsson Tommy, Campbell Cameron, Lee James, et. Al., *Life Under Pressure: Mortality and Living Standards in Europe and Asia, 1700-1900.*, Harvard Ms., Massachussets Institute of Technology Press.

Busset, Thomas (1995), "La mise en place du Bureau fédéral de la statistique", *Revue suisse d'histoire*, (1995)1, 7-28.

Caldwell, John (1980), "Mass Education as a Determinant of the Timing of Fertility Decline", *Population and Development Review*, 6 (1): 225-255.

Derozas, Renzo and van Poppel, Frans (eds.) (2006), *Religion and the Decline of Fertility,* New York/Dordrect, Springer, pp. 104-132.

Derozas, Renzo (2000) "When culture matters: Differentials infant mortality of Jews and Catholics in nineteenth century Venice", *International Congress of Historical Sciences,* Oslo 6-13 August 2000.

Goldscheider, Calvin (2006), "Religion, family and fertility: What do we know historically and comparatively?" in Renzo Derozas and van Frans Poppel (Eds.), *Religion and the Decline of Fertility,* (pp. 41-58), Dordrecht, The Netherlands: Springer.

Kertzer, David I. (1995), "Political-economic and cultural explanations of demographic behavior", in Greenhalgh, S. (Ed.), *Situating fertility. Anthropology and demographic inquiry*, (pp. 29-52), Cambridge: Cambridge University Press.

Lee Robert and Vögele Jörg (2001), "The Benefits of Federalism? The Development of Public Health Policy and Health Care Systems in nineteenth-century Germany and their Impact on Mortality Reduction", *Annales de démographie historique*, (2001)1, 65-96.

Lesthaeghe, Ron (1991), "Moral control, Secularisation and Reproduction in Belgium (1600-1900)", in *Historiens et populations*, Liber amicorum Etienne Hélin, Louvain-la-Neuve: Academia, 257-279.

Lorenzetti, Luigi and Perrenoud (1999), Alfred, "Infant and Child Mortality in Switzerland in the 19th and 20th centuries", working paper, University of Geneva.

McQuillan, Kevin (2004), "When does religion influence fertility?" *Population and Development Review*, 30, 25-56.

Noonan, John T. (1969), "Contraception et mariage. Evolution ou contradiction dans la pensée chrétienne", Paris : Cerf.

North, D.C. (1981), *Structure and Change in Economic History,* New York and London, W.W NortonandCompany.

Perrenoud, Alfred (1974), "Malthusianisme et Protestantisme", *Annales ESC*, 29/4, 975-988.

Praz, Anne-Françoise (2005), *De l'enfant utile à l'enfant précieux – Filles et garçons dans les cantons de Vaud et Fribourg, 1860-1930*, Lausanne: Editions Antipodes.

Praz, Anne-Françoise (2006), "State institutions as mediators between religion and fertility. A comparison of two Swiss regions (1860-1930)." in R. Derozas and van Frans Poppel (Eds), *Religion and the Decline of Fertility* (pp. 104-132), Dordrecht, The Netherlands: Springer.

Praz, Anne-Françoise (2007), "Four Swiss Villages, 1860-1930: Putting Gender back into Historical Demography", *Gender and History,* 19, 242-259.

Reher, David (1999), "Back to the basics: mortality and fertility interactions during the demographic transition", *Continuity and Change*, 14 (1), 9-31.

Reid, Alice (1997), "Locality or class? Spatial and social differences in infant and child mortality in England and Wales, 1895-1911", in Corsini, Carlo A. and Viazzo, Pier Paolo (Eds.), *The Decline of Infant and Child Mortality. The European Experience: 1750-1990,* (pp. 129-154), The Hague, The Netherlands: Martinus Nijhoff Publishers.

Servais, Paul (2001), "The Church and the Family in Belgien", *Revue belge d'histoire contemporaine*, 31(3-4): 621-647.

Sevegrand, Martine (1995), *Les enfants du bon Dieu - Les catholiques français et la procréation au XXe siècle*, Paris: Albin Michel.

Schofield, R., Reher, D, and Bideau, A. (1991), *The decline of mortality in Europe,* Oxford: Clarendon Press.

Smith, Herbert L. (1989), "Integrating Theory and Research on the Institutional Determinants of Fertility", *Demography*, 26 (2), 621-647.

van de Walle, Etienne (1992), "Fertility Transition, Conscious Choice, and Numeracy", *Demography* 4, pp. 487-502.

van de Walle, Francine (1977), *One Hundred Years of Decline - The History of Swiss Fertility from 1860 to 1960*, Philadelphia, (dactyl., Bibliothèque universitaire de Neuchâtel/Suisse).

van Poppel, Frans, Schellekens, Jona, and Liefbroer, Aart C. (2002), "Religious differentials in infant and child mortality in Holland", *Population Studies*, 56, 277-289.

van Poppel, Frans (1992), "Religion and Health: Catholicism and Regional Mortality Differences in Nineteenth-Century Netherlands", *Social History of Medecine, 5/2, 229-253.*

In: Religion
Editors: P. Bellamy and G. Montpetit

ISBN 978-1-61470-382-2
©2012 Nova Science Publishers, Inc.

Chapter 2

FREE WILL PERCEPTIONS AND RELIGION IN PATIENTS WITH SCHIZOPHRENIA AND THEIR CAREGIVERS

Amy Weisman de Mamani, Michael Mejia, Kayla Gurak, and Stephen Sapp*
University of Miami

ABSTRACT

This chapter explores how free will perceptions relate to religious beliefs and values and psychological functioning in patients with schizophrenia and their family members. The paper begins with a discussion of what free will means and where laypeople stand on the question of its existence (from the literature, it appears that the overwhelming majority of the general public do subscribe to a free will perspective). Next we review psychological research on free will. Studies suggest that belief in free will has benefits to both the individual (e.g., greater self-esteem) and to society (e.g., lower rates of aggression and crime). Next we discuss components of free will and our premise that free will subsumes the following constructs: locus of control, self-efficacy, motivation, and meaning-making coping. We then turn to an overview of

---

* Amy Weisman de Mamani, Ph.D. Associate Professor, Dept of Psychology, University of Miami. 5665 Ponce de Leon Blvd, Coral Gables FL 33146. Phone: (305)284-3477. Fax: (305)284-3402.

how free will and religion interact. We contend that a free will perspective is compatible with most Western religious views because most of these religions are founded on the premise that free will exists. The second section of the paper addresses how free will relates to functioning in patients with schizophrenia and their caregivers. Two case examples are presented. Drawing from the literature, our own empirical studies, and the numerous patients and caregivers we have treated as part of our Schizophrenia Family Project, we propose the following hypotheses: For both patients and their relatives, those who endorse greater free will beliefs (toward self) will experience greater psychological well-being and greater quality of life. For patients, we also propose that the severity of their psychiatric symptoms will be less severe. Finally, this chapter will examine how free will perceptions may relate to religious beliefs and values to impact mental health in schizophrenia patients and their relatives. Implications from this review suggest that mental health practitioners in contact with individuals with schizophrenia and their caregivers may better serve them by fostering the notion that, despite the illness, they are still free to assume an active, autonomous role in the course of their lives. More empirical research in this area is clearly needed.

INTRODUCTION

"...Forces beyond your control can take away everything you possess except for one thing, your freedom to choose how you will respond to the situation. You cannot control what happens to you in life, but you can always control what you will feel and do about what happens to you." (2006, Kushner, foreword, to Viktor Frankl's Man's Search for Meaning, p. X)

This quotation (written by Harold Kushner) poignantly summarizes Viktor Frankl's philosophy. In his renowned book, *Man's Search for Meaning*, Frankl notes that concentration camp workers who were able to retain a sense of dignity and maintain a purpose for which to live were likely to survive longer and keep apathy at bay. Many were highly devout Jews who found in their religion a purpose for living and resisting their oppressors. Frankl's viewpoint is clear: He believes that people cannot always control their circumstances but they can control how they view or react to them. Philosophers, psychologists, and other scholars can be found with opinions that both support and refute the claim that humans can control their fate in this way. Although some attention will be paid to the validity of this viewpoint, this chapter will focus primarily on the advantages (and in some cases, potential consequences) of holding the perspective that one always retains the freedom to choose how to respond to events, particularly in the face of adversity. The interplay among free will, religion, and related constructs (e.g., locus of control, self-efficacy) will also be addressed.

The "adversity" under scrutiny in this chapter is a serious mental disorder known as schizophrenia. Specifically we will examine how free will perceptions may relate to psychiatric symptoms and the course of illness in patients with the disorder. We will also examine the impact of free will beliefs on caregivers of individuals afflicted with schizophrenia. Two clinical case examples from our own research will be provided. The last section of the chapter addresses the complexity of addressing free will in self versus other and briefly describes where our research is heading to disentangle this issue.

WHAT IS FREE WILL AND DO LAYPEOPLE BELIEVE IN IT?

Free will has been defined in many ways but it is generally considered to be the ability of agents to make choices that are free from constraints. Baumeister, Crescioni, and Alquist (2011) describe it as a unique form of action control that came about to meet the increasing demands of human life, especially moral action and the pursuit of enlightened self-interest. There are multiple ways of thinking about free will, and when viewed from different perspectives, its meaning can change dramatically (Howard, 1994). It is a multifaceted construct that in our view includes (but is not limited to) the following dimensions: locus of control, self-efficacy, meaning-making coping, and motivation.

It is important to point out that many psychologists and philosophers who assert that free will exists do not argue that it is absolute. That is, they believe that people have some say in who they are, how they respond to things, or what they do (Dweck and Molden, 2008). Proponents of free will emphasize the possibility that, in almost any given situation, a person can act or react in more than one manner. In his experiences in four concentration camps, Viktor Frankl observed that great variability existed in the manner in which prisoners reacted to the stress of internment. Some became completely detached, helpless, and hopeless, just waiting to die. Others became "animals," treating fellow prisoners even worse than the guards did. On the other hand, there was a small, albeit noteworthy, number of men who, despite all of the excruciating physical and mental controls that were placed on prisoners, managed to act with kindness, humor, and in solidarity with other prisoners. Frankl notes that the minority who were able to remain positive and optimistic were those who used the tragedy as an opportunity to reflect on their lives, find meaning in the experience, and maintain hope and dignity regardless of the real possibilities. The following quotation pertaining to these observations sums up Frankl's free will perspective: "...in the final analysis it becomes clear that the sort of person the prisoner became was the result of an inner decision, and not the result of camp influences alone. Fundamentally, therefore, any man can, even under such circumstances, decide what shall become of him—mentally and spiritually. He may retain his human dignity even in a concentration camp" (Frankl, p. 66).[1]

Free will is often viewed as the antagonist of determinism. The deterministic position leaves no room for free human choice. From this perspective, everything that happens is the unavoidable product of prior causes (Baumeister, 2008). Psychologists tend to be divided on whether people have free will. Some believe that freedom of will exists because people make choices and can theoretically choose differently under the same circumstances. Others believe that psychology must explain all behavior in terms of causes. Consequently, if a behavior is caused, then it is not truly or fully free (Baumeister and Bushman, 2008). Ultimately, the definition of free will and the validity of this view are philosophical issues. However, whether people believe they possess free will and the consequences of this belief (or lack of it) fall squarely within the purview of psychology. This topic will be addressed further below.

According to most contemporary scientists, belief in the notion of free will is widespread. For example, based on their research, Baumeister, Crescioni, and Alquist (2011) offer evidence for the following four hypotheses:

1) Laypeople generally believe in free will.
2) Belief in free will has favorable social consequences, which include increases in socially and culturally desirable behavior.

---

[1] Stemming from this philosophy, Frankl developed logotherapy, an existential analysis based on the premise that a person's primary motivational force is to find meaning. Logotherapy has the following three primary tenets: 1) life has meaning under all circumstances, even the most miserable; 2) one's main motivation for living is to find meaning in life; and perhaps most important, 3) people have freedom to find meaning in what they do, what they experience, or at least in the stand they take when faced with a situation of unchangeable suffering.

3) Laypeople are able to differentiate free actions from less free actions reliably.
4) Actions that are viewed to be free are thought to emerge from the following inner processes: planning, initiative, self-control, and rational choice.

The idea that ordinary people believe in free will is not new. Philosophers such as Arthur Schopenhauer (1883) have long espoused the view that belief in free will is extensive. For example, in *The World as Will and Idea* Schopenhauer wrote, "Everyone believes himself *a priori* to be perfectly free, even in his individual actions, and thinks that at every moment he can commence another manner of life (p. 147)."[2]

Most of the research to date that has examined people's free will beliefs has been conducted in Western cultures. However, a recent study by Sarkissian, Chatterjee, de Brigard, Knobe, Nichols, and Sirker (2010) examined intuitions about free will and moral responsibility in college students from four countries: the United States, India, China, and Colombia. Interestingly, they found a striking degree of cultural convergence in line with the views presented by Baumeister, Crescioni, and Alquist (2011) and their predecessors. In other words, in all four cultures the majority of participants espoused the view that free will exists. As research outlined throughout this chapter will support, many mental health benefits may result from espousing this view.

THE STUDY OF FREE WILL IN PSYCHOLOGY

The topic of "free will" has received the most attention in the disciplines of religion and philosophy (Stroessner and Green, 1990). This is, no doubt, in part because the most debated question regarding free will, namely, whether people have it, does not lend itself readily to the empirical methods required in disciplines such as psychology. On the other hand, beliefs and perceptions

---

[2] It is important to point out, however, as the rest of the quotation implies, that Schopenhauer himself was a determinist: "...But a posteriori, through experience, he finds to his astonishment that he is not free, but subjected to necessity, that in spite of all his resolutions and reflections he does not change his conduct, and that from the beginning of his life to the end of it, he must carry out the very character which he himself condemns." (An ellipsis is not necessary at the beginning and end of quotations because it is assumed something precedes and follows. I have left them at the beginning here, though, to indicate the "attachment" to the part in the text.)

about free will can be studied empirically. Yet psychological explanations rarely mention free will as a factor (Baer, Kaufman, and Baumeister, 2008), and the topic has been empirically investigated in only a handful of psychological studies.

Despite the scarcity of empirical research directly examining free will beliefs, the findings are compelling. For example, studies have shown that inducing disbelief in free will tends to increase aggressive behavior and reduce willingness to help others (see Baumeister et al., 2009) and to increase dishonest behavior such as cheating on a test (Vohs and Schooler, 2008). Rakos, Laurene, Skala, and Slane (2008) found that a strong sense of free will was associated with higher self-esteem in both adolescents and adults. The authors argue that, as humans evolved, people who believed they possessed free will were better at manipulating their environment in choice situations. In turn, they were better at decision making and problem solving and had more self-restraint, all of which are characteristics associated with improved psychological and physical health. Thus it appears that free will perceptions have important behavioral, emotional, and societal ramifications and are therefore highly worthy of further scientific research in psychology.

FREE WILL AND UNDERLYING CONSTRUCTS

Notions of free will and determinism are closely linked to and include related psychological constructs such as self-efficacy and locus of control and more general psychological factors such as moral and effortful choice, motivation, and meaning-making coping. Following Baumeister, Bauer, and Lloyd (2010), we view free will as a higher order process that subsumes and synergizes many of these related constructs. All of these factors share an underlying commonality pertaining to the question of whether people have the capacity to exert control over their environment and bring about desired emotional and behavioral outcomes.

An internal locus of control and a confident self-efficacy are two essential elements of free will (Waller, 2004). The construct of Locus of Control (Rotter, 1966) refers to the perception that a person holds regarding which factors control positive and negative reinforcements for their actions and whether these factors are internal or external to the person. A determinist would likely hold a view that favors an external locus of control, believing that people do not have control over the outcome of their actions but rather that they are the result of luck, chance, fate, or powerful others. Free will proponents, however, generally hold a position favoring an internal locus of control, characterized by the perception that outcomes are a result of their own actions or other internal forces (e.g., thoughts). These relationships may have implications for a person's understanding of moral responsibility, another aspect of free will perceptions. If people hold the view that they and/or others are capable of acting in a responsible or correct manner, then they are also likely to believe that they and others ought to behave in the approved manner. In this way free will subsumes both locus of control and moral and effortful choice.

In addition to an internal locus of control, free will supporters also believe that they are generally able to exercise control effectively. In other words, free will requires self-efficacy (Waller, 2004). The construct of self-efficacy was introduced by Albert Bandura (1977) and refers to perceiving a sense of competence to carry out a task successfully and achieve a desired result. According to this theory, self-efficacy beliefs can influence motivation in that the greater people's belief that they will be able to carry out certain behaviors efficaciously, the more likely they are to undertake challenging tasks to begin with. Thus, free will subsumes self-efficacy beliefs and motivation as well.

A free will perspective implies perceived control not only over behaviors but also over thoughts and emotions. Free will proponents generally believe they are in control of their emotional reactions to events and are able to construe their emotions adaptively. To achieve this aim, free will believers tend to be adept at a meaning-making coping style that allows them to reframe suffering and other potential adversities in a manner that is beneficial, or at the very least, tolerable. In fact, we believe that it is the ability to reconstrue events adaptively and take control of one's emotions that makes a free will perspective particularly adaptive.

FREE WILL AND RELIGION

Free will and religion have much in common, with both constructs educing questions regarding human choice, willpower, and self-control. The notion of free will whereby people are seen as authors of their own actions is at the heart of the "Western" (or more accurately, Abrahamic) religions of Judaism, Christianity, and Islam. For example, these religions assume that people can freely choose to perform sinful or virtuous acts (Baumeister, Masicampo, and DeWall, 2009), though reconciling such freedom with God's omnipotence is a particularly vexing theological challenge for these religions.

Baumeister et al. (2010) note that regardless of whether free will exists, belief in it appears to benefit society. Religion, by way of promoting this belief, can improve functioning within a civilization and therefore benefit the society itself.

There is strong empirical evidence that religion is associated with both mental and physical health. For example, studies have linked greater interest in religion and religious practices with better self-esteem, greater personal adjustment, less alcohol and drug abuse, and less sexual permissiveness and suicide (Waite, Hawks, and Gast, 2000; Pargament, Kennell, Hathaway, Grevengoed, Newman, and Jones, 1988; Pargamant, Koening, Tarakeshwar, and Hahn, 2004). McCullough et al. (2000) conducted a comprehensive meta-analysis and found that greater religious involvement was associated with much lower odds of dying prematurely.

In this chapter we follow Baumeister, Baer, and Lloyd (2010) by proposing that religion may benefit individuals and society in part by supporting belief in free will. Specifically, most organized religions encourage followers to believe that they can choose to resolve dilemmas by controlling selfish impulses and thoughts that might cause harm to themselves or others. Many religions encourage followers to resist immediate temptations in favor of more significant long-term goals to bolster inner restraints and to curb aggressive inclinations, and to replace these with prosocial behaviors that appear to benefit most members of society.

APPLYING THE STUDY OF FREE WILL TO SCHIZOPHRENIA PATIENTS AND THEIR CAREGIVERS

Schizophrenia Patients

Schizophrenia is generally considered to be one of the most severe forms of mental illness. It is marked by general disorganization in thinking, behaving, and perceiving. People who have this illness are often unable to think logically, perceive what is happening around them accurately, and, unfortunately for many, hold a job and live a normal everyday life (Beidel, Bulik, and Stanley, 2010). In many respects, the onset of the disorder is often associated with an afflicted person's loss of sense of control over his or her destiny. Family members often try to inflict constraints and limits on patients' daily activities and behaviors. Psychiatrists frequently impose medications.

Mental health practitioners oblige or encourage psychotherapy and other sorts of behavioral controls. Even the symptoms themselves seem to belie a free will perspective. For example, delusions of influence are frequent in patients with schizophrenia. Common themes include beliefs that thoughts are being removed from one's head, that government or alien forces are stealing one's thoughts, or that one's private thoughts are being transmitted over the television or radio (Beidel, Bulik, and Stanley, 2010). Patients with schizophrenia often have great difficulty discriminating between self- and other-generated information and actions and often attribute self-generated information to others. In other words, many patients believe they are not free to control something as private and fundamental as their own thoughts. Interestingly, in a qualitative analysis of recovery from schizophrenia, Davidson (2003) observed that people with schizophrenia often identify reestablishing their sense of agency as a key component in recovery. It is worth quoting a summary of his observations that are based on several in-depth interviews aimed at capturing patients' own phenomenological experiences of their illness. Davidson eloquently writes:

> Being unable to retain a sense of oneself as the source of the direction of one's own awareness may thus deprive the person with schizophrenia of the most fundamental sense of ownership of his or her own experiences. Without this basic self-awareness, people may then lose their secondary sense of themselves as agents active in and affected by the world. The impact of voices and cognitive disruptions in this way reverberates throughout the person's experience of self leading to the constitution of a sense of personal identity built more on feelings of being controlled by and vulnerable to external influences than of being the agent of one's own thoughts, perceptions, and feelings as well as actions (p. 141).

As the preceding passage illustrates, helping patients capture or recapture a free will perspective may be useful in rebuilding their confidence, happiness, and health after schizophrenia strikes. We now turn to a clinical case example of a patient that we will call Marcia [3] who, one could argue, had overwhelming and largely irreparable consequences as the direct result of her illness. Her worldview, however, which is very much in line with a free will perspective, appears to have allowed her to live a meaningful and happy life.

---

[3] Pseudonyms are used for both clinical case examples provided in this chapter and a few demographic facts have been altered to protect participants' identities.

Marcia, a devout Christian, is a woman in her late 70's suffering from schizophrenia. She first came into contact with our research laboratory approximately five years ago and has been steadily involved in different aspects of our schizophrenia intervention research. Members of our research team know her very well. Marcia experienced her first bout with serious mental illness in her late 30's. Prior to this, she was happily married with three children and a satisfying and thriving career. During this bout she became highly paranoid and suspicious of everyone, including her loved ones. She also became highly disorganized, complained of hearing voices, and became exceedingly anxious to the point of being largely unable to leave the house. Less than a year following the first psychotic episode, Marcia's husband, fearing for his and their children's safety, filed for divorce and moved to a new state, taking their young children with him.

Shortly thereafter, Marcia lost her job and was never again able to resume work. Following the psychotic break (and subsequent divorce and job loss) one of Marcia's siblings stepped in and took on a primary role as her caregiver and guardian, accompanying Marcia to all psychiatric appointments and treatments and overseeing most of her daily activities for approximately forty years. Since her psychotic break, Marcia has had almost no contact with her children (aside from a few isolated phone conversations and a handful of visits). Sadly, over a year ago Marcia's sibling (who was also her caregiver and closest friend and confidant) died after a long bout with cancer.

Given the circumstances of her life, another person in Marcia's shoes might have become dejected and felt bitter after losing (and never managing to regain fully) the things that the majority of people report as the most meaningful and important to their wellbeing (e.g., children, marriage, and a career).[4] However, from the beginning (as much as we would like to take credit for a change in her outlook), what was most striking about Marcia was her pervasively optimistic stance toward life and an uncanny ability to find the good in every situation, even those that most people would experience as devastating.

To cite a few representative examples, following the death of her brother, Marcia displayed deep and appropriate grief over her loss. However, within a few short weeks she was also able to transform her grief and energies into a profound sense of gratitude. This went far beyond feeling appreciative for having had such a kind and wonderful brother and also went past feeling

---

[4] Research corroborates that these factors (marriage, family, meaningful work) are among those most closely related to happiness (Myers, 1993).

indebted to him for the care that he had given her. Instead of viewing his illness and death as another major life blow, she focused on what the situation had to offer her, namely, the opportunity to reverse roles and tend to her brother's physical and emotional needs during his final hours. In other words, she reported and continues to report comfort in knowing that she was able to reciprocate the extensive care that he had provided to her over the years. This opportunity appears to have given her a deep sense of satisfaction and purpose and helped her to find a greater meaning in his illness and in his death. Marcia also expressed gratitude that her brother had gone first and therefore did not have to deal with the pain of her eventual death.

Marcia was similarly able to construe the loss of her children and her failed marriage in a productive manner. Although she does express occasional sadness and guilt over not having been a regular part of her children's lives, she focuses much more of her energy on feelings of thankfulness that the father of her children had the good sense to take them away when she was psychotic. She also reports feeling grateful that he was in a position to provide them the kind of loving and consistent care that she herself, during the acute stage of her illness, could not.

It is important to convey that Marcia's outlook goes well beyond life's great challenges. In her day-to-day living she is able to address her setbacks head-on and also provide care, support, and a sense of meaning to the difficulties of others in her therapy group. Though she is in late life, she continues to reinvent herself, taking on and even embracing new responsibilities and activities that she once believed were beyond her capacities (e.g., buying a new house and living alone). She continually creates new friendships and most importantly remains vocal and adamant in her stance that life is beautiful and worth living at any age or under any circumstance. Marcia recently declared that this year she had the "best holiday season since her psychotic break." She explained that for so many years she had just been managing her symptoms and trying to offset the chances of another episode, but that now she is finally able to experience joy again. She honored the holidays in small but meaningful ways, by buying herself eggnog and fruit cake and listening to holiday music in her apartment. She is taking control of her illness with more confidence each and every year. Marcia also recently joined Weight Watchers®. This was a major and very carefully planned step for her because over the past forty years all of her social activities, save family functions, have been defined by her illness. When Marcia first told her therapy group that she had joined, she said, "It's time for me to get control of this" ("this" being her weight). Marcia reported wanting to work on gaining self-esteem and feeling self-control in areas other than managing her symptoms. She continues to have minor psychiatric symptoms (though most are well controlled on medication and in recent years have been more in the realm of anxiety than psychosis). However, the manner in which she chooses to cope with her illness and all of her life's setbacks has allowed her to lead a life that she views as worthwhile and happy, while several of our other patients in similar (or in many cases even more favorable circumstances in an objective sense) have not thrived nearly as well.

Schizophrenia Caregivers

Schizophrenia is an incapacitating mental illness that takes its toll not only on the person who suffers from it but on family members as well, resulting in high levels of caregiver distress and burden. Family members report experiencing an array of difficulties, including grief over losses experienced by the patient, family conflict caused by the illness, financial strain, restricted leisure and social activities, feelings of stigma, and shock over witnessing bizarre symptoms in a loved one (Friedman-Yakoobian, Weisman de Mamani, and Mueser, 2009).

Although most family members report experiencing disruption in their lives as a result of the illness, we once again see remarkable variability in family members' emotional and behavioral responses to the disorder. We turn now to an example of one caregiver who we believe exemplifies what a free will perspective can do.

Miriam is the mother of Max,[3] a 30-year-old male with schizophrenia. Max is an attractive, personable young man of superior intelligence. Miriam and her family had exceptionally high hopes for Max both professionally and personally. Max was a college student during his first psychotic break. However, the symptoms of his illness were severe enough to prevent him from completing college, dating, or holding down a professional job (he has been able to earn money from some manual labor and other blue-collar jobs occasionally). Initially, Miriam was devastated that despite Max's intellectual and other gifts, he would not be able to reach his full potential. However, instead of turning inward in despair, Miriam and Max took control of the illness. A primary mission in Miriam's life became "not to let the illness control Max or me." Miriam sought family and group therapy, joined family member support groups, and became actively involved in political organizations that champion the rights of mentally ill patients. She also utilized services around her Jewish faith to help her cope with the illness. In addition, she learned as much as she could about the illness and ways of interacting with Max that have also helped him to thrive. As part of her family treatment in our project, she became fascinated by a body of work called expressed emotion (frequently referred to as EE; see Weisman de Mamani, Dunham, Aldebot, Tuchman, and Wasserman, 2009, for a review). This area of research shows that patients with loving and supportive relatives fare better and keep symptoms at bay more effectively than those whose family members express high levels of hostile and critical attitudes toward them. Miriam embraced this knowledge, and we have been struck by how competent she became at responding to Max's symptoms in a calm and patient manner, where previously she had reacted with anger and frustration. She held great faith that she could change, and in essence she did. As tension in the household subsided, so did the severity of Max's symptoms.

Over the years, both Miriam and Max have been able to find great meaning in his illness. Max, a talented artist, has used his symptoms as inspiration for his music, photography, and art (which he frequently performs and displays live). Miriam would still like to see Max "conquer" his illness and she continues to dedicate her life to finding both better treatments for schizophrenia and a cure. However, she has also come to the realization that Max would never have become the wonderfully complex person that he is today without having had schizophrenia. For instance, both Miriam and Max strongly believe that Max never would have realized his full artistic potential without the illness. This is significant in that Max's art represents one of his greatest sources of pleasure and pride (and is also a source of pride and joy for the rest of the family). In essence, for many caregivers the illness becomes nothing more than an encumbrance. For Miriam, however, finding a way to construe it and react to it helped her and her son feel stronger about themselves. In fact, in many ways they report feeling stronger as individuals and more cohesive as a family than prior to Max's first psychotic break.

RELIGION AND SCHIZOPHRENIA/SEVERE MENTAL ILLNESS

Much like the research above demonstrating benefits of belief in free will in normative populations, the preponderance of evidence in schizophrenia, though complex, generally indicates that being more religious has mental health benefits for patients and their caregivers (see Weisman de Mamani, Tuchman, and Duarte for a review, 2010). For example, in a sample of psychiatric inpatients, Pieper (2004) found that religion had a positive impact on the manner in which patients dealt with mental health problems. Greater general religiousness and greater religious coping were both associated with greater existential well-being. In a study of caregivers of patients with mental illness, greater religiosity was correlated with less depression and better self-esteem and self-care (Murray-Swank, et al., 2006). In another study, religiosity was found to be inversely related to symptoms of depression among caregivers (Magana, Ramirez, Hernandez, and Cortez, 2007).

On the other hand, using the Moral Religious Emphasis subscale of the Family Environment Scale (Moos and Moos, 1981), Weisman, Rosales, Kymalainen, and Armesto (2005) found no relationship with general emotional distress in schizophrenia caregivers. The authors note that the absence of a correlation may be due to the measure used in the study, which is designed to assess institutional religiosity (e.g., going to church) as opposed to more intrinsic elements (e.g., holding religion as a master framework for living). This explanation is supported by a meta-analysis of 34 studies which found that, overall, religiosity appears to be positively correlated with mental health (Hackney and Sanders, 2003). However, measures of institutional religiosity were shown to have the weakest predictive ability in this context. Hackney and Sanders (2003) concluded that the contradictory findings observed in previous research on religiosity and mental health can be explained by differences in operationalization.

The importance of having clear operational definitions also appears in research examining religious meaning-making coping styles, which addresses control-related beliefs about one's relationship with God. For example, in a sample of patients with serious mental illness, Phillips and Stein (2007) examined the following three religious meaning-making coping styles: benevolent religious reappraisals (attempts to redefine a stressor as having religious benefits), punishing God reappraisals (redefining the stressor as a punishment from God), and reappraisals of God's power (redefining God's ability to influence stressful events such as viewing God as incapable of altering a stressful situation). They found that benevolent religious reappraisals were associated with more positive mental health, whereas reappraisals of God's power and punishing God reappraisals were associated with poorer mental health. This line of research suggests, and many researchers concur (e.g., Weisman et al., 2005; Payne et al., 1991), that it is more important to understand *how* a person is religious than *whether* a person is

Free Will Perceptions and Religion in Patients ... 47

religious. Consequently, studies that examine religiosity as a construct should rely on varied and multi-dimensional methods of assessment.

In our experience, religious patients and caregivers who view God or another higher power as an aid to assist them in selecting the best course of action when other alternatives are available or to accept adversity with dignity and calm when other alternatives are not available fare far better than those who passively turn to God or religion for answers.[5] We recently conducted a pilot study that assessed the connection between attributions of God control and psychological distress (using the Depression, Anxiety, Stress Scale; Lovibond and Lovibond, 1995) in 81 family members of individuals with schizophrenia (Tuchman, Mejia, and Weisman de Mamani, 2010). Those who agreed with the statement "God controls most things that happen to us, including mental illness" reported greater distress than those who disagreed. In other words, the perception that God controls a loved one's illness (i.e., that free will is limited) may cause distress because it suggests that even with serious planning, initiative, and wise choices, patients and their relatives do not have the power to control mental illness (this perception may have a detrimental impact on mental health similar to that of holding punishing God reappraisals observed by Phillips and Stein [2007] and discussed in the previous paragraph). Because freedom and choice are deeply woven into the fabric of human relations (Baumeister, 2008) and Western societies place a high premium on them, it is not surprising that mental health may deteriorate when perceptions of free choice and control are challenged or lacking. In short, religion may be useful to individuals in coping with schizophrenia partially because it supports both the exercise of and the belief in free will (Baumeister, Bauer, and Lloyd 2010).

Self Versus Other Free Will Perspective in Schizophrenia Caregivers

A potential disadvantage to a robust free will perspective may be that unfair blame is placed upon others (and perhaps oneself) when things go wrong. Some of our own data and those of colleagues suggest that there may be circumstances for which increasing free will views in caregivers could be

---

[5] In fact, this message is strongly espoused by theologian Reinhold Niebuhr's famous Serenity Prayer, perhaps best known through its association with Alcoholics Anonymous: "God grant me the serenity to accept the things I cannot change; courage to change the things I can; and wisdom to know the difference."

associated with detrimental attitudes toward patients. For example, the first author of this chapter and colleagues (e.g., Weisman et al., 1993, 1997, 1998) and others (Brewin, MacCarthy, Duda, and Vaughn, 1991) offer data that suggest that family members who perceive patients with schizophrenia as having greater control over their illness and the associated symptoms are more likely to be blaming, hostile, and critical toward them. As noted earlier, high EE attitudes in relatives are associated with a poor course of illness for patients (Weisman de Mamani et al. 2009; Breitborde, López, and Nuechterlein, 2009) also reported finding that high-EE caregivers perceive the expression of symptoms as stemming from their ill relative's agency more frequently than did low-EE caregivers. This study is well-written and offers interesting insights. However, it is important to note that "agency" was measured by only one item: "How did (ill relative) come to contact the hospital this most recent time?" This item was confounded with EE in that it was derived from the opening passage of the Camberwell Family Interview (the same interview used to assess EE) and the agency coder was not blind to EE status. Furthermore, from the description of the open-ended rating system described in the paper, it is unclear how the construct of "agency" is different from the construct of "control" used in prior studies (e.g., Brewin, MacCarthy, Duda, and Vaughn, 1991; Weisman et al., 1993, 1997, 1998).

In this paper we have proposed that caregivers who hold a greater free will view are also likely to be happier and healthier. As illustrated above in the case of Miriam, we believe this view may translate into behaviors that also benefit patients. On the other hand, research described in the preceding paragraph complicates this issue and raises the question of whether the adaptive benefit of free will perceptions may vary depending on whether the agent is self or other. This topic is worthy of additional investigation.[6]

One aim of our future research will be to examine directly how free will relates to agency (self versus other) in caregivers' reactions toward symptoms in a loved one. An existing scale by Rakos, Laurene, Skala, and Slane (2008) includes items that may serve as a useful tool in evaluating this interesting question. For example, this scale contains two subscales: beliefs about oneself ("I am in charge of my actions even when my life's circumstances are

---

[6] Although most people subscribe to a free will perspective, people are generally able to distinguish free from unfree situations. For example, the United States legal system is based on the view that free will exists. However, the insanity defense, which views a defendant as incapable of distinguishing between right and wrong, is an exception. Thus even caregivers who are avid free will proponents may be able to judge culpability accurately when reacting to bonafide symptoms of schizophrenia in their loved one (particularly those who have been properly educated about the illness and its symptoms).

difficult") and beliefs about people in general ("Life experiences cannot eliminate a person's free will)." Our research team is also currently developing a "Free Will Beliefs in Schizophrenia Scale." This instrument will be combined with existing scales to examine more explicitly patients' and caregivers' free will beliefs in direct response to the illness. More research is clearly needed to tease apart the self versus other distinction in free will beliefs toward schizophrenia. We hope that our new scale in conjunction with existing measures will allow us to speak more directly to these interesting questions.

CONCLUSION

In summary, this chapter reviewed the literature on free will perceptions and religion in patients with schizophrenia and their caregivers. Stemming from the studies reviewed above, we conjecture that both patients and their relatives who endorse greater free will beliefs (toward self) will experience lower levels of depression and anxiety and greater quality of life. Extrapolating from the research above, we also theorize that patients with schizophrenia who endorse greater free will beliefs (toward self) will display less severe psychiatric symptoms. We hope that we have conveyed our belief that instilling a free will view in patients with schizophrenia and their caregivers would likely help them to manage and cope with the illness more effectively. More research is needed to validate these claims empirically.

In closing, we turn once more to Frankl (2006):

"An incurably psychotic individual may lose his usefulness but yet retain the dignity of a human being. This is my psychiatric credo. Without it I should not think it worthwhile to be a psychiatrist" (p. 133).

"..... a seemingly hopeless madman has the potential to transcend evil or insanity by making responsible choices" (p. 162).

REFERENCES

Baer, J., Kaufman, J. C., and Baumeister R. (Eds.) (2008). *Are we free? Psychology and free will.* New York, NY: Oxford University Press. (excerpt from jacket).

Bandura, A. (1977). Self-efficacy: Toward a unifying theory of behavioral change. *Psychological Review, 84*(2), 191-215.

Baumeister, R. F. (2008). Free will in scientific psychology. *Perspectives on Psychological Science, 3*(1), 14-19.

Baumeister, R. F., Bauer, I. M., and Lloyd, L. A. (2010). Choice, free will, and religion. *Psychology of Religion and Spirituality, 2,* 67-82.

Baumeister, R. F. and Bushman, B. J. (2008) Social Psychology and human nature (p. 126). Belmont: Thomas Wadsworth.

Baumesiter, R., Crescioni, A. W. and Alquist, J. L. (2011). Free will as advanced action control for human social life and culture. *Neuroethics, 4,* 1-11.

Baumeister, R. F., Masicampo, E. J., and Dewall, C. N. (2009). Prosocial benefits of feeling free: Disbelief in free will increases aggression and reduces helpfulness. *Personality and Social Psychology Bulletin, 35,* 260-268.

Beidel, D. C., Bulik, C. M., and Stanley, M. A. (2010). *Abnormal Psychology.* Boston: Prentice Hall

Blaire, R. J. (2007). Aggression, psychopathy and free will from a cognitive neuroscience perspective. *Behavioral Sciences and the Law, 25,* 321-331.

Breitborde, N. J. K., Lopez, S. R., and Nuechterlein, K. H. (2009). Expressed emotion, human agency, and schizophrenia: Toward a new model for the EE-relapse association. *Culture, Medicine and Psychiatry, 33,* 41-60.

Brewin, C. R., MacCarthy, B., Duda, K., and Vaughn, C. E. (1991). Attribution and expressed emotion in the relatives of patients with schizophrenia. *Journal of Abnormal Psychology, 100,* 546-554.

Davidson, L. (2003). *Living Outside Mental Illness: Qualitative Studies of Recovery from schizophrenia.* New York, NY: University Press.

Dweck, C. S. and Molden, D. C. (2008). Self theories: The construction of free will (pp44-64). In J. Baer, J. C. Kaufman, and R. Baumeister R. (Eds.) *Are We Free? Psychology and Free Will.* New York, NY: Oxford University Press.

Frankl, V. (2006). *Man's Search for Meaning.* Boston Beacon Press.

Friedman-Yakoobian, M., Weisman de Mamani, A., and Meuser, K. (2009). Predictors of distress and hope in relatives of individuals with schizophrenia. *Israel Journal of Psychiatry, 46,* 130-140.

Gorsuch, R. L., and McPherson, S. E. (1989). Intrinsic/extrinsic measurement: I/E-revised and single-item scales. *Journal for the Scientific Study of Religion, 28,* 348-354.

Hackney, C. H., and Sanders, G. S. (2003). Religiosity and mental health: A meta-analysis of recent studies. *Journal for the Scientific Study of Religion, 42*(1), 43-55.

Howard, G. S. (1994). Some varieties of free will worth practicing. *Journal of Theoretical and Philosophical Psychology, 14,* 50-61,

Lovibond, P. F., and Lovibond, S. H. (1995). The structure of negative emotional states: Comparison of the depression anxiety stress scales (DASS) with the Beck depression and anxiety inventories. *Behavior Research and Therapy, 33,* 335-342.

Magana, S. M., Ramirez Garcia, J. I., Hernandez, M. G., and Cortez, R. (2007). Psychological distress among Latino family caregivers of adults with schizophrenia: The roles of burden and stigma. *Psychiatric Services, 58*(3), 378-384.

McCullough, M. E., Hoyt, W. T., Larson, D. B., Koenig, H. G., and Thoresen, C. (2000). Religious involvement and mortality: A meta-analytic review. *Health Psychology, 19,* 211-222.

Moos, R. H., and Moos, B. S. (1981) Family environment scale manual (2nd ed). Palo Alto, CA: Consulting Psychologist Press.

Myers, D. (1993). *The Pursuit of Happiness: Discovering the Pathway to Fulfillment, Well-Being, and Enduring Personal Joy.* New York: First Avon Books.

Murray-Swank, A. B., Lucksted, A., Medoff, D. R., Yang, Y., Wohlheiter, K., and Dixon, L. B. (2006). Religiosity, psychosocial adjustment, and subjective burden of persons who care for those with mental illness. *Psychiatric Services, 57,* 361-365.

Pargament, K. I., Kennell, J., Hathaway, W., Grevengoed, N., Newman, J., and Jones, W. (1988). Religion and the problem-solving process: Three styles of coping. *Journal for the Scientific Study of Religion and Spirituality, 27,* 90-104.

Pargament, K. I., Koenig, H. G., Tarakeshwar, N., and Hahn, J. (2004). Religious coping methods as predictors of psychological, physical and spiritual outcomes among medically ill elderly patients: A two-year longitudinal study. *Journal of Health Psychology9,* 713-730.

Payne, I. R., Bergin, A. E., Bielema, K. A., and Jenkins, P. H. (1991). Review of religion and mental health: Prevention and the enhancement of psychosocial functioning. *Prevention in Human Services, 9,* 11-40.

Phillips, R. E., and Stein, C. H. (2007). God's will, God's punishment, or God's limitations? Religious coping strategies reported by young adults living with serious mental illness. *Journal of Clinical Psychology, 63*(6), 529-540.

Pieper, J. Z. (2004). Religious coping in highly religious psychiatric inpatients. *Mental Health, Religion and Culture, 7*(4), 349-363.

Rakos, R. F., Laurene, K. R., Skala, S., and Slane, S. (2008). Belief in free will: Measurement and conceptualization innovations. *Behavioral and Social Issues, 17,* 20-39.

Rotter, J. B. (1966). Generalized expectancies for internal versus external control of reinforcement. *Psychological Monographs, 80*(609), 1-28.

Sarkissian, H., Chatterjee, A., de Brigard, F., Knobe, J., Nichols, S., and Sirker, S. (2010*)*. Is belief in free will a cultural universal? *Mind and Language, 25,* 346-358

Schwarzer, R., and Jerusalem, M. (1995). Generalized Self-Efficacy Scale. In: J. Weinman, S. Wright and M. Johnston (Eds.), *Measures in Health Psychology: A User's Portfolio. Causal and Control Beliefs* (pp.35-37). Windsor, UK: NFER-NELSON.

Schopenhauer, A. (1883). Second Book *The World as Will-* First Aspect. In R. B. Haldane and J. Kemp (Trans.), The World as Will and Idea (Vol. 1, p. 147). London: Trubner.

Stroessner, S. J., and Green, C. W. (1990). Effects of belief in free will or determinism on attitudes toward punishment and locus of control. *The Journal of Social Psychology, 130*(6), 789-799.

Tuchman, N., Mejia, M. G., and Weisman de Mamani, A. (November 2010). God control attributions and psychological distress in relatives of patients with schizophrenia. Poster presented at the annual meeting of the Association for Behavioral and Cognitive Therapies, San Francisco.

Vohs, K. D., and Schooler, J. W. (2008). The value of believing in free will: Encouraging a belief in determinism increases cheating. *Psychological Science, 19*(49), 49-54.

Waite, P. J., Hawks, S. R., and Gast, J.A. (1999). The correlation between spiritual well-being and health behaviors. *American Journal of Health Promotion, 13,* 159-162.

Waller, B. N. (2004). Neglected psychological elements of free will. Philosophy, *Psychiatry and Psychology, 11,* 111-118.

Weisman de Mamani, A., Dunham, R., Aldebot, A., Tuchman, N., and Wasserman, S. (2009). Family-focused psychoeducational programs for minorities with serious mental illness. In S. Loue and M. Sajatovic (Eds.) *Determinants of Minority Mental Health and Wellness (255-272).* New York: Springer.

Weisman de Mamani, A. G., Tuchman, N., and Duarte, E. A. (2010). Incorporating religion/spirituality into treatment for serious mental illness. *Cognitive and Behavioral Practice, 17,* 348-357.

Weisman, A., Nuechterlein, K. H., Goldstein, M. J, and Snyder, K. (1998, August). Expressed emotion, attributions, and schizophrenia symptom dimensions. *Journal of Abnormal Psychology*, *107*, 355-359. *Featured in the Clinician's Research Digest: Briefings in Behavioral Science.*

Weisman, A., Rosales, G., Kymalainen, J., and Armesto, J. (2005). Ethnicity, family cohesion, religiosity and general emotional distress in patients with schizophrenia and their relatives. *The Journal of Nervous and Mental Disease*, *193*(6), 359-368.

Weisman, A., and López, S. (1997). An attributional analysis of emotional reactions to schizophrenia in Mexican and Anglo cultures. *Journal of Applied Social Psychology*, *27*, 224-245.

Weisman, A. G., López, S. R., Karno, M., and Jenkins, J. (1993). An attributional analysis of expressed emotion in Mexican-American families with schizophrenia. *Journal of Abnormal Psychology*, *102*(4), 601-606.

In: Religion
Editors: P. Bellamy and G. Montpetit

ISBN 978-1-61470-382-2
©2012 Nova Science Publishers, Inc.

Chapter 3

"DO BELIEFS REALLY HAVE SOCIETAL EFFECTS? IMPLICATIONS FOR THEORIES OF RELIGION"

Craig T. Palmer,[1] Ryan O. Begley,[1]
Kathryn Coe,[2] Ryan M. Ellsworth,[1]
and Lyle B. Steadman[3]
[1]University of Missouri
[2]Indiana University School of Medicine
[3]Arizona State University

ABSTRACT

It is typically assumed that religious beliefs have important societal effects, and that these effects include the promotion of cooperative behavior among people who hold the same religious beliefs. This chapter will argue that although there is indeed abundant evidence for an association between religion and cooperative behavior, the assumption that this societal effect is the result of religious *beliefs* is unwarranted. The chapter will first describe the problematic nature of assuming that the societal effects of religion are the result of shared religious beliefs. It will then argue that this assumption can, and should, be replaced by a focus on certain behavior, specifically talk; that is, communicating acceptance of supernatural claims. It will then describe how such talk, as a form of communication, may produce the societal effect of increased cooperation that so often is attributed to shared religious beliefs. It will then respond to criticisms of this shift from studying the societal effects of religious beliefs to the study of the societal effects of religious talk. Finally, to demonstrate the strength of this proposition, and its importance in current debates regarding religion, it will apply the theoretical issues raised in the paper to the example of asserting that the deadly societal effect of suicide bombings are caused by religious beliefs.

INTRODUCTION

It is typically assumed that religious beliefs have important societal effects, and that these effects include the promotion of cooperative behavior among people who hold the same religious beliefs (Wilson, 2002; Bulbulia, 2004; Irons, 2001; Shariff and Norenzayan, 2007; Soler, 2008; Sosis and Ruffle, 2004). This chapter will argue that although humans regularly talk about beliefs and the fact that there is indeed abundant evidence for an association between religion and cooperative behavior among people, the assumption that this societal effect is the result of religious *beliefs* is unwarranted. After first examining the nature of this assumption, we will present an alternative approach that focuses on the societal effects of certain forms of talk that appear to distinguish behavior as religious. We then respond to some of the counter-arguments that have recently been put forth against this alternative approach. Finally, we will illustrate the importance of the debate over the identifiableness of religious beliefs, and thus whether religious beliefs can be the basis of testable explanations of societal effects, using the example of suicide bombings.

THE PROBLEMATIC NATURE OF ASSUMING RELIGIOUS BELIEFS HAVE SOCIETAL EFFECTS

The study of religion has always claimed to focus on the causes and effects of religious beliefs, especially the societal effects that religious beliefs in the supernatural are claimed to have. This long-standing focus on religious belief is seen in the statement by Wells (1921) who, after referring to the similar emphasis on supernatural belief in the definitions by Plato, Kant, and

"Do Beliefs Really Have Societal Effects? Implications ..."   57

James, concluded that "regard for correct usage of the term requires that religion be defined in such a way as to include supernatural belief" (p. 275). Indeed, "Probably the most widely accepted definition of religion is something like 'belief in the supernatural.'" (Steadman and Palmer 2008, p.9; see also Steadman and Palmer 1995; Steadman et al. 2009; Palmer et al. 2008). There is, however, a fundamental problem with this definition. Although someone who says "I believe in God" may believe in God, he or she may not.

The unacceptable nature of this "simplistic approach to religious belief" (Hilty, 1988, p. 243), that assumes that what people say is equivalent to what they believe, has been pointed out by numerous authors (see Hahn, 1973; Saler, 1973; Kirsch, 2004). Those who recognize this problem usually assume that it can be solved by using non-verbal behaviors to identify religious beliefs (see Boyer, 2001, p. 305; Barrett, 2004). The observation of nonverbal behaviors, however, fails to solve the problem. If a person says that he/she believes in a taboo and also follows the taboo, we still cannot assume that the behavior is a result of the belief, even though this assumption is routinely made in the supposedly scientific study of ritual taboos (see Mullen, 1969; Poggie et al., 1976; Tunstall, 1962; Poggie and Pollnac, 1988; van Ginkel, 1987; Zulaika, 1981). The flaw in this assumption is revealed in studies, such as Palmer's (1989) study of Maine lobster fishermen, that find a situation in which claims of beliefs were regularly contradicted by behavior. Some fishermen practiced taboos that they claimed not to believe in, while other fishermen did not practice taboos that they claimed they did believe in. This forces us to confront the question of whether a belief is revealed through the verbal or the nonverbal behaviors. We contend that there is no evidence that could answer this question.

Not only is there no way to definitively answer whether or not a person does or does not hold a religious belief, there is not even any way to calculate the probability that someone holds a religious belief. Empirical observations could determine the frequency with which the statement "I believe in God" is followed by going to church, or giving to a charity. These results would not, however, provide a probability that the individual does or does not believe in God. Without a way to identify the presence or absence of religious beliefs, all hypotheses about the societal effects of such beliefs must be deemed untestable. Thus, we now describe an alternative approach that focuses on the societal effects of religious behavior instead of alleged religious beliefs.

AN ALTERNATIVE APPROACH: STUDYING THE SOCIETAL EFFECTS OF RELIGIOUS BEHAVIOR

Although religious beliefs cannot be identified, talk about the supernatural is identifiable. Thus, the societal effects of such talk can be scientifically studied. Toward this end, Steadman and Palmer (2008) asked ". . . exactly what is the talk that distinguishes behavior as religious?" (p. 15) They went on to state, "Although a claim of the existence of something unidentifiable by the senses appears necessary for behavior to be distinguished as religious, such a claim alone is not sufficient" (p. 15). This is because some acts of uttering supernatural claims may be taken as something other than religious, for example an indication of mental illness. Thus, they propose ". . . that religious behavior is distinguished, and hence can be defined as, the *communicated acceptance of a supernatural claim*" (p. 16).

Steadman and Palmer (2008) then put forth a hypothesis about why this particular form of communication has the societal effect of promoting cooperation between the individuals communicating acceptance of the supernatural claim and the one(s) asserting the claim. The first part of this hypothesis states that

> The explicit, communicated acceptance of a claim that cannot be verified by the senses communicates *a willingness to suspend skepticism*, to suspend the critical use of the senses to examine the accuracy of an assertion. To communicate acceptance of a claim whose truth cannot be demonstrated communicates *a willingness to accept another person's influence nonskeptically*, without regard to one's own senses." (p. 40; emphasis in original)

They then propose that this is why "the most significant effect of religion, the effect that can account for its persistence through time, is that it encourages 'close' kinship behavior between either distant kinsmen or, more recently (in the last few thousand years), people said to be like kinsmen" (Steadman and Palmer 2008, p. 44).

Given the enormous implications of this argument about the identifiability of religious beliefs for the future of the scientific study of religion, it is not surprising that it has received rebuttals. We now examine, and respond to, the two most detailed responses to this argument.

RESPONSES TO STEADMAN AND PALMER

The following two counterarguments to the position just presented argue that the need for shifting the study of religion from the study of religious beliefs to the study of certain talk is not needed because religious beliefs actually can be identified and studied scientifically.

Dominick Johnson

We start with the review of Steadman and Palmer (SP) (2008) by Dominick Johnson (2009). In this review, Johnson (2009) states that:

> When one considers the big picture, SP's claim that science in general cannot study phenomena that are beyond the human senses is clearly wrong. Otherwise, we would put out of work physicists who study dark matter or engineers who make infrared lights. Evolutionary biologists cannot "see" natural selection either, but it hardly prevents us (or SP) from studying it. As long as there are tools to test difficult concepts, they are open to scientific enquiry. The human senses are obviously limited, but it does not mean that we cannot study phenomena that lie beyond them. We have been successfully doing so for centuries. (p. 226)

Interestingly, Johnson actually agrees with Steadman and Palmer that to be scientifically acceptable, hypotheses (or what he calls "concepts") must be empirically testable. Leaving aside the fact that natural selection has been observed in quickly reproducing species, Johnson attempts to avoid agreeing with Steadman and Palmer, by constructing a straw man, arguing that they suggest that science cannot study phenomena beyond the human senses *unaided* (without the use of "tools"). Of course, it is the case that science often uses instruments, which, among other uses, can amplify the human senses. Because a cell is invisible to the naked eye, for instance, it does not mean that the use of a microscope cannot make it visible, and thus, subject to scientific inquiry. To use Johnson's own examples, engineers who make infrared lights can rest assured such light, though it falls outside of the visible spectrum, is observable by means of images created through the use of instruments (e.g., night vision devices; thermal imaging), which allow for verification by the human senses. The only relevant question here, however, is whether "tools" exist to empirically test who does or does not hold certain religious beliefs (e.g., whether or not one believes in God)?

An affirmative answer to the previous question is all that is needed to falsify the Steadman and Palmer position, but Johnson (2009) fails to provide such an answer, neither in his discussion of infrared lights nor in his section on the "importance of cognition" (p. 226). This is evidently because Johnson cannot state how cognitive psychology, even when combined with brain imaging or other physiological tests, allows its researchers to identify, for instance, who does and does not believe in God. This is because cognitive psychology studies patterns of behavior, usually in carefully controlled environments, in order to identify correlations between specific environmental stimuli and specific behaviors. The reason the methods of cognitive psychology have been unable to identify who does or does not hold a religious belief is that they have failed to identify correlations between identifiable behaviors and identifiable stimuli that would be produced by a "believing brain," but not produced by a "non-believing brain." This is because every conceivable pattern of behavior, such as saying "I believe in God," or "I do not believe in God," going to church, wearing a cross, following a taboo, or even choosing to be killed instead of publicly renouncing one's belief, could be the product of either a believing brain or a non-believing brain.

The failure to find a way to identify the people with the believing brains also means that experiments purported to study correlations between believing brains and certain physiological aspects of the brain (measured through imaging, chemical analysis, etc.) do not actually include the claimed "belief/non-belief" variable. What is actually being studied is a correlation between some behavior (e.g., saying "I believe in God;" going to church; saying "religion is very important") and brain physiology.

Unable to state how to identify religious beliefs, Johnson (2009) can only assert that "whatever problems the various existing theories of religion may have, it seems implausible that such diverse theories would all fall because of exactly the same flaw" (p. 226). This is a hollow argument. If each theory of religion, diverse as they may be, makes the same basic assumption (that religion is defined as belief in the supernatural), and this assumption is false, unfounded or untestable, then the only conclusion that can be reached is that they all fall under the weight of the same criticism. The fact that Johnson would find such a universal flaw inconvenient for his own explanation of religion and career does not in itself make the reality of the flaw "implausible."

Benjamin Purzcki et al.

Like Johnson, Purzycki et al. (2008) grasp what is at stake concerning the Steadman and Palmer argument, in this case describing how acceptance of the SP position will lead to an "overhaul of the study of religion" (p. 629). Also like Johnson, Purzycki et al. proclaim with the utmost confidence that SP are wrong about the unidentifiability of religious beliefs: "The evolutionary and cognitive study of religion is flourishing, and research programs examining the structure and retention of religious *beliefs* and behaviors are producing novel and exciting results at a remarkable pace" (p. 629; our emphasis). Purzycki et al. build upon this statement with the assertion that the SP argument to exclude untestable assertions about religious beliefs from the scientific study of religion places "an unnecessary limitation that ignores *vital* progress in cognitive science" (p. 629; our emphasis). Indeed, they even use an exclamation point when they praise the power of the "scientific study of religious beliefs!" (p. 630) As is the case in Johnson's review, all that remains to be provided is a description of exactly how to tell whether someone, say S or P for example, believes in God or does not believe in God.

Their answer, such as it is, comes later in the review, but only after they make a number of statements that raise serious questions about just how certain they are about their own argument that SP are wrong. For example, Purzycki et al. state "While the question of whether or not people actually believe their religious claims is an interesting one, none of the current research programs examining the evolution of religion rely on this, contrary to SandP's claim" (p. 630). This statement leads us to wonder why the question of identifying whether or not someone actually believes in God is "interesting" if there are well known ways to easily determine the answer? Further, if none of the evolutionary explanations of religion rely on knowing whether or not someone actually believes in God, why would acceptance of the SP argument lead to an overhaul of the study of religion?

Leaving such issues unresolved, Purzycki et al. reverse their position again, and reassert that the study of religious belief is both possible and solves such an important problem as to warrant another exclamation point:

> More importantly, we have evidence of the inconsistency of *stated* religious beliefs and *actual* cognitions of religious concepts, meaning that not only are there at least two levels of processing for such propositions, but also that a science of religious beliefs can detail this very problem!" (p. 630)

Despite the certainty suggested by the exclamation point, if there really is a way to test if a person's *stated* religious beliefs are or are not the same as their *actual* beliefs, it would be simple enough to just describe what that test would entail. Further, if such a test actually existed there would be no need to talk about "cognitions of religious concepts" instead of beliefs, and "detailing a problem" instead of testing a claim about those beliefs.

Purzycki et al.'s own word choice is also inconsistent with their supposed certainty regarding their ability to identify religious beliefs. For example, they write "Skepticism is a cognitive act which *may* inform behavior (e.g., "He's a fraud! Charlatan!") . . ." (p. 630; our emphasis). The use of the word "may" implies an uncertainty about whether or not the identifiable act of saying "He's a fraud! Charlatan!" is or is not the result of disbelief. If they have ways of telling whether or not someone believes in God by their claims to believe or not believe in God, why don't they apply them to their own example and state that "Skepticism (i.e., disbelief) is a cognitive act which can be identified whenever someone says "He's a fraud! Charlatan!"? The answer, we suggest, is that both a believer and a disbeliever could say "He's a fraud! Charlatan!" just as both a believer and a disbeliever could say "God exists" or "God does not exist."

Purzycki et al.'s own apparent *inability* to identify what people believe is also revealed in their statement that "In a Christian service (C), for instance, fermented grape juice (X) represents the blood of Christ (Y). Surely there is variation in how individual congregants conceive of this, yet all participate in rites to partake in consuming the 'blood of Christ'" (p. 630). Here, Purzycki et al. assert that people saying the same words "blood of Christ" "surely" have different ways of conceiving of this (i.e., different beliefs). If indeed Purzycki et al. were "sure" of this assertion, they could state exactly which individuals conceived of this in which way (i.e., which person had which beliefs). Instead of demonstrating such an ability, Purzycki et al. adopt the exact approach championed by SP and state that the identifiable talk, not the beliefs, would produce identifiable consequences "Violating the expectations congregants have in others' participation (e.g., loudly proclaiming that the wine tastes cheap) would likely result in scolding or sanction." (p. 630).

Purzycki et al. (2008) finally reveal their ace in the hole on page 631, when they proclaim that experimental studies can identify religious beliefs through the behaviors they cause: "In experimental studies, believing that supernatural agents are watching has been shown to change the way subjects make moral decisions (Bering, McLeod, and Shackelford, 2005) and influence

"Do Beliefs Really Have Societal Effects? Implications ..." 63

conduct in economic transactions (Shariff and Norenzayan, 2007)." Once again, the problem in these studies is that "belief in supernatural agents" is only assumed, not demonstrated. The identifiable variables in the experiment do not include anyone's beliefs, but instead only consist of someone *telling* a subject there are supernatural agents watching them and the subject's subsequent behaviors. It cannot be shown that the participants in the study actually believe that a supernatural agent was watching them. To falsify SP's position it is necessary to demonstrate that the talk about the presence of watchful supernatural agents could *only* have a particular influence on the behavior of someone who believed the supernatural claim. As Steadman and Palmer argue, supernatural claims can be a form of powerful communication that influences people's behavior because it provides indications of likely future consequences of behavior. In this example, telling participants that a supernatural agent is observing them is likely to increase moral behavior because participants have been reminded of the potential negative consequences of immoral behavior – participants are simply behaving according to a learned association between breaking the rules and the consequences of doing so. It is no different than the societal effects of a warning sign of any kind. The ironic aspect of this supposed criticism of the SP position is the fact that identifying correlations between talk and other behavior is exactly what SP argued should be studied. Indeed, SP's entire explanation of religion is based upon the argument that communicating acceptance of supernatural talk influences behavior.

Instead of acknowledging that the SP position is perfectly consistent with what is actually observed in such experiments, Purzycki et al. criticize SP for ignoring the literature that shows "The distinction between what people *claim* they believe (theologically correct) and what people *actually* think . . . [i.e., peoples "real-time beliefs"]" (p. 632). However, instead of showing "real-time beliefs," the studies described in this literature merely show the previously discussed point that there are often inconsistencies between what people say they believe and their other behavior. Again, what is needed is identification of exactly what behavior could be performed if and only if someone believed in God (or someone who did not believe in God). If such a behavior is known, it would only take one sentence to state what it is. Instead of providing such a sentence, Purzycki et al. (2008) simply assert that they have now proved their point: "That we can test for differences between stated beliefs and real-time computations *and* the influence of beliefs on behaviors suggests that we should not abandon the focus on our evolved minds" (p. 631; emphasis in original). We agree that our evolved minds, or at least brains, should be studied. However, we can only scientifically study things we can empirically identify, and at this point in time religious beliefs do not fall into that category.

A SPECIFIC EXAMPLE: RELIGIOUS BELIEF AS A CAUSE OF SUICIDE BOMBINGS AND SUPPORT FOR SUICIDE ATTACKS

Immediately after the attacks of September 11, 2001, the acts were blamed on the religious beliefs of Islamic extremists (Dawkins, 2001; 2003). Since that time a string of articles have continued to be published on the topic of suicide attacks from an evolutionary psychological perspective (Atran, 2003; 2006; Ginges, Hansen, and Norenzayan, 2009; 2010; Liddle, Machluf, and Shackelford, 2010; Liddle, Bush, and Shackelford, in press). Given the striking increase in the frequency of suicide attacks in the last few decades (Atran, 2004), it is certainly a problem deserving serious attention from behavioral scientists. As first argued by Palmer (2003), many, if not all, of these efforts at understanding suicide terrorism contain the fundamental flaw we have discussed in this paper: the untestable assumption that the suicide attacks are a societal effect of religious belief.

This role of untestable assumptions about religious belief is most clearly seen in the *"the religious-belief hypothesis"* (Ginges et al., 2009, p. 224), which proposes that "devotion to religious belief might facilitate support for suicide attacks (Harris, 2005) because certain religious beliefs denigrate people of other faiths (Dawkins, 2003), promise martyrs the reward of an afterlife (Hoffman, 1998), or contain narrative traditions that glorify acts of combative martyrdom (Gambetta, 2005; Rapoport, 1990), such as suicide attacks" (ibid.). This hypothesis is contrasted with a second hypothesis referred to as *"the coalitional-commitment hypothesis,"* which suggests that "religion's relationship to suicide attacks may be independent from belief *per se*, but derive instead from religion's ability to enhance commitment to coalitional identities (Atran, 2003; Irons, 2001) and within-group cooperation (Norenzayan and Shariff, 2008; Sosis and Ruffle, 2003) or parochial altruism (Choi and Bowles, 2007) via collective ritual" (ibid.). However, this second hypothesis also contains untestable assumptions about who does, or does not, hold certain religious beliefs.

In two studies of Palestinian Muslims living in the West Bank and Gaza, and using prayer frequency as an index of "religious devotion", itself a proxy

"Do Beliefs Really Have Societal Effects? Implications ..." 65

for religious beliefs, and frequency of mosque attendance as an index of coalitional commitment, Ginges et al. (2009) found that mosque attendance, but not frequency of prayer, was a significant positive predictor of support for suicide attacks. As the results of all four studies carried out by Ginges et al. (2009) found support for the coalitional-commitment hypothesis, but not the religious-belief hypothesis, the authors conclude that "the relationship between religion and support for suicide attacks is real, but is orthogonal to devotion to particular religious belief, or indeed religious belief in general", and that "[i]t appears that the association between religion and suicide attacks is a function of collective religious activities that facilitate popular support for suicide attacks and parochial altruism more generally" (p. 230).

In a commentary on these studies, Liddle et al. (2010) accuse Ginges et al. (2009) of premature dismissal of the religious-belief hypothesis, claiming that their testing of the hypothesis was conceptually flawed because Ginges et al. did not examine actual beliefs held by participants, but only devotion to some unspecified set of religious beliefs as measured by prayer frequency. Liddle et al. argue that a proper test of the relationship between religious beliefs and support for suicide terrorism would involve assessing *particular* beliefs, such as belief in an afterlife (p. 345). In a published rejoinder to the commentary of Liddle et al. (2010), Ginges et al. (2010) defend their method of testing the religious-belief hypothesis, claiming that devotion to religion entails believing a core set of beliefs, and thus a measure of devotion to Islam should account for the influence of the specific beliefs mentioned by Liddle et al. (2010) as potentially important in explaining support for suicide attacks.

Rather than go into any more detail of the debate between these two groups of authors, we wish here to point out that *all* of them make unverifiable claims regarding methods for investigating the role of religious belief in explaining support for suicide terrorism. In their studies, what Ginges et al. (2009) were measuring by using prayer frequency as an index of religious devotion was not the beliefs held by participants, but rather the association between participants' reported frequency of prayer and their responses to a question regarding how important religion is in their lives. Thus, Liddle et al. (2010) are correct in their claim that Ginges et al. did not conduct a proper test of the religious-belief hypothesis. However, Liddle et al.'s suggestions for how to go about providing justifiable confirmation or disconfirmation of the hypothesis are equally flawed. This is because what Liddle et al. would actually be empirically investigating is not the specific beliefs held by individuals and the relation of these specific beliefs to support for suicide attacks, but rather the association between participants' *statements* and their support, or nonsupport, for suicide attacks.

Liddle et al. (in press), remarking on the state of affairs with regard to the status of the religious-belief hypothesis, state that "[a]s it stands, the direct link between specific religious beliefs and one's willingness to engage in suicide terrorism is open for debate, since there is no evidence strong enough to effectively confirm or disconfirm this hypothesis." What is puzzling about this statement is that in the very same paper Liddle et al. (in press) make the unwarranted claim that "suicide terrorism is so often performed by individuals with strong religious beliefs." Liddle et al. are partly correct in their assessment of the evidence bearing on the religious-belief hypothesis; the whole truth, however, is that *there is no evidence at all pertaining to the influence of religious beliefs on behavior.* Assigning causality of behavior to putative underlying beliefs amounts to little more than speculation and assumptions. Speculations and assumptions are not evidence that can be be brought to bear on hypotheses of the causal role of belief.

Despite the fundamental flaw of assumptions about belief, some aspects of the work of Ginges et al. (2009), and Liddle et al. (in press) are potentially promising avenues of research contributing to understanding of religion's association with behaviors such as suicide terrorism. The coalitionary-commitment hypothesis of Ginges et al. (2009), stripped of its assumptions about belief, might be productively combined with the ideas of Liddle et al. (in press) concerning the possibility that evolved inclusive fitness mechanisms designed to benefit kin might be manipulated by involvement with religious sects composed of "fictive kin."

Several researchers have noted the power of religious behavior's ability to promote commitment and cooperation between co-religionists (e.g., Bulbulia, 2004; Irons, 2001; Shariff and Norenzayan, 2007; Soler, 2008; Sosis and Ruffle, 2004). Indeed, the cooperation-enhancing and promoting effects of religious behavior are arguably the reason that religious behavior was favored by selection (see Steadman and Palmer, 2008).

According to the evolutionary scenario first laid out by Steadman and Palmer (1995), religious behavior was favored by natural selection because it promoted the descendant-leaving success of ancestral individuals through traditions that encouraged cooperation between individuals who communicated acceptance of the same supernatural claims. Steadman and Palmer (2008) propose that ancestor worship was the primordial form of religious behavior; thus, those communicating acceptance of the same supernatural claims would have been co-descendants of the same ancestors, and thus relatives. It was the mutually beneficial cooperation between descendant relatives that increased the descendant-leaving success of the ancestors who were successful at transmitting these traditions to descendants (who would themselves become ancestors). Religious behavior was originally a kin-centered and kin-directed behavior.

The cooperation-enhancing effects of religion continue to operate today, although not confined to the kin-based social contexts in which it evolved. Modern world religions, although not primarily kin-centered or kin-directed, involve a striking amount of kin terminology—creating communities of fictive kin—and encourage kinship-like behavior, including sacrifice and altruism, toward others identified as co-religionists (Batson, 1983; Qirko, 2004; Steadman and Palmer, 2008). Thus, it is entirely plausible that the cooperation- and commitment-enhancing qualities of modern religions result from manipulation of inclusive-fitness mechanisms (Liddle et al., in press), causing individuals to treat others as if they were kin—including, in some circumstances, sacrificing one's life for the perceived benefit of others. Rather than debating the existence or nonexistence of certain beliefs, research should be concentrated on the societal effects of religious talk, and how such talk might influence individuals to support, and in some cases commit, such devastating acts of violence.

CONCLUSION

Perhaps the most important lesson to be learned from the counter arguments put forth in response to the claim that religious beliefs cannot be identified is the necessity of clear language in order to fairly evaluate the question of whether or not religious beliefs can or cannot be studied scientifically. Thus far, the counter arguments have lacked such clarity. For example, consider the ambiguity of the assertion that "entertaining particular religious beliefs . . . radically alters" other behaviors. Does "entertaining particular religious beliefs" refer to what people say or what they believe? In a debate focused on the potential difference between stated religious beliefs and actual religious beliefs, avoiding such ambiguity is obviously essential. Even more striking is Purzycki et al.'s (2008) wording of the following assertion:

> Bulbulia (2004; 2008) and Sosis (2003) both argue that the presence of religious post-mortem delayed payoffs (e.g., blissful afterlife, honor, etc.) predicts prosocial behavior, and various studies have supported this

prediction (Bulbulia and Mahoney, 2008; Johnson, 2005; Johnson and Kruger, 2004; Soler, 2008; Sosis and Alcorta, 2008; Sosis and Bressler, 2003; Sosis, Kress, and Boster, 2007). (p. 631).

Here the authors are not asserting that it is the presence of unidentifiable religious beliefs in an afterlife that can scientifically explain social behavior, they assert that it is the actual presence of a "blissful afterlife" that "predicts prosocial behavior" (p. 631).

Studies that purport to measure some behavior as a proxy for belief are merely examining are the effects of one behavior on another behavior. As such, these studies cannot possibly be proven to have demonstrated any effect of belief on behavior. Although the arguments made in this paper have, for the past several years, fallen on largely deaf or obstinate ears, researchers of religion need to carefully consider that behavior is not always a transparent window into the mind (Palmer and Steadman, 2004; Palmer, Coe, and Wadley, 2008; Steadman and Palmer, 1995). They need to take seriously the question of whether belief can be given a causal role in behavior with any degree of certainty for any individual. The study of religion, when focused on or concerned with belief, is a futile endeavor if one seeks scientific validity.

As it stands, we must conclude that there is currently no method by which to empirically verify beliefs, much less assign them a causal role in any given instance of behavior. Until a time comes when religious beliefs can be empirically identified, researchers purporting to conduct scientific studies should refrain from using what amounts to nothing more than assumption and speculation to build theory and "test" hypotheses. Further, even if a satisfactory "religious belief" test were invented, it would still mean that every assertion of religious belief made without the supporting evidence of the test (which would include every assertion of religious belief that has thus far been made) would have been made without supporting scientific evidence.

REFERENCES

Alexander, R. D. (1979). *Darwinism and human affairs.* Seattle, WA: University of Washington Press.

Atran, S. (2003). Genesis of suicide terrorism. *Science, 299,* 1534-1539.

Atran, S. (2004). Mishandling suicide terrorism. *The Washington Quarterly, 27,* 67-90

Atran, S. (2006). The moral logic and growth of suicide terrorism. *The Washington Quarterly, 29,* 127-147.

Barkow, J. H., Cosmides, L., and Tooby, J. (Eds.) (1992). *The adapted mind: evolutionary psychology and the generation of culture.* Oxford: Oxford University Press.

Batson, C. D. (1983). Sociobiology and the role of religion in promoting prosocial behavior: an alternative view. *Journal of Personality and Social Psychology, 45,* 1380-1385.

Bulbulia, J. (2004). Religious costs as adaptations that signal altruistic intent. *Evolution and Cognition, 10,* 19-42.

Buss, D. M. (Ed.) (2005). *The handbook of evolutionary psychology.* Hoboken, NJ: John Wiley and Sons, Inc.

Crawford, C. B., and Krebs, J. L. (Eds.) (1998). *Handbook of evolutionary psychology: ideas, issues, and applications.* Mahweh, NJ: Lawrence Erlbaum Associates.

Dawkins, R. (2001, September 15) Religion's misguided missiles: Promise a young man that death is not the end and he will willingly cause disaster. *The Guardian.* Retrieved from http://www.guardian.co.uk/world/2001/sep/15/september11.politicsphilosophyandsociety1.

Dawkins, R. (2003). *A devils chaplain: reflections on hope, lies, science, and love.* Boston: Houghton Mifflin.

Ginges, J., Hansen, I., and Norenzayan, A. (2009). Religion and support for suicide attacks. *Psychological Science, 20,* 224-230.

Ginges, J., Hansen, I., and Norenzayan, A. (2010). Religious belief, coalitionary commitment, and support for suicide attacks. *Evolutionary Psychology, 8,* 346-349.

Johnson, D. (2009) Beyond belief – A review of "The Supernatural and Natural Selection: Religion and Evolutionary Success" *Evolution and Human Behavior,* 30, 225-228

Irons, W. (2001). Religion as hard-to-fake sign of commitment. In R. Nesse (Ed.), *Evolution and the capacity for commitment* (pp. 292-309). New York: Russell Sage Foundation.

Liddle, J. R., Machluf, K., and Shackelford, T. K. (2010). Understanding suicide terrorism: premature dismissal of the religious-belief hypothesis. *Evolutionary Psychology, 8,* 343-345.

Liddle, J. R., Bush, L. S., and Shackelford, T. K. (in press). An introduction to evolutionary psychology and its application to suicide terrorism. *Behavioral Sciences of Terrorism and Political Aggression.*

Palmer, C. T. (1989). The ritual taboos of fishermen: an alternative explanation. *Maritime Anthropological Studies, 2,* 59-68.

Palmer, C. T. (2003). "War, Terrorism, and Religion." Invited Panelist, New England Institute, Conference on Religion and Evolutionary Psychology. August, 2003.

Palmer, C. T., Coe, K., and Wadley, R. L. (2008). In belief we trust: why anthropologists abandon skepticism when they hear claims about supernatural beliefs. *Skeptic Magazine, 14,* 60-65.

Palmer, C. T., Ellsworth, R. M., and Steadman. (2009). Talk and tradition: why the least interesting components of religion may be the most evolutionarily important. In E. Voland, and W. Schiefenhövel (Eds.), *The biological evolution of religious mind and behavior* (pp. 105-116). New York: Springer.

Palmer, C. T., and Steadman, L. B. (2004). With or without belief: a new approach to the definition and explanation of religion. *Evolution and Cognition, 10,* 138-147.

Purzycki, B., Swartwout, P. and Sosis, R. (2008). Searching for Darwin: Metaphor, Collusion, and Natural Selection: Review of "The Supernatural and Natural Selection" by Lyle Steadman and Craig Palmer. *Evolutionary Psychology, 6,* 628-636.

Qirko, H. (2004). Altruistic celibacy, kin-cue manipulation, and the development of religious insititutions. *Zygon, 29,* 681-706.

Shariff, A. F., and Norenzayan, A. (2007). God is watching you: priming god concepts increases prosocial behavior in an anonymous economic game. *Psychological Science, 18,* 803-808.

Soler, M. (2008). Commitment costs and cooperation: evidence from Candomble, an Afro-

Brazilian religion. In J. Bulbulia, R. Sosis, E. Harris, R. Genet, C. Genet, and K.

Wyman (Eds.), *The evolution of religion: studies, theories, and critiques* (pp. 167-174). Santa Margarita, CA: Collins Foundation Press.

Sosis, R., and Ruffle, B. J. (2004). Ideology, religion, and the evolution of cooperation: field experiments on Israeli kibbutzim. *Research in Economic Anthropology, 23,* 89-117.

Steadman, L. B., and Palmer, C. T. (1995). Religion as an identifiable traditional behavior subject to natural selection. *Journal of Social and Evolutionary Systems,18,* 149-164.

Steadman, L. B., and Palmer, C. T. (2008). *The supernatural and natural selection: the evolution of religion.* Herndon, VA: Paradigm Publishers.

Steadman, L. B., Palmer, C. T., and Ellsworth, R. M. (2009). Towards a testable definition of religious behavior. In J. Feierman (Ed.), *The biology of religious behavior* (pp. 20-35). Santa Barbara, CA: Praeger.

Wells, W. R. 1921. Is Supernaturalistic Belief Essential in a Definition of Religion? *Journal of Philosophy*, 18, 269–74.

In: Religion
Editors: P. Bellamy and G. Montpetit

ISBN 978-1-61470-382-2
©2012 Nova Science Publishers, Inc.

Chapter 4

SPIRITUALITY, SECULARITY, AND WELL-BEING

Karen Hwang

Department of Outcomes Research, Kessler Foundation Research
Center, University of Medicine and Dentistry of New Jersey,
West Orange, New Jersey, USA

ABSTRACT

The last few years have seen a great deal of research on the association between religion, spirituality and medical outcomes. This research has not been without controversy however, in terms of methodological and analytical issues. One particular under-researched area concerns the increasingly visible sub-population of individuals who identify themselves as "nonreligious," a group that includes atheists, agnostics and individuals who believe in god(s) but do not identify with one particular religion. As a result, relatively little is known about the health and quality of life within this particular group, not only in comparison to religious individuals, but also within nonreligious populations as well. The proposed chapter plans to cover three major issues: 1) a brief summary of the controversies concerning religion-health research; 2) reasons for the neglect of nonreligious individuals to date and reasons for increasing attention to them; and 3) what the current research does indicate about the nonreligious, particularly about affirmative atheists (as opposed to simply "nonreligious").

SUMMARY OF RESEARCH ON RELIGION/SPIRITUALITY AND QOL

The topic of religion and quality of life (QOL) has been the focus of much empirical research, particularly within the past two decades. While findings remain highly controversial, the majority of these studies have reported a "small, robust" association between religiosity and/or spirituality (R/S) and various indicators of physical and psychological well-being (Waite and Lehrer, 2003). For instance, regular church goers were generally happier (Ferris, 2002) and healthier (Waite and Lehrer, 2003). Positive associations between religious practices and physical and mental health have been documented among population samples of adolescents (Wong, Rew, and Slaikeu, 2006), veterans (Chang, Skinner, and Boehmer, 2001), and medically compromised older adults (Koenig, 2004; Yohannes, Koenig, Baldwin, and Connolly, 2008). Religious practices are thought to enhance recovery from coronary transplant (Harris, et al. 1995); cancer (Laubmeier, Zakowski, and Bair, 2004; Nairn andMerluzzi, 2003), vision loss (Brennan, 2004), spinal cord injury (Johnstone, Glass and Oliver 2007; Matheis, Tulsky, and Matheis, 2006), and HIV (Ironson and Hayward, 2008; Vance, Struzick, and Raper, 2008), among others (see Dyer, 2007; Jantos and Kiat, 2007; McCullough, et al,. 2000; McCullough and Koenig, 2001; Pesut, et al., 2008).

However, this link has not received universal empirical support (Blumenthal, et al., 2007; Powell, Shahabi, and Thoresen, 2003; Stefanek, McDonald, and Hess, 2006; Thuné-Boyle, et al, 2006). Sloan and Bagliella (2002) reviewed 266 studies gathered via MEDLINE search. Of the articles that related directly to religion and health, the majority contained significant inaccuracies in representation and methodology, including construct validity (using church attendance as a proxy variable for religiosity); sampling difficulty (non-equivalent subject samples or unequal treatment procedure); and problematic analyses (inferring causality from correlation, only reporting positive effects). These problems, the authors argue, severely compromised the validity of the findings.

Other studies have suggested that QOL is not related to religiosity but spirituality. Ho and Ho (2007) have argued that atheism does not exclude spirituality. Even in largely atheistic countries, such as mainland China, people still considered spirituality to be a positive, meaningful value. Although the word "spiritual" is traditionally associated with religious experience (and for that reason objectionable to many secularists), the word itself is difficult to define. Interpretations range from "search for the sacred," (which may occur outside of an established religious tradition) (Pargament, 1999) to "subjective self-fulfillment" (Sheldrake, 2007) and has often been conflated with elements of physical and mental health to the point where they are no longer separate and discrete domains (Koenig, 2008). It is for this reason that conducting research in the area of spirituality and health research is difficult.

Of course, there is no empirical support for the implication that certain essential elements of human experience are limited exclusively to the religious or "spiritual". Norman (2006) describes five such distinct kinds of experiences: 1) the experience of the moral 'ought'; 2) the experience of beauty; 3) the experience of meaning conferred by stories; 4) the experience of otherness and transcendence; and 5) the experience of vulnerability and fragility (p. 474). He argues that these are meaningful components of any human life, and contests claims by some theists that such experiences are by nature essentially religious and so the nonbeliever's participation in these experiences is in some way lacking.

DIFFERENCES WITHIN THE NONRELIGIOUS POPULATION

Although much media attention has focused on the so-called "New Atheists" (most notably such authors as Richard Dawkins, Christopher Hitchens, et al), these individuals make up only a small subset of the nonreligious population. Individuals self-identifying as "nonreligious" can range in beliefs, from hardcore atheists to believers who choose not to affiliate with any identified religious groups to those describing themselves as "not religious but spiritual", and everything in between.

The American Religious Identification Survey (Kosmin et al, 2008) describes religious "nones" as a "diverse group of people who do not identify with any of the myriad of religious options in the American religious marketplace" (Kosmin et al 2008, p.i). This group has increased in number from 14 to 34 million adults between 1990 and 2008. Individuals self-identifying as "atheist" comprised only 9% of the population, in contrast to agnostics (40%), deists (21%), and unchurched believers (21%). Demographically, "nones" are disproportionately male (60%), young (30% are under age 30) and are more likely to be single and never married (largely due to their young ages). Nones are also more likely to be Caucasian non-Hispanic, although they are becoming increasingly similar to the general U.S. population and more highly educated. Using data from the 2005 Baylor University Religion Survey, Baker and Smith (2009) found that nonreligious individuals were also more likely to have been raised by nonreligious parents, less likely to have attended religious services as children and more likely to associate with nonreligious peer groups and marry nonreligious spouses.

ATHEISTS, DEFINITION OF, DEMOGRAPHIC CHARACTERISTICS

At its most basic level, the word atheist refers to a person who does not believe in God or gods. This is not necessarily to say that the individual is actively opposed to God or religion, although a certain subgroup of atheists (the so-called "New Atheists ") do hold this view. According to Michael Martin's (1980) taxonomy, variations among the godless range from strong or explicit atheism, the explicit denial of any gods, to weak or implicit atheism (sometimes regarded as default atheism), a simple lack of belief. An atheist may accept the idea of God as a psychological or metaphorical construct, without independent existence. A related position, agnosticism, does not refer to the belief or disbelief in a god, but to the impossibility of ever answering the question.

It is often difficult to determine the actual numbers of atheists in the world, mainly because some nonbelievers reject the word "atheist" and instead opt for designations such as freethinkers, secular humanists or "Brights". According to Zuckerman (2007), the number of nonbelievers worldwide is estimated to be between 500 million and 750 million. The greatest concentrations of atheists live in richer, industrialized democracies such as Japan, Canada and most of Europe, and are lowest in South America, Africa and the Middle East. Among developed countries, the US remains something of an anomaly, where only 6-12% of the population does not believe in god (Kosmin and Keysar, 2009). It is difficult to pinpoint future population distributions, but there appear to be two concurrent trends: rates of belief within developed countries are falling, while the numbers of religious believers worldwide is increasing, due largely to higher birth rates in highly religious countries (Zuckerman, 2007).

Within the United States population, results from the American Religious Identification Survey (Kosmin and Keysar, 2009), a recent nationally representative telephone survey of more than 50,000 respondents, estimates the percentage of American adults who are without a belief in god or gods to be about 2.3% (compared with 31%-44% in Britain; see Zuckerman 2006). An additional 10% of the American population are hard ("there is no way to know"; 4.3%) and soft ("I'm not sure"; 5.7%) agnostics. Another 12.1% are deists or hold a New Age pantheistic notion of god (i.e., "There is a higher power but no personal God. Importantly, only 21% of those who are atheists by belief self-identify as atheists when asked "What is your religious affiliation, if any?" The balance self-identify as: no religion or none (59%), agnostic (5.7%), or report a religious affiliation (14.3%).

WHAT WE DO KNOW ABOUT ATHEISTS?

American atheists (by belief) are predominantly male (77%) and young (58.8% are under the age of 49). In part due to their youth, 27% are single and 9.8% have no more than a high school education. Compared with the general adult population, Atheists are less likely to be African American and more likely to be Asian or Caucasian (non-Hispanic). A majority of atheists identify as political independents and are less likely to identify as Republicans compared to the general population, and more likely to live in the West and Northeast as opposed to the South. Smaller studies have found parallel demographic patterns (James and Wells, 2002; Beit-Hallahmi and Argyle, 1997; Hayes, 2000; Bainbridge, 2005; Jenks, 1986). Among a random sample of 1,021 American adult individuals who self-identified as religious nones, those who were atheists (by belief) were better educated, wealthier, more likely to be white, male, and older than other individuals with no religious affiliation (Hunsberger and Altemeyer 2006; Kosmin and Keysar, 2009). The greatest proportion of respondents reported little or no religious emphasis during their childhoods. About one quarter had experienced at least a moderate religious influence in their homes. Compared to religious believers, atheists are less dogmatic, less authoritarian (Galen 2009xxx), and less likely to be obese (Cline and Ferraro 2006).

FACTORS AFFECTING QOL AND ATHEISTS

Conversion and Apostasy

Apostasy can be defined as the moving away from a religious belief, sometimes referred to as "de-conversion". While there is a substantial body of research describing the phenomenon of religious conversion (see Paloutzian, Richardson, and Rambo, 1999; Halama, 2005; Jindra, 2008), much less information exists on the topic of religious apostasy. Of the few investigations specifically focused on apostasy, there is evidence that apostates tend to have higher levels of education and to have attended elite colleges (Zelan, 1968). Apostates are also more likely to have an intellectual orientation (Hunsberger and Brown, 1984) and prefer academic careers (Zelan, 1968) compared to religious non-apostates. Apostates also show high levels of intellectual autonomy, complex thought (Jindra, 2008) and personality trait "openness to experience" (Shermer, 1999).

There is also some evidence that home life is a relatively important influence in religious development (Hunsberger and Brown, 1984. The Catholic scholar Paul Vitz (1999) has proposed that atheism is a result of disrupted attachment, particularly from absent or deceased fathers; however, there is no empirical evidence to support this theory. Parental conflict is often associated with the rejection of familial religion (Galen 2009), although one should be cautious not to assume a causal relationship between the two. Indeed, apostates often experience a loss of familial approval and support as a result of their rejection of their family's religion (Altemeier and Hunsberger, 1997).

Some investigators (Exline et al, 2011) have proposed that, at least for some atheists, rejection of religion results from an angry withdrawal from god, largely shaped by problematic attachment relationships with parents. Samples of atheists recruited from the 1) general US population; 2) college undergraduates; 3) people adjusting to bereavement and 4) cancer were asked about their reactions to a hypothetical god, while comparison groups of religious believers completed similar measures regarding their relationships with god. Results showed that some atheists held images of God as extremely cruel and responsible for negative events. These so-called "angry atheists" were more likely to have difficulty adjusting to bereavement and cancer, and exhibited more psychological problems than either believers or simple unbelievers. However, the reported results may have resulted from a methodological artifice: while religious believers were asked to describe

Spirituality, Secularity, and Well-Being   79

relationships with an actual god, atheists were asked to react to a hypothetical god, two entirely different tasks involving different cognitive processes.

Discrimination

Attitudes toward atheists have been used as measures of religious intolerance for many years (Bloesch, Forbes and Curtis, 2004). Despite their increasing numbers in the United States population, discrimination against atheists remains high. Because of their relatively higher mean levels of education and income, atheists are not often recognized as a target of prejudice. Nevertheless, both academic studies and national polls have reported significant levels of anti-atheist prejudice in the US. A 2003 survey by the Pew forum on religion and public life reported that a majority of Americans surveyed held "mostly unfavorable" attitudes about atheists (52%, vs. only 34% "mostly favorable"). The same poll revealed that 52% of the respondents would refuse to vote for a well-qualified atheist for President. White evangelicals (63%) and African Americans (51%) indicated there were reasons why they "might not vote for an atheist if one received their party's presidential nomination". A similar Gallup poll in 2007 found that 53% of those surveyed said they would refuse to vote for an atheist for president. This represents a 5% increase from a previous survey conducted in 1999, which is (probably) outside the margin of error. Comparing the results over the past 50 years revealed that the largest drop in anti-atheism occurred between 1959 and 1978 (74%-53%) but that this figure has been hovering around 48-53% since then. In fact, in both surveys atheists were the only minority demographic for whom less than 50% of survey respondents would be willing to support for President. This was far lower than for Jewish (92%), African-American (94%), Catholic (95%), female (88%), or gay (55%) candidates. Disapproval of atheists is higher among religious conservatives; a 1995 national telephone survey conducted by the evangelical Christian Barna research group reported that 92% of born-again Christians held negative views about atheism, as opposed to 50% of non-Christians. Additionally, 47.6% of respondents also they would disapprove of their child marrying an atheist. This is also higher than for other racial or religious minorities. According to the researchers, atheists are thus a "symbolic representation of one who rejects the basis for moral solidarity and cultural membership in American society altogether."

An internet-based cross-national survey of 8200 atheists (Acaro, 2010) revealed that a majority (55%) of US respondents felt that atheists were "very stigmatized" in their culture, in stark contrast to atheists in Western Europe (3%), Australia (4%), UK (4%) and Canada (17%).

PARTICULAR STEREOTYPES OF ATHEISM AND ATHEISTS

Atheism is Immoral

One popular stereotype states that if religion and God are commonly used as the basis for individuals' moral code, then nonbelievers must also be morally unmoored. A 2008 survey of 1003 American adults conducted by the evangelical Christian Barna Group research organization found that atheists and agnostics were significantly more likely than religious persons – particularly evangelicals – to engage in such activities as "inappropriate" (i.e. premarital) sex, gambling or profanity (or were at least willing to admit to engaging in such activities), leading the authors to conclude that lacking a solid moral foundation in religious faith left individuals free to construct a "moral system based on convenience, feelings, and selfishness" (Barna, 2008). In other research, Farmer, Trapnell, and Meston (2009) found that nonreligious women reported more sexual activity than conservative religious women; the same was not found for nonreligious men.

Atheism is Anti-Religious or Anti-American

Because of the increasing profile of the so-called "New Atheists", many have assumed that atheism is anti-theistic or anti-religious. In contrast to the "New Atheists," however, most seculars are relatively neutral to religion. Many secular individuals are quite well informed about the teachings of world religions. A recent Pew Forum survey (2010) found that atheists outscored religious believers on surveys of knowledge of both biblical teachings and world religions.

In a similar vein, many Americans harbor doubts about atheists' patriotism. Although former president George H.W. Bush's alleged statement that, "No, I don't know that know that atheists should be considered as citizens, nor should they be considered patriots. This is one nation under God" is largely unverified. A well-publicized study by Edgell, Gerteis and Hartmann (2006) found that nearly 40% of a nationally representative sample of 2081 American adults felt that atheists were a group that "does not at all agree with my vision of American society". This was a greater proportion than for Muslims (26.3%), gays (22.6%) or Hispanics (20%). Other national polls from the Pew Research Group (Jones, 2007) and Newsweek (2007, cited in Cline, 2011) report that 50-62% of American voters would refuse to vote for any presidential candidate who admitted to being an atheist.

Atheism is a Result of Disrupted Attachments to Parents, Particularly Fathers

This theory was advanced by Vitz (1999), based on the idea that if religious belief functions as a symbolic representation of parental attachment, then atheism must come from a disruption of attachment, particularly paternal attachment. In his book *Faith of the Fatherless*, he supports his thesis using biographical accounts of ten prominent historical atheist thinkers, all of whom had deceased or emotionally distant fathers, in contrast to ten Christian thinkers, all of whom enjoyed warm, loving relationships with their fathers. Similarity, Vetter and Green (1932) reported relatively high rates of parental death and abandonment among a sample of 308 members of an atheist advocacy group. However, this study was conducted in 1932, and without more contemporary replication, would have limited relevance to modern-day atheists.

Atheism is Pathological

If R/S has positive effects on well-being, does that mean atheism is bad for you? Studies looking at the relationship between R/S and health often rely on self-report measures of religiosity or spirituality that measure the construct of R/S simply as global indices on a range from "low" to "high" religiosity or spirituality. While there may be some merit to the idea that higher scores on these measures indicate greater levels of R/S, one cannot by extension infer that low scores on religiosity or spirituality can automatically be reverse-coded to indicate greater secularity (as recently alleged by Hall, Koenig, and Meador, 2009).

Atheism does not appear to have deleterious effects on mental health. Hunsberger, Pratt and Pancer (2001) conducted two studies investigating possible links between religious and nonreligious socialization and adjustment, comparing (a) "no religion," (b) mainline Protestant, (c) conservative Protestant, and (d) Catholic families along 11 measures of mental health and adjustment. None of the scales revealed any significant differences among the four groups. This was replicated in samples of college undergraduates and high school students. In sum, the results failed to support any claim that religious socialization has positive implications for adjustment among youth. In a survey of atheists and religious believers conducted in Germany, Buggle, et al. (2001) found that both highly religious people and strongly atheistic people reported lower rates of depression than either wavering agnostics or half-hearted believers.

A majority of the US atheists reported that they would face at least minor repercussions in their families, workplaces and local communities – most severely in the Midwest and the so-called "Bible belt" region of the South – and at least some level of discomfort when religion is invoked (as in a group prayer) during intimate social situations or public settings. Atheistic individuals may be targeted for religious harassment, loss of child custody or job opportunities, or having personal property vandalized (Downey 208; Ritchey 2009). Nonbelievers may also be subject to religious micro-aggressions, in which religious individuals either consciously or unconsciously transmit messages that derogate or invalidate the psychological experiences of their target, such as aggressive proselytizing, pathologizing, or denying that prejudice exists (Sue, 2010). Atheists also typically lack the social institutions akin to churches that offer affirmation and solidarity with like-minded people. As a result, individual atheists and other individuals without strong religious beliefs are more likely to report feeling lonely (Lauder, 2005).

There is evidence to support the idea that simply being a member of a socially marginalized minority group can in itself predispose its members to increased physical and psychological distress, a phenomenon identified as minority stress (Meyer, 2003), whereby stigma, prejudice, and discrimination create a stressful social environment that can lead to physical and mental health problems in people who belong to stigmatized minority groups (Friedman, 1999). Minority stress has been observed among racial minorities and LGBT individuals. Of these groups, the most likely to serve as a model for atheist minority stress is the LGBT population, since LGBT individuals – like atheists – do not constitute a visually identifiable group (unlike racial or sexual minorities). As a consequence, LGBT individuals often feel "closeted" and unable to fully express their own identity in anticipation of negative social repercussions (Silverman, 1998). This can lead to social hyper-vigilance and internalized self-hatred ("I'm not one of those gays..."), substance abuse, affective disorders, and even suicide. On the other hand, membership within an atheist or secularist organization can help to foster a sense of belonging and collective affiliation (Ritchey, 2009).

QUALITY OF LIFE

Research Findings on QOL in Atheists

The results of the body of research linking religion/spirituality to more positive medical and psychosocial well-being has led at least one researcher to infer that a corresponding "small, robust health liability" must be associated with secularity (Hall, Koenig and Meador, 2009). Specifically, existing measures of religiosity may be reverse coded to demonstrate the detriments seen in exclusively secular individuals. However, there is no empirical evidence to support this idea; in fact, there is some evidence that affirmatively atheistic individuals have levels of depression comparable to those of strong religious believers. In one study investigating depression rates among atheists and religious believers in Germany (Buggle et al., 2001), both strong believers and strong atheists suffered the lowest rates of depression, compared to both wavering agnostics and half-hearted believers. A study of atheists living with spinal cord injuries (Hwang, 2008) found that all of the interviewees reported feeling "moderately happy "or "extremely happy" with their lives. In addition, all 10 atheists indicated that their atheism had either a positive effect or no effect on their ability to adjust to their injuries. Sociological studies show that some of the countries that report the greatest quality of life are also the least religious (Zuckerman, 2009). High rates of atheism in countries is generally correlated with greater levels of public health, education, gender equality and economic equality, as well as higher IQ scores (Kanazawa, 2010). While it may be tempting to conclude from this association that a secular ideology promotes economic equality and social comfort, it is just as likely that greater social comfort breeds greater secularity.

In Conclusion: Why Study the Secular? Challenges in Conducting Research with Nonbelievers

The exploration of the impact of religion and spirituality on physical and psychosocial well-being is an enduring area of professional interest. Numerous studies have reported an association between religion/spirituality and aspects of medical and psychological well-being. However, nonreligious individuals in these studies have largely been treated as a statistical outlier. The category of nonreligious persons encompasses a variety of beliefs, from hardcore atheists to believers who do not identify with any religion, and as a comparison group are too heterogeneous to draw any meaningful conclusions.

Like religion, atheism can be regarded as an orienting world view that is consciously chosen by its adherents (Whitley, 2010). However, there has been relatively little to no research dealing with the impact of atheism – especially affirmative atheism – on physical and mental health. The data that do exist is often fraught with biases and assumptions regarding secularity and seculars, such as assuming a direct and causal association between secularity and health deficits based on purely correlational findings, or interpreting an individual's atheism as indication of anger, rebellion or spiritual conflict rather than its own stable and cohesive worldview, with potential effects in the atheist's social environment, including possible stresses associated with prejudice and stigma. Despite increasing acceptance of nearly all social minorities, about half the US population still remain deeply distrustful of atheists and harbor many false stereotypes about them.

Although there are many survey measures designed to assess religious or spiritual development, there is a marked lack of assessment measures that can accurately capture the range and depth of worldviews held by religious nonbelievers. Current measures of religious and spiritual well-being, which typically measure spirituality only in terms of "high" to "low" spirituality, do not provide an accurate enough picture of people at the low end of the scale to differentiate between the spiritually conflicted and the affirmatively atheist. This may be partly due to possible biases of the researchers or simply because of difficulties in recruiting an adequate number of secular participants. There are also currently no assessment measures that describe a model of secular identity development. What does it mean to be secular in a highly religious society? How do people develop secularity over their lifetimes? How is secularity experienced by young versus old individuals, or between men and women? At present, these remain uninvestigated questions.

REFERENCES

Acaro, T. (2010). The stigma of being an atheist: An empirical study on the New Atheist movement and its consequences. *Skeptic , 15*, 50-55.

Baker, J., and Smith, B. (2009). None too simple: Examining issues of religious nonbelief and nonbelonging in the United States. *Journal for the Scientific Study of Religion , 48*, 719–733.

Barna, G. (2008). *Young adults and liberals struggle with morality* Ventura, CA: Barna Research Group.

Beit-Hallahmi, B., and Argyle, M. (1997). *The psychology of religious behaviour, belief and experience*. New York: Routledge.

Bloesch, E., Forbes, G. B. and Adams-Curtis, L. E.(2004). A Brief, Reliable Measure of Negative Attitudes Toward Atheists. *Psychological Reports, 95*(3,Pt2), 1161-1162.

Blumenthal, J. A., Babyak, M. A., Ironson, G., et al. (2007). Spirituality, religion, and clinical outcomes in patients recovering from an acute myocardial infarction. *Psychosomatic Medicine, 69*, 501-8.

Brennan, M. (2004). Spirituality and religiousness predict adaptation to vision loss in middle-aged and older adults. International *Journal for the Psychology of Religion, 14*, 193-214.

Buggle, F., Bister, D., Nohe, G. et al. (2001). Are atheists more depressed than religious people? A new study tells the tale. *Free Inquiry, 20*, 4.

Chang, B. S. (2001). Religion and mental health among women veterans with sexual assault experience. *International Journal of Psychiatry and Medicine, 31 ,* 77-95.

Cline, K., and Ferraro, K. (2006). Does religion increase the prevalence and incidence of obesity in adulthood? *Journal for the Scientific Study of Religion , 45*, 269–281.

Downey, M. (2004). Discrimination Against Atheists: The Facts. *Free Inquiry , 41* (3).

Dyer J. (2007). How does spirituality affect physical health? A conceptual review. *Holistic Nursing Practice, 21*, 324-8.

Edgell, P., and Gerteis, J. (2006). Atheists As 'Other': Moral boundaries and cultural membership in American society. *American Sociological Review ,71*, 211-234

Exline, J. J., and Martin, A. M. (2005). Anger toward God: A new frontier in forgiveness research. In E. Worthington, *Handbook of Forgiveness* (pp. 73-88). New York: Routledge.

Farmer, M.A., Trapnell, P.D and Meston, C. M. (2009). The relation between sexual behavior and religiosity subtypes: A test of the secularization hypothesis. *Archives of Sexual Behavior, 3,8* 852-865.

Ferris, A. (2002). Religion and the quality of life. *Journal of Happiness Studies , 3*, 199-215.

Galen, L. (2009). Profiles of the Godless: Results from a survey of the nonreligious. *Free Inquiry , 29*, 41-45.

Harris, R., Dew, M., and Lee, A. (1995). The role of religion in heart-transplant recipients' long-term health and well-being. v. *Journal of Religion and Health, 34 ,* 17-22.

Ho, D., and Ho, R. (2007). Measuring spirituality and spiritual emptiness: Toward ecumenicity and transcultural applicability. *Review of General Psychology , 11*, 62-74.

Hunsberger, B., and Hunsberger, B. (1984). Religious socialization, apostasy, and the impact of family background. *Journal for the Scientific Study of Religion , 23*, 239-251.

Hunsberger, B., Pratt, M., and Pancer, S. (2001). Religious versus nonreligious socialization: Does religious background have implications for adjustment? *International Journal for the Psychology of Religion , 11*, 105-128.

Hwang, K., Hammer, J. H., and Cragun, R. (in press). Extending the religion-health research to secular minorities: Issues and concerns. *Journal of Religion and Health.*

Ironson, G., Stuetzle, R., and Fletcher, M.A. (2006). An increase in religiousness/spirituality occurs after HIV diagnosis and predicts slower disease progression over 4 years in people with HIV. *Journal of General Internal Medicine, 21 S*uppl 5, S62-8.

Jantos, M., Kiat, H. (2007). Prayer as medicine: how much have we learned? *Medical Journal of Australia*, 21, S51-3.

Jindra, I. (2006). Religious stage development among converts to different religious groups. *International Journal for the Psychology of Religion , 18*, 95–215,.

Johnstone, B., Glass, B.A, and Oliver, R.E. (2007). Religion and disability: Clinical, research and training considerations for rehabilitation professionals. *Disability and Rehabilitation, 15*, 1153-63.

Jones, J. M. (2007). Some Americans reluctant to vote for Mormon, 72-year old presidential candidates. Gallup, Inc. Retrieved January 6, 2009, from http://www.gallup.com/poll/26611/Some-Americans-Reluctant-Vote-Mormon-72YearOld-Presidential-Candidates.aspx

Koenig, H. (2008). Concerns about measuring "spirituality" in research. *Journal of Nervous and Mental Disease, 196,* 349-355.

Koenig, H. (2004). Religion, spirituality, and medicine: research findings and implications for clinical practice. . *Southern Medical Journal, 97* , 1194-200.

Kosmin, B., Keysar, A., Cragun, R., and Navarro-Rivera, J. (2008*). Nones: The profile of the no religion population: A report based on the American Religious Identification Survey* 2008. Hartford, CT: Trinity University.

Laubmeier, K.K., Zakowski, S.G., and Bair, J.P. (2004). The role of spirituality in the psychological adjustment to cancer: a test of the transactional model of stress and coping. *International Journal of Behavioral Medicine, 11*, 48-55.

Lauder, W., Mummery, K., and Sharkey, S. (2006). Social capital, age and religiosity in people who are lonely. *Journal of Clinical Nursing, 15*, 334-340.

Matheis, E. N., Tulsky, D.S. and Matheis, R. J. (2006). The relation between spirituality and quality of life among individuals with spinal cord injury. *Rehabilitation Psychology, 51*, 265-271.

McCullough, M.E., Hoyt, W.T., Larson, D.B., et al. (2000). Religious involvement and mortality: a meta-analytic review. *Health Psychology, 19*, 211-22.

Nairn, R. C. and Merluzzi, T. V. (2003). The role of religious coping in adjustment to cancer. *Psychooncology, 12*, 428–441.

Norman, R. (2006). The varieties of non-religious experience. *Ratio , 19*, 474–494.

Pargament, K. (1999). The psychology of religion and spirituality? Yes and no. *International Journal of Psychology and Religion , 9*, 3-26.

Pesut, B., Fowler, M., Taylor, E.J., et al. (2008). Conceptualising spirituality and religion for healthcare. *Journal of Clinical Nursing, 17*, 2803-10.

Pew Research Center for the People and the Press (2005). Views of Muslim-Americans hold steady after London bombings. Pew Research Center.

Retrieved January 6, 2009, from http://people-press.org/report/252/views-of-muslim-americans-hold-steady-after-london-bombings

Powell, L.H., Shahabi, L. and, Thoresen, C.E. (2003). Religion and spirituality. Linkages to physical health. *American Psychologist, 58*, 36-52.

Ritchey, J. (2009). "One nation under God": Identity and resistance in a rural atheist organization. *Journal of Religion and Popular Culture , 2*, 1-13..

Sheldrake, P. (2007). *A brief history of spirituality.* Marston, MA;. Blackwell;

Shermer, M. (1999). How we believe: *The search for God in an age of science* New York: Macmillan.

Silverman, D. (2002). Coming out: The other closet. American Atheists. Retrieved January 6, 2009, from http://atheists.org/atheism/coming_out

Sloan, R. P., and Bagiella, E. (2006). Science, medicine, and intercessory prayer. *Perspectives in Biological Medicine, 49*, 504-14.

Stefanek, M., McDonald, P.G. and Hess, S.A. (2006). Religion, spirituality and cancer: Current status and methodological challenges. *Psychooncology, 14, 450-63..*

Sue, D. W. (2010). *Microaggressions and marginality: Manifestation, dynamics, and impact.* Hoboken, NJ: Wiley.

Thuné-Boyle, I.C., Stygall, J.A., Keshtgar, M.R. and Newman, S.P. (2006). Do religious/spiritual coping strategies affect illness adjustment in patients with cancer? A systematic review of the literature. *Social Science and Medicine, 63*, 151-64.

Vetter, G. B., and Green, M. (1932). Personality and group factors in the making of atheists. *Journal of Abnormal and Social Psychology, , 27*, 179-194.

Vitz, P. (1999). *Faith of the fatherless: The psychology of atheism.* Dallas, TX: Spence Publishing Company.

Vance, D.E., Struzick, T.C., Raper J.L. (2008). Biopsychosocial benefits of spirituality in adults aging with HIV: implications for nursing practice and research. *Journal of Holistic Nursing, 26*, 119-25.

Waite, L., and Lehrer, E. (2003). The benefits from marriage and religion in the United States: A comparative analysis. *Population and Development Review , 29* (2), 255-75.

Whitley, R. (2010). Atheism and mental health. *Harvard Review of Psychiatry, 18* (3), 190-94.

Wong, J., Rew, L., and Slaikeu, K. (2006). A systematic review of recent research on adolescent religiosity/spirituality and mental health. *Issues in Mental Health Nursing, 27*, 161–183.

Yohannes, A. M., Koenig, H., Baldwin, R., and Connolly, M. (2008). Health behavior, depression and religiosity in older patients admitted to intermediate care. *International Journal of Geriatric Psychiatry, 23* , 735-740.

Zelan, J. (1968). Religious apostasy, higher education and occupational choice. *Sociology of Education , 4*, 370-379.

Zuckerman, P. (2009). Atheism, secularity, and well-being: How the findings of social science counter negative stereotypes and assumptions. *Sociology Compass , 36*, 949–971.

Zuckerman, P. (2007). *Atheism: Contemporary numbers and patterns.* Cambridge, UK.: Cambridge University Press.

In: Religion
Editors: P. Bellamy and G. Montpetit

ISBN 978-1-61470-382-2
©2012 Nova Science Publishers, Inc.

Chapter 5

MAIMONIDES' VIEWS

Leonard Angel
Douglas College, British Columbia, Canada

ABSTRACT

Maimonides (1135 – 1204) is generally regarded as a great philosopher. But most of the twenty-five propositions that he listed and regarded as indubitable are rejected or doubted by almost all philosophers today. The way most philosophers reject or doubt these supposedly indubitable propositions is reviewed in the following pages. Contemporary theologians may want to be clearer than they have been about whether they agree or disagree with the propositions that Maimonides thought to be indubitable. There are enough issues, often buried issues, in the shift from Maimonides' time to our time so that attention to the gap between what seemed indubitable in Maimonides' time, and what seems incorrect or dubitable now may provoke a useful conversation at a general theological level.

1. INTRODUCTION: THE PROBLEM AND THE PLAN

Maimonides (1135 – 1204) is often regarded as one of the best theologians of the past. Yet there is an intriguing problem. At the beginning of Part II of his important work, *The Guide To The Perplexed*, Maimonides articulated

92 Leonard Angel

twenty-six propositions of which twenty-five are, he says, indubitable. Yet most of these propositions are either out and out rejected, or regarded as dubious, by most philosophers today. Religious philosophers today should be a bit more willing than they have been to say whether they agree with most contemporary philosophers or with a medieval representative of the Aristotelian position, as Maimonides was. The reason is that important religious views result from Maimonides' twenty-five or twenty-six propositions.

In this Chapter there will be a review of the twenty-five supposedly indubitable propositions (section 2), a review of why or how they are out and out rejected, or doubted, by the majority of philosophers today (section 2), and a presentation of the many questions that this huge gap generated in regard to the pursuit of spirituality between what was accepted in the 12th century as indubitable, and what is highly doubted or rejected now (sections 3 and 4).

2. MAIMONIDES' TWENTY-FIVE SUPPOSEDLY INDUBITABLE PROPOSITIONS

In the beginning of Part II of *Guide To The Perplexed*, Maimonides organized twenty-six theses, and of them, the first twenty-five, he informed us, have been fully established. "Their correctness," he said, "is beyond doubt" (Introduction, Part II, *The Guide*). The twenty-six principles are enunciated and briefly explained, and then, in Part II, Ch. 1, from the twenty-five reportedly indubitable ones, Maimonides developed his account of the philosophical proofs for the existence of God, the immateriality of God, and the unity of God. In fact, Maimonides developed two proofs for the existence of God. In addition to his proof in Part II Ch. 1, in Ch. 2 he proved the existence of God using the twenty-sixth thesis (which he did not accept).

These twenty-six principles were drawn from Aristotle's views on space, time, astronomy, causality, the nature of being, qualities, properties, and Aristotelian mathematics in regard to the nature of the infinite. Without the application of Aristotelian views on such secular or worldly matters, the development of much of Maimonides' synthesis for his time would have been impossible.

In first response, many would say that Maimonides' principles are Aristotelian, and Aristotle's system has been long superceded; nonetheless, there are alternate proofs for the three propositions: God exists, God is

Maimonides' Views 93

immaterial, and God is a unity; after all, these are the three propositions that Maimonides supposedly proved using the twenty-five propositions.

However, of these three propositions, the second proposition, that God is immaterial, has much going against it in contemporary evidence. In fact, many philosophers today would not accept the immateriality of any being in interaction with the universe. Otherwise the rules, laws, forces, or however they are regarded, of physics would be broken, and they are not. So, it seems, either God is immaterial but not in interaction with the universe – a Deist sort of God – or God is not immaterial, or there is no God. Theologians, though, reject the last view, so the choice for a contemporary science-accepting theologian seems to be between a Deist god, or a God that is not immaterial. Or perhaps there is some other concept of God that can be proposed; but its details, of course, would need to be specified. In other words, the modern point of view indicates a critique of central concepts that people, including Aristotle, used and use, namely that there are purposes fundamentally or basically in or behind nature.

In this way, assessing Maimonides' twenty-five supposedly indubitable propositions provides the beginnings of a useful conversation. Each thinker can figure out whether she or he agrees or disagrees with each of the twenty-five propositions that Maimonides says is indubitable. Equally important, each thinker would figure out what about God can be systematically developed, and on what basis. Only then can meaningful conversation about the different systems be had. That is little other than a specific approach to doing theology. Here it has a focus on what is accepted and what is rejected in Maimonides' system; it looks at what used to be considered indubitable, and how what used to be considered indubitable is now regarded. That is particularly instructive because of the next point to be observed, about the then up-to-date-ness of Maimonides and the sciences of his time, and the desire of thinkers today, including theologians, to be currently up-to-date with the sciences of our time.

Maimonides asks us to use the best of current mathematics, logic, science and so forth. Maimonides tells us that we must "study all mathematical sciences, and (be) well acquainted with Logic." We must also "have a thorough knowledge of Natural Science... (and) understand the nature of the objections (to any given theory)" (*Guide to the Perplexed* II: XXIII). Of course new fields have been added in mathematics and in logic since Maimonides' time; also, the natural sciences have become quantified since the 17th century. That quantification brings the natural sciences into the realm of mathematical notions. It is important to note that no mathematical proofs have been once accepted but later, generally, altogether rejected; this has been true for thousands of years. Perhaps this doesn't matter much to philosophical concerns; on the other hand, perhaps the mathematization of physics, beginning in the 17th century has. Let us find out.

Let us begin through looking at the twenty-five supposedly indubitable propositions that Maimonides lists and at the attitudes towards their contents that developed in subsequent centuries.

Maimonides' first proposition states that "the existence of an infinite magnitude is impossible." This proposition adopts the Aristotelian view that an infinity is only a potential infinity. Magnitudes are measured in numbers, and an infinite magnitude, says, Maimonides, would be a measure of some kind of actual infinity. But, according to the Aristotelian view, there is no actual infinity, and so an infinite magnitude would be impossible. In assessment of Maimonides' first proposition one remembers that Newtonian physics assumed that there is an actually infinite space; and modern set theory inaugurated by Georg Cantor in the last three decades of the nineteenth century, depended on the acceptance of sets with actually infinitely many members. Maimonides' first proposition is generally rejected.

Maimonides' second proposition states that "the co-existence of an infinite number of finite magnitudes is impossible" (*ibid.*) However, one consensus refutation of Zeno's paradoxes of motion, such as the Achilles and the Tortoise paradox, depends on the rejection of this second proposition. The development of the calculus, first by Newton and Leibniz, and then by Cauchy and Weierstrass through the theory of limits, and through the development of the understanding of infinite series that finitely limit, requires that we are able to view a finite line segment, for example, as a collection of infinitely many segments, each of which has non-null, finite magnitude. Elsewhere I have shown how Newtonian physics provides for models of various Zeno paradoxes (Angel 2001, 2002) using the falsity of the second point, a point that Maimonides took to be indubitable.

Maimonides' third proposition states that "the existence of an infinite number of causes and effects is impossible even if these were not magnitudes; if, e.g., one Intelligence were the cause of a second, the second the cause of a third, the third the cause of a fourth, and so on, the series could not be continued ad infinitum (*ibid*)." Once again, this principle is not accepted in Newtonian physics. It is even possible to present examples of Newtonian 'billiard ball' causal sequences in which there are an infinite number of causes and effects, even within a finite period of time. The supertask literature has some intriguing examples. For example, imagine an infinite series of revolving baseball bats at every milepost in an actually infinite Euclidean space. The bats revolve in such a way as to increase the speed of the baseball, doubling its speed each time the baseball is struck. The ball is thrown to the first bat, and then, in a finite amount of time, and an increasingly shorter amount of time, to the next bat, so the baseball will travel an actually infinite corridor. The consequence is that in a finite amount of time, there will be infinitely many causes and effects, all happening to a single object, the baseball. This is a fanciful modelling of José Benardete's thought experiment (1964: 149). (See also, Perez Laraudogoitia (1997).)

The fourth proposition states that four sorts of things, or four types of things, are subject to change, and one such type is 'substance.' In being subject to change, Maimonides did not mean something like 'acquires different properties.' Instead, he meant only that substances can be created and destroyed or undergo genesis and destruction. Some philosophers afterward disagreed. Spinoza, for instance, held that a substance undergoes neither genesis nor destruction; it is, rather, in Spinoza's view, self-caused. The key question has to do with the notion of 'substance.' Also, since 1905 or so there has been a mass-energy conservation law in physics. Whatever system is closed will follow this law above the Planck scale. It would seem that there cannot be many human-scale-substances properly within such a closed system. Maimonides' fourth proposition is dubious, at least.

Fifth: "Motion implies change and transition from potentiality to actuality." Transition from potentiality to actuality is a kind of goal-satisfaction, or teleological transition. Maimonides accepted this inherent goal-satisfaction in motions. But that was altogether abandoned by Newton, who built on what is called Galilean relativity and who employed the inertial principle. Another way to put this is to say that Newton analyzed motions by non-teleological mathematical descriptions. Others since the 17th century have taken that mathematical-description approach entirely. Maimonides' fifth proposition is generally rejected.

Sixth: Maimonides distinguishes between essential and accidental (non-essential) motions. But since the quantification of the natural sciences beginning in the 17th century, all motions are analyzed together through uniform mathematical descriptions. In one main way, at least, the distinction between essential and accidental (non-essential) motions has been abandoned.

Seventh: "Everything that moves is divisible, and, consequently corporeal; but that which is indivisible cannot move, and cannot therefore be corporeal." This was hypothetically rejected by Boscovitch's work (in the 18th century) on moving point particles; it has been practically rejected by approximate references to moving point particles; it was rejected in chemistry by Dalton's work on atomic chemistry. Dalton's atoms were supposed to be indivisible. Dalton's notion was not satisfied, yet there is still a notion of quantum indivisibles. What they are is not known, but that they would have (non-continuous) changes of location (only to a degree of measurement) is taken for granted. In fact, Richard Feynmann said that the atomic hypothesis is the most useful hypothesis of all hypotheses about the world (quoted in Bilodeau 1998: 224).

Eighth: "A thing that moves accidentally must come to rest ... hence accidental motion cannot continue forever." Maimonides' 'accidental' required his proposition to be about earthly motions. But Newton's first law of motion rejected the eighth proposition. In Newton's first law of motion, a thing's straight-line motion continues forever, unless the thing is affected by a force action of some sort.

Ninth: "A corporeal thing that sets another corporeal thing in motion can only effect this by setting itself in motion at the time it causes the other thing to move." This would be abandoned if there is no special framework in which a thing sets itself in motion at a given time. And we have, since special relativity in 1905, rejected the notion of absolute frameworks. Hence there is no special framework in which the thing sets itself in motion. This is part of how what is now called Galilean relativity has eliminated absolute frameworks.

Tenth: "A thing which is said to be in a corporeal object... is a force existing in a corporeal object." This is dubious, in part because of the 'essential' versus 'accidental' language the full statement in the original employs.

Eleventh: "... among the things which form the essential elements of an object, there are some which cannot be divided in any way, as, e.g., the soul and the intellect."

The 'essence' versus 'non-essence' contrast is dubious. The use of it to generate formal non-physical atomism is even more dubious, or, by very many thinkers at least, has been wholly abandoned or rejected.

Twelfth: "A force which occupies all parts of a corporeal object is finite, that object itself being finite." The gravitational force occupies all parts of any corporeal object. On what grounds Maimonides asserts that all corporeal objects are finite is not stated. Indeed, he had no grounds other than the Aristotelian reasons for thinking that the cosmos is finite. Of course that the cosmos is finite for Aristotelian reasons has long been abandoned. Newton took the cosmos to be infinite. Now its measured portion is regarded, since the Big Bang, as finite. But within what context the Big Bang occurred is

Maimonides' Views

97

unknown, or is being figured out. This, Maimonides' twelfth proposition, is dubious at best.

Thirteenth: "None of the several kinds of change can be continuous, except motion from place to place, provided it be circular." This was rejected in several ways. Here is one: In Newton's first law of motion, root motions were taken to be linear and continuous.

Fourteenth: Maimonides states that locomotion comes first, then transformation (genesis and corruption, and if genesis or corruption, increase or decrease). The contemporary picture doesn't temporally relate these supposedly different forms of change. Instead, classically, locomotion is found in all actual change; quantum-wise there are merely different position-locations within a degree of precision. Maimonides' thesis is dubious.

Fifteenth: "Time is an accident that is related and joined to motion..." That time is an accident is dubious or rejected; that it is related to motion is accepted, though the statement would be put differently now, given that though time is mathematically different from space, objects are found only in spacetime. Maimonides' acceptance of the pre-relativistic point of view on time makes the proposition dubious.

Sixteenth: "...purely spiritual beings, which are neither corporeal nor forces situated in corporeal objects, cannot be counted, except when considered as causes and effects." That purely spiritual beings can be considered as causes of any change in the natural world has been rejected by just about all mind-body philosophers after, say, 1970, since the existence of such purely spiritual beings interacting with the world or in the world has been rejected due to the mathematization of physics, the physicalization of chemistry, and the physio-chemicalization of biology. (These three processes will be discussed below in section 3.)

Seventeenth: "When an object moves, there must be some object that moves it..." This was rejected by Newton's first law of motion. There are, as well, other important features of the proposition that have been rejected, e.g., that "when a living being dies... the soul has left the body." That has been rejected by what follows "due to" in comments on the sixteenth proposition.

Eighteenth: "Everything that passes over from a state of potentiality to that of actuality is caused to do so by some external agent..." This is wholly rejected. Often, there is no obvious external agent; physics, for instance, was quantified in the 17th century. Take a stone rolling off a hill. There is a movement from potentiality to actuality there, according to anyone who accepts such a metaphysics. But since Newton's accounts as interpreted through Lagrange's work in the late 18th century, the mathematical

98   Leonard Angel

descriptions alone suffice to account for the changes. There need be no external agent in such an analysis. This was emphasized in the publication of Emmy Nöther's Theorem in 1918.

Nineteenth: "A thing which owes its existence to certain causes has in itself merely the possibility of existence..." This proposition survives.

Twentieth: "A thing which has in itself the necessity of its existence cannot have for its existence any cause whatever." This is often rejected, since the notion of 'self-cause' is taken to apply to such beings, and the existence of self-causing beings is often rejected. Alternatively, nothing is taken to exist necessarily. Occasionally, though, there are analyses that take it that some assembly or some whole has necessary existence. Maimonides' twentieth proposition is at least debatable.

Twenty-first: "A thing composed of two elements (e.g., substance and form) has necessarily their composition as the cause of its present existence. Its existence is therefore not necessitated by its own essence; it depends on the existence of its two component parts and their combination." Suppose, for the sake of discussion, that an object has necessary existence because it includes all possibles. Compositions are possible. Then the object would have those composing objects. But, according to those who accept the 'essence' versus 'non-essence' notions, its necessity would come from its essential nature, that it has all possibles, not from the mere compositional assembly of elements, or not from the mere compositional assembly of component parts. Maimonides' proposition is dubious.

Twenty-second: "... The two component elements of all bodies are substance and form. The accidents attributed to material objects are quantity, geometrical form, and position." Many thinkers no longer accept the 'substance' and 'form' analyses of bodies.

Twenty-third: "Everything that exists potentially, and whose essence indicates a certain state of possibility, may at some time be without actual existence." This employs many terms no longer in use, but the proposition otherwise survives.

Twenty-fourth: "That which is potentially a certain thing is necessarily material, for the state of possibility is always connected with matter." If one accepts, or translates, 'potentiality/actuality' one will not have difficulty with this proposition. The reasons for accepting the resulting proposition will be different, however, from Maimonides' reasons. For this reason, it is not easy to classify Maimonides' twenty-fourth proposition.

Twenty-fifth: "Each compound substance consists of matter and form, and requires an agent for its existence..." This has been rejected by the analyses

Maimonides' Views 99

actually given of things. Agents have had a problematic status for a few centuries, and since, say, 1970 an even more problematic status, given the results referred to at the end of the comments on Maimonides' sixteenth proposition. The proposition also states that "... Matter does not move of its own accord—an important proposition..." This has been rejected by, for example, Galilean relativity or Newton's first law of motion.

The large majority of the twenty five 'established' principles which are, in Maimonides' opinion, 'beyond doubt', and on which – see the Guide, Part II, Ch. 1 – he bases his philosophical demonstrations, have been outright rejected by modern achievements in mathematics, physics, and philosophy, or are debatable, or dubious in their strength.

3. OPTIONS IN THE PRESENT DAY CONTEXT

Thinkers are likely to readily accept that many of Maimonides' propositions are no longer acceptable, and, also, to think that their unacceptability no longer affects much in theological thinking. That sets up our next topic, how following Maimonides' advice, stating that we must "study all mathematical sciences, and (be) well acquainted with Logic;" and that we must also "have a thorough knowledge of Natural Science... (and) understand the nature of the objections (to any given theory)" affects one's theology.

By about 1970, three processes had occurred in the natural sciences: a very high plateau level was reached in the mathematization of physics; (a good way to date this is to say that it happened by 1918, the date of publication of Nöther's Theorem; it is also useful to note that the plateau level has only raised since then, for example, as it has in string theory); chemistry was physicalized (by roughly 1930, through the application of quantum work on electron orbits to chemical relations); and biology was physio-chemicalized (by some time from the 1930's or so to about 1970, often through the DNA and RNA research of the 1950's and '60's along with hundreds of years of previous research).

If one accepts the mathematization of physics, the physicalization of chemistry, and the physio-chemicalization of biology, then one is required to accept a consequence of the position sometimes referred to as physical closure. The consequence states that events in nature do not themselves alter the effects of suitably restricted physics. 'Physical closure' is an unfortunate name, since it has the term 'closure' in it. Perhaps we need a new term for 'physical closure.' And perhaps we need a new term for the consequence of physical closure as well. I will use the new term 'phystriology' for the consequence (thanking educational historian Eric Damer who in conversation coined the neologism).

'Phystriology' can be taken to refer to the nesting of biology in physio-chemistry and chemistry in physics; it can also be taken to refer to the non-violation in any change of any physics' outcome, as long as mathematical formulas are taken as approximative, are used only in original contexts of research, and are applied in short term time periods. There is, in this way, a suitable restriction for physics. In any case, 'phystriology,' presupposes the mathematization of physics. It is also worth noting that naturally selective evolution, in one form or another, is implied by phystriology.

And the statement that the world is phystriological does not help the spiritual quest; rather, phystriology deeply challenges many theological notions. Yet it does follow Maimonides' advice on combining one's theological thinking with the best available natural science, mathematics, and logic. Theologians prior to a few hundred years ago definitely took stands on issues; Maimonides is a good illustration of that. I will now note some issues, and for each issue noted, there will be a readily available question or several readily available questions that I will then pose to contemporary thinkers. The conclusion of this chapter, then, in regard to spirituality pursuits, is a questioning one.

CONCLUSION: A BUNCH OF QUESTIONS

As was just said, anyone who likes spirituality pursuits and accepts the current sciences, will face many questions. Maimonides is the philosopher we are looking at, so it will be convenient to use his views as examples in formulating the questions.

Maimonides definitely took the stand that God is immaterial. This means that he denied the idea that God is material. Later, there were some philosophers who said that God is as much material as immaterial. Spinoza, for instance, was such a philosopher.

What, then, is your view? Is God immaterial? Or is God as much material as God is immaterial? Or is God specially material? Or does God underlie the material world, and if so, how?

Maimonides' Views

Maimonides definitely took the stand that many motions on earth require God as a causal agent. What is your view? Do many motions on earth require God as a causal agent? And how does your answer to that question harmonize with your view on whether the world is phystriological?

Maimonides definitely took the stand that for each human being, there is an afterlife. (That is, Maimonides definitely thought there is a conscious afterlife; it is not just that each human being is remembered, or is survived by buildings he or she had built, and so on). This meant that Maimonides denied the view that there is no afterlife.

What, then, is your view? "Is there an afterlife? Or is there no afterlife?" Perhaps this is a childish question. Religious leaders often work among lay practitioners. They are, then, very familiar with people in states of grief after events like the loss of a beloved family member. For this reason, they tend to take a mature, non-judgmental view of the matter. Indeed, they may resist coming to their own view or resist expressing their own view of the matter. They would prefer to say something like, "Let everybody come to her or his own decision." The tendency towards public hesitancy is understandable. A religious leader is a member of a group of people. Nonetheless, there are the private views of the leaders of religious institutions.

Without being under any obligation to state one's view, does one, privately, let us suppose, have an opinion on the matter of an afterlife? If one's privately held opinion is 'There is an afterlife,' then that might need a defense; what would that defense be? If the privately held opinion is 'There is no afterlife,' this privately held opinion might not be expressed, but two question follow: First, could one's private opinion on the matter be publicly expressed in such a way as not to offend those in mourning? If so, what would it be? If not, why not? Second, there is the central question, "What are the implications of contemporary science in regard to whether there is an afterlife?" This would need to be considered in the light of the view described above, that phystriology obtains.

Maimonides certainly took the stand that there was prophetic revelation, and law revealed through the prophetic revelation. This, on the face of it, means that he denied the view that at the literal level, there is no prophetic revelation and that there is no obligation that is not a cultural product.

What, then, is your view on the matter? At the literal level, is there prophetic revelation? Religious leaders often say slippery things that can be interpreted both ways on the clear question. They say things like, "Sacred matters can be understood in such a way that the source is transcendental, and they can be understood in such a way that the source is non-transcendental..." Perhaps there are positive uses of such remarks. But the root question is relatively clear: Is there a *supreme personal God* who literally gives prophesy? Can you express your view on this question in a non-slippery manner?

Maimonides certainly took a stance on the unity of God. He denied any plurality in God.

What, then, is your view? And if you accept the unity of God, what does it mean, and how do you account for it? Is it possible to experience transcendental unity, or not, and if so, how?

Further to the second question posed above, Maimonides seems to have taken the view that God is, or has an aspect as, an agent.

What, then, is your view? What is an agent? And is God an agent? Or does God merely have an aspect as an agent?

This is the beginning of what may become a fruitful conversation.

REFERENCES

Angel, L. (2001). A Physical Model of Zeno's Dichotomy. *British Journal for the Philosophy of Science, 52*, 347 – 358.

Angel, L. (2002). Zeno's Arrow, Newton's Mechanics, and Bell's Inequalities. *British Journal for the Philosophy of Science, 53*, 161 – 182.

Benardete, J. (1964). *Infinity*. Oxford: Clarendon Press.

Bilodoeau, D. (1998). Physics, Machines, and the Hard Problem. in J. Shear (Editor) *Explaining Consciousness*. Cambridge Mass: Bradford MIT: 217 – 234. (First in *Journal of Consciousness Studies, 3*, 1996 5/6, 386 – 401.)

Maimonides, M. (R'). (1956, (English, 1904)). *Guide For the Perplexed*. M. Friedlander, translator. NY: Dover.

Perez Laraudogoitia, J. (1997). Classical Particle Dynamics, Indeterminism and a Supertask. *British Journal for Philosophy of Science, 48*, 49-54.

Spinoza, B. (1982 (Latin, etc., ~1677)). *The Ethics and Selected Letters*. Shirley, S., translator; Feldman, S., editor, Indianapolis: Hackett.

In: Religion
Editors: P. Bellamy and G. Montpetit

ISBN 978-1-61470-382-2
©2012 Nova Science Publishers, Inc.

Chapter 6

THE ARCHITECTURE OF NONCONFORMIST CHRISTIAN RELIGION AND NATIONAL IDENTITY

Stephen Roy Hughes
Royal Commission on the Ancient and Historical Monuments of Wales,
United Kingdom

It has often been simplistically asserted that the elaboration or simplicity of a Christian religious building depends on the type of Christian worship practised there. That a Catholic Church exhibits a very elaborate edifice, an Anglican or Episcopalian Church a very traditional and impressive structure and that nonconformist chapels are simple prayer-halls reflecting Puritan worship practices inspired by Calvin and others. Others see dense areas of nonconformist worship as nothing more than an expression of newly found and expressed worker independence lacking the expression of any particular minority or cultural grouping. The following article seeks to show that rather different causal factors determined the degree of elaboration of a religious structure and that the overall density of a type of non-state religion was equally determined by resurgent ideas of cultural and national identity within small nations. These trends are largely, but not exclusively, explored using the details available from a long-term large-scale study of religious buildings of Wales and also of the religious buildings of the global Welsh diaspora (Royal Commission; Coflein).

Within Great Britain nonconformist religious worship had a brief flowering under the impetus of the revolutionary movements fostered by the freedom allowed by the republican, or Commonwealth, period following the mid seventeenth-century civil war. The mountainous area of western Britain, Wales, being about one-fifth of the area of England and retaining the use of the earlier British Celtic language (now called Welsh), was naturally conservative and largely Royalist and not then a natural breeding-ground for religious radicalism.

Figure 1. Maesyronnen Congregational Chapel, Radnorshire, mid eastern Wales, showing simple conversion from a byre or cattle housing (Crown copyright, RCAHMW).

The first nonconformist gatherings were naturally held with a few people gathered-in to the main living-area, or parlour, of the houses of principal supporters or worshippers. In this ideas were no different to the early days of Christianity in Rome where some church sites originated as ad-hoc worship rooms in the houses of Roman citizens (for example the 2-3rd house of St. Cecilia in the Trastevere area of Rome). As these congregations grew in size in

The Architecture of Nonconformist Christian Religion ...   105

rural areas meetings transferred to available barns & byres (cow-houses) and in urban areas the structure of workers' houses, sometimes with the neighbouring properties, might be converted into simple chapels (Hughes, 2000, 285-86). In early industrialised areas the open areas provided in works or colliery offices, or market halls, might also be used.

In time some of these barns or cow-houses might be rebuilt on the same site but in a form that reflected their new function. The seventeenth-century meetings at Maesyronnen Farm in the eastern mid-Welsh uplands of rural Radnorshire were held in the cow-house built onto the end gable of the late-Medieval farmhouse which still retains its oaken cruck-frame timbers. Meetings in the vicinity are supposed to have started in the Civil War period led by the Welsh Puritan Vavasour Powell from 1640 and the Commonwealth State Protector Oliver Cromwell (whose *real* rather than *adopted* surname was the Welsh surname 'Williams') is supposed to have attended a meeting at Maesyronnen Farm. Ministers are recorded before 1658 and between 1672 and 1682 the farm of Henry Maurice and the chapel was formally adapted for worship for dissenters when registered at the nearby border town of Presteigne in 1696. At that time the front wall of the chapel seems to have been rebuilt with doorways at either end: that adjacent to the house may have been the original access into the cow-house. In between, and on the gable away from the house, were a series of simple domestic-style windows to light the interior and on the facing back wall was a pulpit and reader's desk, with the preacher and reader back-lit by irregular rear windows.

The interior was furnished with simple backless benches, some of which still remain in an interior which is now preserved as a museum. The chapel was leased to this congregational group by the landowner in 1720. A second example of this type of conversion of an agricultural building into a chapel, but this time probably a free-standing barn, is Pen-Rhiw Unitarian Chapel. This was erected at Dre-fach Felindre in Carmarthenshire, south-west Wales, and formally acquired by the Unitarians as a meeting-house in 1777. The size and design of the box pews on the bottom floor varied as they were built for different families, each of whom commissioned a design for their own pews. In 1953 it was re-erected as an exhibit in St. Fagans Museum near Cardiff. In the same period (in 1796) uncomfortable benches, with no back support were being replaced with pews elsewhere in other chapels such as Libanus Independent Chapel in what was then the main urban centre of Wales at Swansea and the lower Swansea Valley (Hughes, 2000: 285). That chapel was rebuilt 14 years after its original construction as a simple barn-like construction in 1782, with earthen floors. For the previous 100 years this had been a small rural house-church congregation using a small squatter-cottage established on nearby common-land. While in 1796 the congregation was establishing a second more elaborate and comfortable purpose-built worship-space it transferred from the Independent, or Congregationalist, denomination to the Methodist cause operating under the more austere edicts of Calvin. It was clearly not Puritan ideals, but lack of numbers, and of poverty, that determined the simplicity of early meeting-houses in such cases.

Figure 2. Simple chapel of 1771 from Dre-fach Felindre in Carmarthenshire, south-west Wales, originally built as a barn (Crown copyright, RCAHMW).

Within an urban area the equivalent of such agricultural conversions would be the adaption of a worker's dwelling-house used for meetings to accommodate worship. Such workers' house premises were generally too small to accommodate a growing congregation. One room used in for the Welsh language Wesleyan cause at Cwm Shon Mathew, near the Rhymney Ironworks in south-east Wales in 1851, could accommodate a congregation of 32 and measured only 13ft by 13ft (Jones & Williams, 1976: 63). One possibility for expansion exercised in the early purpose-built workers'

The Architecture of Nonconformist Christian Religion ...   107

settlement of Morriston in south-west Wales (founded 1779 near Swansea) was to acquire the neighbouring house and convert the two properties into a place of worship.

The Methodist Revival in Welsh worship actually pre-dated that promulgated by John and Charles Wesley with such effect in England and the United States. Howell Harris, Daniel Rowland and William Williams started a mid-eighteenth century Revival (1735 on (Williams 1737 on)) which had a massive effect among the still largely monoglot Welsh-language community of Wales (Welsh Biography: Rowland). The first conference to organise local societies, or congregations, was the gathering of Welsh evangelical nonconformist Christians who met at Watford, near Caerphilly, in south-east Wales on January 5-6 1743 under the chairmanship of the Bristol-born charismatic preacher George Whitefield. This first Methodist Association was held eighteen months before the first conference held by John Wesley in England (June 25, 1744). Whitefield had been at Oxford University with John & Charles Wesley and it was the loan of a book from the former that largely led to Whitefield's conversion experience in 1735.

In many ways the influence of George Whitefield was central to the Great Spiritual Awakening in Wales, England and what was to become the United States of America. He was one of the founders of Methodism and of the evangelical movement generally. Whitefield was at the core of the promotion of open-air preaching to huge previously unreached audiences and of the tolerance and acceptance of this by the authorities of Wales and of England. While preaching as an Anglican clergyman in the church at Bermondsey in London he was touched by the size of the 1,000 plus people outside who were unable to enter the packed church. John Wesley thought Whitefield's idea of outside preaching 'insane' and the Conventicle Act in fact banned outside preaching in Wales and England except at public hangings. However Whitefield was the first to spot the opportunity this presented for reaching a mass working-class audience when a programmed public execution in front of the coalmining community of Kingswood in east Bristol was foiled by the suicide of the prisoner. Whitefield, one of the most charismatic and gifted preachers of the eighteenth-century, spotted his opportunity and exploited it to great effect. A consequent result being the continued use and promotion of these mass evangelisation practices as he was subsequently banned from preaching inside most Anglican, or Episcopalian, Churches. On Thursday June 14 1739 John Wesley noted that 'I went with Mr. Whitefield to Blackheath, where were, I believe, twelve or fourteen thousand people. He a little surprised me, by desiring me to preach in his stead; which I did (though nature recoiled)

... I was greatly moved with compassion (Bewes, 2003, 1739). It was Whitefield who similarly encouraged William Williams to leave his curacies, when ordained into the Anglican Church in his native Wales, and to pursue itinerant outdoor evangelisation.

Figure 3. Horeb Welsh Baptist Chapel, at Blaenavon, a simple round-headed style, or Italianate Chapel, built by the local ironworks engineer, Thomas Thomas in 1862 (Crown copyright, RCAHMW).

Whitefield was a Calvinist and the two strands of Methodism subsequently separated. The Wesleyan Methodists in England were the first to break with the Anglican Church of England, the first step being when John Wesley gave legal status to his conference. He was also prompted to ordain ministers for America, as there was a drastic shortage of clergy to administer the sacraments following the War of Independence. Wesley felt obliged to act as the Bishop of London had refused to ordain ministers for this purpose. Further disputes about travelling preachers and the administration of the sacraments resulted in the Wesleyans decisive break with the Church of England under the Plan of Pacification (1795). The Welsh Calvinists followed to independence from the Anglicans in 1811.

The Architecture of Nonconformist Christian Religion ...   109

The end product of this movement was a late nineteenth-century Wales in which more than double the proportion of the population was non-conformist even compared to the industrial textile belt of Lancashire and Yorkshire in northern England or the fellow Celts employed in the staunchly Methodist copper and tin-mining areas of Cornwall. Although all British worker communities in the industrial period in England and Wales expressed their radicalism through the foundation of Nonconformist congregations this was particularly marked in Wales where there was no Welsh-speaking bishop in post over the Established Church in Wales between the mid-eighteenth century and 1870. This was despite the great majority of the population speaking that language almost exclusively. In Wales, at the time of the religious census in 1851, only 19.3 *per cent* of the population worshipping on a Sunday did so in an Anglican Church whereas between one-third and two-thirds did so in English counties (Coleman 1980, p. 8). This situation was reinforced after the Great Religious Revival of 1858–59 which was brought to Wales from North America but had a particular resonance in Wales where Welsh workers built many new and more elaborate places of worship (Hughes 2003, p. 88).

There was a second difference, as well, in that membership of a Welsh chapel was central to much of Welsh cultural identity, providing a rich linguistic, musical, social cultural experience throughout the week and not just a weekly religious experience. As the Industrial Revolution in Swansea and Blaenavon boomed in the first half of the nineteenth century the population of Wales also boomed but the number of places of worship almost trebled from 1,369 to 3,805 (Jones 1994, p. 273). Revealingly, the rate of increase in the established Anglican Church was only 16 *per cent* while the workers' Nonconformist chapels increased by 51 *per cent*. By 1851 no less than 82.6 *per cent* of the population in the thirteen counties of Wales attended a place of worship on a Sunday whereas in England the average was considerably lower with only 37 *per cent* in London and 41.9 *per cent* in the northern English counties attending a church or chapel. The latter area is often compared to Wales in the density of worker chapels but in fact that was much less as the total attending any place of worship on a Sunday was much lower. The building landscape of the Welsh worker communities of the late eighteenth and nineteenth centuries to a great extent reflected the linguistic divide, for as noted, the Anglican churches of the landowners and capitalists had had no Welsh-speaking bishops for over a century before 1870 and some three-quarters of the worker Nonconformist chapels remained Welsh-speaking until the end of the nineteenth century (*ibid.*, p. 273).

Interestingly, the religious townscapes after the great religious revival of 1857–58 and the growing status of the Welsh-speaking Nonconformist population meant that Welsh towns such as Blaenavon and Morriston came to have a density of workers chapels unequalled in the rest of the United Kingdom. Increasingly in the nineteenth century, as English-speaking immigrants combined with the, at first, bilingual and then later monolingual English-speaking students produced by the iron and coppermasters' English-language schools in Wales, it was necessary to add English-language chapel equivalents to the multiple denominations of the earlier Welsh-language chapels. Works' schools to educate the children of workers were established at Swansea in 1806 and Blaenavon in 1813 and grew in size and range throughout the nineteenth century (Hughes 2005, p. 159).

Figure 4. Bible Christian Chapel built by English-language Cornish copper smelters in simple gothic style in the Welsh copper smelting community of Hafod, Swansea, in south Wales, in 1873 (Crown copyright RCAHMW).

Sometimes the denominations of the chapels denoted the origin of the various worker groups. In the lower Swansea valley the large and numerous

The Architecture of Nonconformist Christian Religion ... 111

Welsh-language worker congregations formed the great majority of worshippers and their buildings. However by the end of the nineteenth-century many of the Welsh congregations gave their old buildings to new English-language causes within their denominations, made up partly of the younger local population who spoke English in preference to Welsh and also to newcomers from England. Swansea town itself had always been more Anglicised than the surrounding area and by the mid nineteenth-century Cornish managers at the Cornish-owned Hafod and Morfa Copperworks were playing a leading role in the English-language Wesleyan Methodist chapel in Swansea Town. Later Cornish migrants to the Hafod Copperworks founded an English-language Bible Christian Chapel and Sunday School in Trevivian, the workers' settlement adjacent to the works.

At Blaenavon there were thirteen worker-built chapels by 1901 (Figure. 3), and only one (ironmaster-built) Anglican church. By this time only 8 *per cent* of the town's population of 10,010 was composed of Welsh-speakers (Barber 2002, p. 111). At Morriston, largest of the Lower Swansea Valley worker townships, there were sixteen Nonconformist chapels by the end of the nineteenth century, two holding congregations of 1,500, completely dwarfing the two Anglican churches (Hughes 2000, p. 286).

Mining and manufacturing districts in Cornwall and the Lancashire/Yorkshire area also came to have townscapes with a strong presence of chapels but many of the townscapes at Blaenavon and Morriston had (and to an extent still have) such a density of Nonconformist chapels that often two, or more, would dominate the surroundings.

As already noted the Welsh population were also twice as likely to actually attend a place of worship on Sundays as their English contempories.

The reasons for this were partly cultural and linguistic. Ironically the Protestant Established Church – of the Anglicans or Episcopalians – was founded by the first Monarchs of England of Welsh descent, the Tudors. However, although Queen Elizabeth commissioned a translation of the bible into Welsh by the eighteenth century the language of the established church was primarily English and the appointment of English Bishops who could speak no Welsh was commonplace. Additionally it can be argued that Wales was the first industrial nation in the world for the 1851 census shows that Wales was the first state where the proportion of the population employed in agriculture was exceeded by the proportion employed in industry. This transformation in society meant that migrant workers who might formerly have been firmly attached to a local Anglican parish church, as their forbears before them, were suddenly transplanted to a new social milieu where in the words of one of them 'we were suddenly alone and it did not matter who approached us first but the nonconformists were first to greet new workers.'

Figure 5. Tabernacle Welsh Independent Chapel, Morriston, Swansea, 'the Cathedral of Welsh Nonconformity' and built by indigenous Welsh entrepreneurs in 1872-73, dominating all local places of worship (Crown copyright, RCAHMW).

The Architecture of Nonconformist Christian Religion ...   113

However, nonconformists should not be seen as one monolithic block. There were no less than four main denominations in Wales: the Calvinistic Methodists were the one denomination unique to Wales but there were also Congregationalists (or 'Independents'); Baptists and Wesleyan Methodists. Initially all these denominations except the Wesleyans of mid Wales operated almost solely in the Welsh language. In the mid-nineteenth century even large Welsh villages could have four large chapel structures, one for each of the main denominations, seating up to 800 while urban chapels commonly seated 1,000 to 1,500. By the end of the nineteenth century a combination of the migration of workers from England and the provision of education for workers' children only through the medium of English meant that even smaller industrial towns now had a minimum of eight chapels with each major denomination having separate buildings for Welsh and English congregations.

Chapels originating as long simple-gabled agricultural buildings with entrances in the side walls set the pattern for the purpose-built structures of the eighteenth-century.

What is interesting is that the Catholic Church that is often considered to always require more elaborate buildings for its more ritualised and elaborate services at first re-emerged from the intolerance and persecution of the Reformation in a similar way using simple buildings. In Brecon, in Powys, mid-Wales, for example a farmhouse was used for services until the church was completed in 1851.

In Wales Monmouthshire had the largest proportion of Roman Catholics within its population in the period 1715-20 with 10-20% of its population belonging to the old faith. At Llanarth Court, in Monmouthshire, south-east Wales a disguised church was built in 1750 in the grounds of a mansion as happened elsewhere in Britain at Lulworth Castle in Dorset and Ugbrooke in Devon (Newman 2000, p. 265). The church at Llanarth was built in the walled-garden with a simple row of round-headed windows along one wall and could have been mistaken as an orangery, or tool-store. It was also aligned north-east to south-west rather than a liturgical east-west and the altar is at the north-west rather than the orthodox east end. None of these disguising features would have been necessary in a structure built after the Second English Catholic Relief Act of 1791. The Jones family of Llanarth Court mansion already had a Catholic priest in residence and when their house was rebuilt in c.1792 they also included a private chapel. The strongly nonconformist chapel feel of the church was enhanced in 1835 when a rear south gallery was added for organ and choir.

Within southern Britain by far the largest population of indigenous Catholics was in Lancashire area of north-west England where over 20% of the population were of that persuasion. Within Lancashire it was the area around the large town of Preston where most Catholics lived. Under the most severe repression occurring after the Reformation of the 16th century, house-churches operated with mass being said in people's homes. A few secret and disguised churches had been built such as the Jesuit Mission in Liverpool which was disguised as a warehouse, complete with a hoisting block and tackle. The need for this subterfuge was shown by the fact that this and other secret chapels in the great port-city of north-western England were destroyed by a Protestant mob.

Figure 6. A simple rural early Catholic Chapel of 1794 in Claughton on Brock Lancashire, north-west England, almost identical externally to a nonconformist Protestant Chapel.

House-churches were partly facilitated in Wales and England by the English Catholic Relief Act of 1778 which freed priests and teachers from prosecution arising from the action of informers. The passing of the Second English Catholic Relief Act on 24 June 1791 allowed Catholics to openly practice their religion but no steeple or bell could be allowed on a Roman Catholic church building.

The Architecture of Nonconformist Christian Religion ... 115

The first new Catholic church openly built in southern Britain since the Reformation was subsequently built as St. Mary's in Mulberry Street in Manchester, north-west England in 1792 (since rebuilt). The later surviving but early catholic churches in Lancashire suggest a close affinity to nonconformist Protestant chapels of the period, following a square or rectangular ground-plan with upper galleries on three sides and lit by tall round-headed windows. At Lancaster, the county town of Lancashire, the former Catholic chapel at Dalton Square (now the City Architect's Office) that opened on 1 March 1799 can be compared with the Congregational Church in the High street of 1772-73, or Chipping Catholic chapel of 1827 with the near-contemporary Congregational chapel, or Goosnargh Chapel of 1835, which is almost identical to a nonconformist chapel, with its round-headed openings to front and sides and with an attached house to rear (Mclintock, 1994).

The village Catholic chapel of Claughton on Brock in Lancashire opened in summer 1794 (only three years after the second Catholic Relief Act) and externally remains much as built. It originally had side galleries (removed probably about 1835), has large round-headed windows down the sides and half-round lunettes flanking the door under a hipped roof with a priest-house attached at right-angles to the rear and still has the external appearance of a plain nonconformist chapel except for the addition of the cross above the door. The reason for the similarity is the basic cost of construction that a poor sparse congregation could afford. A Catholic chapel like Claughton only measured 36ft by 56ft, fitted with 'second-best' glass but with its galleries (it retained the rear one) it could seat 700 people. At the beginning of construction only £230 was available but at what was a fairly average cost for a plain chapel the enterprise was rescued by a £200 donation from a local aristocratic family. The interior was initially as poorly furnished as any nonconformist chapel and people paid for places on benches that were obtained second-hand from the temporarily disused church of St. Mary's Preston.

When money became available for improvement it was the interior that was upgraded for more elaborate forms of worship: at Claughton no less than £1,400 was spent on adding a marble-lined chancel or sanctuary and in raising the roof in line with general Catholic aspirations for grander buildings. A few years later an organ and other improvements were made at a cost of £800. In 1872 two marble altars were added and seven stained glass windows at a cost of £1,300. It was the Catholic Emancipation Act of 1839 that removed any need at all for reticence and allowed much greater external architectural assertion in such features as apses and chancels.

Figure 7. The simple Anglican chapel of St. Andrew, Hatton Garden, of 1687 in London, attributed to Sir Christopher Wren.

Today when what is externally still a rather plain nonconformist-type chapel is entered it comes as bit of a shock to encounter the 4ft high statue of Our Lady in Carrara marble and to see the stations of the cross fixed on the wall.

In the Welsh Catholic stronghold of Monmouthshire a similar process of unobtrusive simplicity was similarly followed by the architectural elaboration of worship. In 1793, only two years after the second Catholic Relief Act, Catholics in the county town of Monmouth built a church in the middle of town but discreetly hidden behind three cottages. In 1871 the need for subterfuge was long gone and the cottages were demolished, the church with its simple sash widows was extended to the street frontage and a show front constructed, not dissimilar to many late nineteenth-century nonconformist chapels. By 1839-40 when the nearby urban Roman Catholic church of Newport was built all new Catholic churches were being built in gothic following the lead of Augustus Welby Pugin, the leading Catholic architect and propagandist from 1836. The ecclesiastical movement ensured that the Anglicans would follow suit and abandon then construction of large Italianate preaching 'boxes' that had dominated the rather sparse urban Anglican church construction since the reformation.

Figure 8. The Italianate Anglican Church of 1736-39 at Worthenbury, Flintshire, north-east Wales (Crown copyright RCAHMW).

Sir Christopher Wren's 52 (31 survive) influential Protestant preaching-box Italianate churches of the late seventeenth-century, built for the Anglican Church after the Great Fire of London are very well known. These usually have a Portland-stone facing and elaborate steeples but two simplified Wren-style religious buildings in red-brick round-headed style with selective Portland-stone dressings also survive and the chapel-like style was obviously used on grounds of cost. The first of these still survives in Hatton Gardens, Islington, London and also replaces an Anglican Church, St Andrew's Holborn. However, it was not included in Wren City Churches Commission but was instead built in 1687 at the initiative of Lord Hatton as a chapel-of-ease to serve the poor populace and is reputedly by Wren. The second was designed by the Quaker nonconformist mason Joseph Avis, who had worked with Wren and was begun in 1699. This is the Bevis Marks Synagogue, Britain's oldest extant Jewish place of worship and was set in east London as no Jewish place of worship was allowed in the central City and this simple box-like building is also set behind other buildings as no synagogue was then permitted to front upon the public street (Krinsky 1996, p. 16). Other synagogues with poor congregations in industrial areas continued producing Jewish places that were indistinguishable from nonconformist chapels such as the nineteenth-century example remaining in the old tinplating centre of Llanelli in south-western Wales.

Figure 9. St. John the Evangelist & Ursula 'Hidden' Catholic Church of 1671 at the Begijnhof in Amsterdam.

The Architecture of Nonconformist Christian Religion ...   119

Across Europe similar processes can be seen at work in countries where at the Reformation Calvinism or Lutheranism became the state Protestant religion and where new Catholic churches and Protestant splinter groups became the new nonconformity. Within southern Britain the Anglican Church, based on a form of Calvinism, continued to produce large churches in a traditional style with a cruciform plan, altar at the east end and very considerable architectural elaboration as shown for example in St. Paul's Cathedral in London (1675-1708) with the only significant detail differing from the pre-Reformation being the lack of statuary and the use of the Italian Renaissance rather than the gothic style. Smaller churches followed a similar process until the ecclesiastical revival of the early Victorian period, being designed in conventional form with nave, eastern chancel and western tower but generally expressed by the use of round-headed and Italianate architectural forms as shown in Wales at Dolgellau, Llanfyllin, Llanfair Caereinion, Bangor Is-coed, Worthenbury, Tredegar, Rhymney and in the Pembroke Dock Garrison Chapel. Some Anglican churches were refitted internally and the pulpit where the Word of God was proclaimed came to assume centre stage as in the St John's Anglican Church rebuilt by the gifted architect William Jernigan in north Swansea, but who also redesigned the nearby Calvinist Chapel of the Countess of Huntingdon's Connection. Galleries were also added to increase the capacity of Anglican Churches as at Blaenavon and whole Medieval churches refitted with box and family pews as in the surviving Manordeifi Church interior where the three-decker pulpit again provided an enhanced auditory focus on the north wall of the church (Lloyd, Orbach & Schofield 2004, p. 207).

By the sixteenth century Amsterdam was the chief trading city of northern Europe, and went through a seventeenth-century golden age as the capital of a vast empire and in the eighteenth century became the world's financial capital. A staunchly Catholic city siding with Spain in the Dutch civil and religious wars, until in 1578 Calvinists took civil power and expelled Catholics from Amsterdam in 'the Alteration' and after 1581 the overt practice of the Catholic religion was officially prohibited. However, many people in Amsterdam remained Catholic. They celebrated mass in their living rooms, places of work and in warehouses, frequently with the tacit consent of the authorities. In the greater toleration of the seventeenth-century this first international financial centre acquired a network of 'hidden' churches of which some notable examples remain. In this period not only were Catholic churches not allowed to have the appearance of churches because Protestantism was the State Religion but they also had to have a secular name. One of the earliest surviving is the 'De Rode Hoed' on Keizergracht which dates from 1630 and is now a cultural centre.

The female Catholic religious order of the Beguines in Amsterdam, taking vows of chastity and caring for the sick, were not nuns but a secular order that lived together in the close of houses that can still be seen (van Heyst 2004, p.3). At the Alteration of faith in 1578 the Amsterdam authorities gave the Begijnhof Church to the English-speaking community for their use. The Beguines continued to worship in the church sacristry until this too was appropriated. Then they worshipped in a variety of houses around the close. In 1665 the new parish priest Van der Mije joined two houses together for worship and subsequently in 1671 his nephew laid the foundation-stone for a new purpose-built chapel. The municipality approved the building plans on condition that the building did not look like a church from the outside (van Heyst 2004, p.9). The outside still resembles two four-storey houses and was designed by the Catholic architect in Amsterdam, Philip Vingboons. This chapel of St John the Evangelist and St Ursula has a ground-floor interrupted by a double row of columns with a space extending into the upper storey above so that the sides of the first upper floor serve as galleries. The present round-headed windows set in the old domestic-style windows of the front were added in the nineteenth-century.

The most famous of the hidden churches of Amsterdam was built in same years in a position close to the Olde Kirk in a house block fronting onto the old Voorburgwal Canal. The house had been bought by the German-born Merchant Jan Hartman in 1661 and he produced the present seven-storey block in the following two years. Jan's canal-side house fronted two others facing onto an alley and three storeys up he built a church, largely in the upper three storeys of the rear houses. At first the church was rented to Father Petrus Parmentier but it was always intended for Jan's son Cornelius, who was training for the priesthood, to officiate there. There are two floors of galleries to the church and it was extended in c.1735. It original non religious name so as not to further provoke the secular authorities was 't Haantje' but in the nineteenth-century it became known as 'Ons' Lieve Heer op Solder - Our Lord in the Attic' and is now the Amstelkring Museum (Blokhiis 2002).

Another hidden church also demonstrates the move from the classical or Italianate of the more modest disguised structure to the more assertive soaring church gothic of a church which had been allowed back into mainstream life. In 1654 the Jesuit priest Fr. Petrus Laurentius, of Franco-Flemish stock, bought three houses on the Singel Canal. In the back part of the largest of these three houses, named 'De Crytberghen' he established a hidden church. In 1677, soon after the construction of the two hidden churches already described, he replaced the church with a larger one accessible via a side alley (van Dael 2004, p.37). The new wider church was situated on the first upper floor and provided with galleries and in 1835 it was extended towards the Singel Canal and the two old houses then fronting the width of the larger church were replaced by the present Renaissance style Presbytery in which were two staircases giving access to the church. That church had classical Tuscan columns carrying the galleries and upper wall in the latter were clerestory windows.

Figure 10. 'Ons' Lieve Heer op Solder – Our Lord in the Attic' Hidden Church of 1661-63 in Amsterdam.

In 1881-83 a large new church was built next door to the presbytery. This conformed with the new ideals of the Catholic art historian Joxef Alberdingk Thijm who considered neo-classicism a pagan style and considered gothic the Christian style. The architect Alfred Tepe accordingly rebuilt the new undisguised assertive church twice as high as the neighbouring Presbytery and canalside houses and flanked by two tall and slender towers capped by spires.

Figuer 11. The elaborate Calvinist state church of the Zuiderkerk in Amsterdam, built by Hendrick de Keyser in 1603-11.

By contrast the large Pre-Reformation Catholic churches carried-on in use for the new Protestant religion but stripped of sculpture and paintings. The great new seventeenth-century churches that reflected Amsterdam's pre-eminent position did not primarily assert the simple precepts of Calvin but instead reflected the pre-eminence of the new state religion at the richest financial centre in the globe. The first of these was the Zuiderkerk designed by Hendrick de Keyser and built in 1603-11 but in form it was very much a traditional great church with western steeple, and two transepts but in the contemporary Renaissance style rather than the earlier gothic (Amsterdam Heritage, Zuiderkerk).

Figure13. The simple Nooderkerk in Amsterdam, designed by Hendrick de Keyser for a poor congregation in 1620-23.

The urban expansion project of 1613 produced the beginning of the new Outer Canal Ring Suburbs (now a World Heritage Site) which initially required two new Protestant churches for the north-western urban development. De Keyser's Westerkerk (1620-31) was a larger and grander version of his Zuiderkerk of 20 years previously. When it was completed by his son Pieter in 1631 it was the largest purpose-built Protestant Church in the world, a position that was overtaken by Wren's St. Paul's Cathedral in London when that church was completed in 1708 (Amsterdam Heritage, Westerkerk). The nave, with much taller windows than the Zuiderkerk (South Church), allowed for the use of clerestory windows, having Florentine-style tracery. The soaring Renaissance-style tiered steeple is 279ft (85m) high.

The fact that it was the relative resources available, usually dependent on the affluence and influence of a congregation, that determined the elaboration of a church structure, rather

Figure 14. Keizergrachtkerk of 1888-90, an mixed gothic and Venetian design for the Gereformeerden splinter group from the state Dutch Reformed Church in Amsterdam.

The Architecture of Nonconformist Christian Religion ...   125

The central plan Protestant church design pioneered at the Noorderkirk was much copied in the Netherlands were built at Maassluis, Groningen, Emden, Blokzijl, Bourtange and Leiden.

By the middle of the nineteenth-century the resurgent Catholic Church had firmly developed a mature gothic architectural style, forgoing the earlier domestic-looking churches with classical interiors. The Dutch State Church – the Dutch Reformed Church – had continued the building of large free-standing structures with a Mannerist or Renaissance guise. It was now up to splinter groups, and also to minority faiths or denominations of foreign origin, to produce modest worship structures set within terraces of canal-side houses and to have what focus of architectural embellishment that could be afforded firmly focussed on the front elevation facing a canal-side street. This form of simple barn -like structure with a show-front facing the street was barely indistinguishable from the thousands of prominently facaded nonconformist chapels built in southern Britain after the 1858-59 Great Revival and into the early twentieth-century.

Many architects in later nineteenth-century western Europe and in north America were trying to establish a new distinctive style which often incorporated disparate elements from the past. Nonconformists were especially keen on the often playful use of patterns of stylistic mixtures on the ornament focussed on their show-fronts which so distinguished them from the great churches of the state church and the resurgent Catholic religion.

One of the main splinter groups from the Dutch Reformed Church was the Gereformeerden who in 1888-90 built a gable-fronted chapel, or church, on the street bordering the wide Keizersgracht in Amsterdam. This Keizersgrachtkerk shows a mixing of the early gothic and Venetian styles in a design design produced by G. B. and A. Salm (Archimon, History & styles: The other neo-styles of the 19th century (ca. 1850-1900)). A classic problem with the profile of single-roofed worship buildings fronting onto a street is how to avoid the impression that the congregation are worshipping in rather an inelegant and ungainly shed. The most grandiose solution for this is to provide the gable with two flanking towers or steeples, in Wales for example there may be some 20 chapels, from 6,000, which
have these 'cathedral facades.' There are other ways of breaking-up the huge wall-surfaces of these great gable ends, and they are often vertically divided-up into three bays, or divisions. Often, in this design concept, either the central bay is recessed under a great arch, the head of which breaks up into the gable, as promoted in Wales by the architect Thomas Thomas in many of the 900 or

so chapels where he produced part or the whole of the design, or the side bays can be recessed as was done by the architect Richard Owens who was responsible for another, 200 or so, chapel designs in Wales (Hughes 2003). The Keisergrachtkerk in Amsterdam uses a form of a gothic pointed version of the great arch design breaking-up into the gable.

The device of a wheel, or roundel, window under the head of the great arch was also commonly used in the chapels of Wales as was the use of a smaller roudel, or quadre-foiled window above the arch near the head of the gable to vent the attic. The façade was also commonly split horizontally with a band or group of windows set above the central door and this device is also used on the Keisergrachtkerk.

Figure15. Gereformeerden Schinkelkerk corner chapel in Renaissance style, Amsterdam, 1890.

Another chapel of the Gereformeerden, the Schinkelkerk, of 1890, also shows some classic chapel design ideas. Like many chapels in Britain, particularly those of Wesleyan Methodism, this occupied a corner site which gave many of the benefits of being able to assert a dominating presence without the costs of having to acquire a larger site which a free-standing structure required. The chapel was executed in Renaissance style and this more modest tower-less structure resembles other nonconformist structures built internationally.

Figure 16. English Episcopal church, Amsterdam, 1827-29, a gothic church in a row of housing, J. Janssen, 1827-29.

Other non-state religious buildings had modest frontages in-scale with the residential terraced rows of houses alongside for a variety of reasons. De Papegaai ('The Parrot') as its name suggests originated as two hidden churches and consequently its frontage, although executed in 1848 in full church gothic with a large correctly traceried window, is very narrow and connected to the adjacent buildings although it widens out towards the rear and has galleries, optimising the available space without elaborate ornamentation as with its predecessors.

Figure 17. Neiuwe Waalse Kerk of 1855-56 & 1861, A. N. Godefroy, Amsterdam.

The Architecture of Nonconformist Christian Religion ... 129

A second gothic church, or chapel, built into a terraced row of buildings and with only its front façade visible is the English Episcopal Church in Amsterdam. Its large-shed profile clearly suggests its origin as a cloth-hall which the architect J. Janssen converted into the present church in 1827-29 (Archimon, Amsterdam (NH) part 2/2). Although this church was built to accommodate the resident congregation of the state Anglican Church of southern Britain it represents in this context a denomination which was nonconformist in relation to the Dutch Reformed Church. Its context is reflected in its architectural style which although a very early and influential use of gothic is divided into three bays by slender spirelet turrets and each bay is filled with three large traceried windows with simple intersecting tracery that would not be out of place in any simplified, or 'chapel gothick' structure in Wales or England.

Other minority denominations also constructed simple buildings in scale with the canalside terraces in which they were set and some minority Catholic denominations even utilised the mixed Eclectic style, the variant used here being classical or Italianate including Florentine tracery being mixed with Romanesque elements such as stepped Lombardic corbelling under the gable. This Nieuwe Waalse Kerk ('New Walloon (i.e. French-speaking south-east Belgian) Church) was built in 1855-56 by the architect A. N. Godefroy and rebuilt by him with variations in 1861. The gable-top of the shed-like profile is modified by the use of a raised central gable which is a device also used in Welsh chapels in a standard chapel design that was used in his 1860s buildings at Bethel Calvinistic Methodist Chapel, Newcastle-Emlyn; Tabernacl Newydd Welsh Independent Chapel; Bala Welsh Independent Chapel and Briton Ferry Welsh Independent Chapel in Wales. The major difference being that the Waalse Kerk raised gable was backed by a raised section of the whole roof: a device not found in Welsh nonconformist chapels.

This relationship between the extravagant, elaborate and sometimes traditional buildings of a state Calvinist or Presbyterian church and the simpler, discreet or hidden buildings of minority denominations is a fairly consistent picture between different states. A similar picture is found in Scotland where the state religion became Presbyterian in the sixteenth century. As elsewhere the internal fittings of former Catholic churches were re-organised to centre on the pulpit where the Word of God was preached. Relatively few new preaching boxes were constructed. However, in urban centres the situation was markedly different, Here, the body of a new church might be a preaching box devoid of statuary but burgh, or town, pride demanded soaring steeples be built in tiered classical guise (MacInnes 1999, p. 53). Here, it was the splinter denominations of the Presbyterians such as the 'wee frees' who constructed plain long-wall façade chapels that were barely distinguishable from their contemporary early nineteenth-century nonconformist counterparts further south in Wales and England.

Figure 18. Prefabricated Wesleyan Chapel, 1854, Fitzroy, Melbourne, Australia.

The determinants of the elaboration and style of religious buildings can also be examined in relation to the effects of migration on the scale and form of religious buildings. The first case study will be in one what the biggest city, Melbourne, of the southern Hemisphere of the British Empire in the later nineteenth century. The city was founded in the 1830s but its size and wealth were hugely increase as it became the main port and supply centre for the hugely rich gold discoveries and supply centre for the hugely rich gold discoveries made from 1856 onwards in its hinterland at such centres as Ballarat, Bendigo and Maldon. By the end of the eighteenth century the population of Melbourne was about half a million.

The expedential well-funded expansion of 'Marvellous Melbourne', and the dearth of local materials meant that much essential accommodation was made of prefabricated materials in Great Britain and shipped out to Australia.

A series of these structures remain from Governor LaTrobe's 'mansion', to the corrugated-iron houses of Coventry Street and a prefabricated Wesleyan Chapel of 1854 remains in use as All Saint's Catholic Hall, Fitzroy (Lewis, 1991, p. 70). A number of iron chapels were imported by the Wesleyans via Morewood and Rogers of England but the prefabricated were made by Edward Maw of Liverpool as a cast-mark on the chapel shows. The side walls have intermittent cast-iron pilaster columns with panels of five inch (130mm) corrugated-iron in between. There is a domestic-style window in the

Figure 19. Maldon, Victoria, Australia, Welsh Congregational Chapel of 1863.

corrugated side-wall and a stuccoed façade was added, probably in the 1860s. This is set between the corner pilasters and has a central round-headed doorway, flanked by domestic-style windows, under a classical pediment pierced by a circular attic vent. The other denominations also used prefabricated iron chapels and churches. A simple gothic Anglican example of 1855, complete with iron tower, and which also had an iron spire, remains at Bacchus Marsh in Melbourne (Lewis 1991, p.92). Another first built at Melbourne in 1855 with domestic-style windows, largely survives at the rural settlement of Bridgewater and is typical of the products of Robertson & Lister of Glasgow (Lewis 1991, p.134). Such prefabricated 'tin tabernacles' were fairly commonly built as first established nonconformist chapels in Wales and England and also as Anglican church missions.

Figure 20. Welsh Baptist Chapel of 1865 at Maldon.

The Australian states did not enforce the dominance of the established Anglican Church in quite the same way as in Wales and England and there was a diversity of denominations with the Catholic Church building gothic cathedrals in the late nineteenth century which exceeded in size those of the Anglicans. This meant that other nonconformist denominations could quickly accept themselves as part of the establishment and quite early on did not feel the need to distinguish themselves from the Anglicans by retaining the use of round-headed or Italianate architecture and switched to gothic. This process is evident on one site where the first smaller chapel quickly become used as a Sunday School to a larger secondary neighbour (a very common process on nonconformist chapel sites the world over). These particular examples were built in the rural settlement of Beechworth, where a simple round-headed Congregational Chapel was built in 1858 using the local granite (Lewis 1991, p.100). Its replacement was built in 1862 but in a polychrome brick gothic style by the Anglican Church architect Leonard Terry. A similar process can be seen in the Victorian gold-mining centre of Castlemaine where a simple round-headed chapel was built in 1855 and then rebuilt in a highly mannered elaborate three-gabled façade 'chapel-gothic' style in 1861-62 with exaggerated pinnacle turrets dividing it front three bays with vigorously patterned coloured glass filling the lancets of its idiosyncratic show façade.

Figure 21. Charles Webb's St. Andrews Anglican Church of 1856-67 in Brighton, Melbourne, Australia (the large brick church behind is later)..

The same process can be seen in the chapels of the Welsh-speaking minority which in 1862 had 20 chapels in the State of Victoria (Australia). However, the true figure of Welsh chapels in the later nineteenth-century maybe nearer fifty because of the transient nature of gold-mining activity and settlements. The Victorian (Australia) gold-mining town of Maldon had a significant Welsh entrepreneurial and mining presence. The Welsh Congregational Chapel of 1863 there is built in simple round-headed style of brick construction (Lewis 1991, p.134). Two years later, in 1865, a rather similar Welsh Baptist chapel was built in the town. A much more elaborate Italianate design with a show-front featuring a central projecting pedimented entrance with side bays topped by flat corbel-tables was built for the Welsh Baptist congregation by the architect R. A. Love who the previous year had built an elaborate be-spired developed gothic design for the Presbyterians in the town (Lewis 1991, p.149).

Figure 22 Welsh Calvinist Chapel by Charles Webb in Melbourne, of 1873.

The well established and wealthier Welsh Calvinistic Methodist congregation of Melbourne had a chapel built in fairly developed gothic by the locally well-established chapel and church architect Charles Webb in 1871. Webb's career possibly began with the design of the simple gothic Wesleyan Methodist Chapel at Brighton (Melbourne) in 1854 and certainly developed with the design of the nearby St Andrews Anglican Church in 1856-57. This already had the Webbian characteristics of corner pinnacles on the main façade with a wide traceried three-light gothic window over the central door (Lewis 1991, p.60). Webb's Welsh Chapel of 1873 has a central three light geometric decorated gothic over the central doorway flanked by pinnacle turrets which divide the show-front into three bays (Lewis 1991, p. 47). In this the design is obviously modelled on Webb's design for John Knox Free Presbyterian Church in Melbourne that was built eight years previously in 1863 (Lewis 1991, p.47). The design of the Welsh Calvinistic Chapel was later

Figure 23 John Knox Free Presbyterian Chapel of 1863, by Charles Webb, Melbourne.

refined by Webb four years later (1867) at the Congregational Chapel in Brighton (Melbourne) which has a circular rose window over the central door, also seen at his Christ Church, Dingley, and elaborate polychrome brickwork (Lewis 1991, p.59).

The development of Welsh chapels in America tells a similar story. There were over 500 Welsh language chapels in the U.S.A. but the greatest concentration were in the anthracite coal and slate quarrying areas of the Wyoming Valley of north-east Pennsylvania. By 1900 21,552 Welsh-borne parents and their children lived in the township of Wilkes-Barre and it surroundings and there were no less than 45 Welsh chapels in the area (Hartmann 1985, p.7). Twelve miles away Lackawanna County around Scranton had another 19,348 of Welsh extraction with another 30 Welsh chapels. Between them, the two areas contained one-fifth of the U.S.A.'s Welsh immigrants, attracted by the need for their skills in coal mining (Hartmann 1985, p.7). This was one of the greatest concentrations of Welsh people outside Wales itself.

Figure 24. Congregational Chapel of 1867 by Charles Webb, Melbourne, using polychrome brick.

The first Welsh chapels were built in simple round-headed style and the design of Moriah Welsh Congregational Chapel at Nanticoke has a show-front design including a triplet of an arched Venetian Window over a central doorway: a design composition that could be found any chapel in Wales

Figure 25. Methodist & Baptist Chapels of 1915 in Hill Street, Santa Monica, Los Angeles, U.S.A.

(Hartmann 1985, p. 13). However, what immediately distinguishes this chapel from one in Wales is the materials used in construction. At Moriah, Nanticoke, the chapel is a massive timber-framed structure clad in timber-plank clap- or weather-boarding set on a stone lower storey. The First Welsh Congregational Church in Pittston was a cathedral-fronted (twin-towered) design completely in timber-framed construction with round-arched double windows along the upper part of the side facades: a design element commonly found in chapels in Wales (Hartmann 1985, p. 37). However, the Welsh in Pennsylvania, away from the institutional dominance of the Anglican Church in Wales, felt no need to distinguish themselves from the gothic of an establishment to which they were rapidly assimilating themselves in a new country. Large timber-framed places of worship were now constructed very largely in gothic style, some with spired towers.

The wealth of America, and the confidence of all denominations in a free environment, meant that increasingly large and ambitious chapels and churches were built. By the early twentieth century a multiplicity of cathedral size edifices were being built in West Coast such as Los Angeles in a multiplicity of styles. Smaller nonconformist congregations here were also building many smaller chapels in sizes and styles not unlike those of the confident medium-sized Anglican churches of Wales and England.

Figure26. Early gothic (1866-67) Welsh Independent Chapel, by Thomas Thomas, Menai Bridge, Anglesey, Wales (Crown copyright, RCAHMW).

Figure 27. Antonio Gaudi's Art Nouveau Churches of Segrada Familia and Colonia Guell expressing the re-assertion of Catalan nationhood in Spain.

Back in Wales although some English-language congregations, principally the English Wesleyan Methodists switched to full church gothic in the 1840s most Welsh-language chapels were reluctant to do so. In England most nonconformists saw themselves as part of the establishment of the new industrialising society and no longer felt a need to distinguish themselves stylistically from the traditional Anglican establishment. In Wales it was a different story with gothic-style chapels built for Welsh-language Congregationalists in Menai Bridge, on Anglesey, in north-west Wales in 1866-67 being an event of considerable note (Hughes 2003). In the Welsh language slate-quarrying stronghold of north-west Wales there was felt to be a need to distinguish themselves from the English-speaking Anglican establishment right to the end of the nineteenth-century and into the early twentieth.

The Catalonian population around Barcelona in north-eastern Spain found an expression of national distinctive in the development of Art Nouveau by Antonio Gaudi, and other modernists, in late nineteenth and early twentieth-century secular and religious Catholic architecture: Sagrada Familia and the chapel at Colonia Guell being two of the most famous examples. Art Nouveau was a far too sinuous and suggestive style for Welsh non-conformity and was little used except for early twentienth-century stained-glass and iron-railings. It was in the use of Italianate architecture that the Welsh-speaking population of Wales sought to establish, retain and re-assert their national and cultural distinctiveness.

CONCLUSION

A predominant causal factor that determined the degree of elaboration of a religious structure was not the religious ideology of the sect or denomination involved but was rather dependent on the monetary resources available to that denomination and whether they were the official state-recognised and funded denomination or represented a splinter group or minority with varying degrees of tolerance and recognition. Within this framework smaller cultural, and national, groups demonstrated their identity by the use of certain distinctive architectural forms developed in their religious buildings.

ACKNOWLEDGMENTS

Informing the research for this article has been the fifteen year long nonconformist chapels recording project of the Royal Commission on the Ancient & Historical Monuments of Wales. One of the fruits of this work can be seen in the database entries for each of these chapels available at www.coflein.gov.uk . Many of these entries have historical accounts accompanied by photographs of the chapels. More international comparisons and an analysis of the distribution of architectural trends will be in the final publication of this work which should be available from 2012-13 at www.rcahmw.gov.uk . My thanks to my colleague Susan Fielding for driving this work forward with the active support of the Chairman of the Royal Commission, Dr. Eurwyn Wiliam and the Secretary (CEO) of the Royal Commission, Dr. Peter Wakelin.

REFERENCES

Amsterdam Heritage, Bureau Monumenten & Archeologie at
  http://www.bmz.amsterdam.nl/adam/uk/groot .
Archimon: The virtual museum of religious architecture in the Netherlands at
  http://noordhollandchurches.tripod.com/amsterdam.html .
Bewes, R., 2003. *Wesley Country: A Pictorial History based on John Wesley's Journal,* (Worthing, Bible Matters & Creative Publishing).
Blokhuis, M.; Boers, T.; de Jong, A.; Kiers, J.; Schillemans, R. & van Soestbergen, A. 2002, *Amstelkring Museum, Our Lord in the Attic, Amsterdam,* Amsterdam, Ludion.
Coflein: the database entries of 6,000 nonconformist chapels of Wales are available at *www.coflein.gov.uk* .
Coleman, B. I. 1980. *The Church of England in the Mid-Nineteenth Century: a social geography*, London, Historical Association.
Hartmann, E. G. 1985. *Cymry yn y Cwm: The Welsh of Wilkes-Barre and the Wyoming Valley,* Wilkes-Barr, St. David's Society of Wyoming Valley.
Hughes, S. R. 2000. *Copperopolis: Landscapes of the Early Industrial Period in Swansea*, Aberystwyth, Royal Commission on the Ancient and Historical Monuments of Wales.

142 Stephen Roy Hughes

Hughes, S. R. 2003. 'Thomas Thomas, 1817–88: the first national architect of Wales', *Archaeologia Cambrensis, 152,* 69-166.

Lewis, M. (Ed.) 1991. *Victorian Churches: Their origins, their story & their architecture,* Melbourne, National Trust of Victoria.

Lloyd, T; Orbach, J.; Scourfield, R. 2004. *The Buildings of Wales, Pembrokeshire,* New haven, Yale University Press, p. 277.

Jones, I. G. & Williams, D. (Ed.), 1976. *The Religious Census of 1851, A Calendar of the returns Relating to Wales, Volume 1, South Wales,* Cardiff, University of Wales.

Krinsky, C. H. 1996. 'Between Europe and the New World: Britain's Place in Synagogue Architecture' in Kadish, S. (Ed.). *Building Jerusalem: Jewish Architecture in Britain,* London, Vallentine Mitchell, pp.18-33.

MacInnes, R.; Glendinning, M.; MacKechie, A. 1999. *Building a Nation: The Story of Scotland's Architecture,* Edinburgh, Canongate).

McClintock, M. 1994. *Church of St Thomas the Apostle, Claughton on Brock, A Brief History. http://www.claughtononbrock.co.uk /church/church_history* .

Newman, J. 2000. *The Buildings of Wales: Gwent/Monmouthshire,* London, Penguin.

Roberts, G. M., 2009, 'Rowland, Daniel' in *Dictionary of Welsh Biography,* Aberystwyth, National Library of Wales at *Welsh Biography Online. http://wbo.llgc.org.uk/en/s-ROWL-DAN-1713.html*

Royal Commission: The 'Nonconformist Chapels project' of the Royal Commission on the Ancient & Historical Monuments of Wales, see *www.rcahmw.gov.uk* and database entries on the 6,000 nonconformist chapels of Wales available at *www.coflein.gov.uk* .

van Dael, P. 2004. *Amsterdam: De Krijtberg,* Amsterdam, Kerckebosch, Zeist.

van Heyst, E. 2004. *Begijnhof Amsterdam: Strength from what is Hidden,* Amsterdam, Begijnhof Chapel.

In: Religion
Editors: P. Bellamy and G. Montpetit

ISBN 978-1-61470-382-2
©2012 Nova Science Publishers, Inc.

Chapter 7

A POSSIBLE NEUROSCIENCE APPROACH TO SOME HEALTH BENEFITS RELATED TO RELIGION

Angelica Rosat Consiglio[*]

Universidade Federal do Rio Grande do Sul, Instituto de Biociências,
Departamento de Biofísica, Av. Bento Gonçalves, 9500,
Porto Alegre, RS, CEP 91501-970, Brazil

ABSTRACT

The 1990s were considered the Decade of the Brain; currently, importance is being given to translational research, in a mutual feedback between basic and applied health sciences. Another tendency, sometimes controversial, is the neuroscience approach of spirituality and religion, mainly triggered by some recognized benefits they bring to mental health. Isolated efforts are being made to identify the biological basis that might help explain these benefits.

Radical opinions avoiding this possible approach may be found among scientists and religious people. However, some individuals from both groups have their mind open to start investigating which viewpoints are shared and which are in disagreement, without interfering with someone´s faith or with the scientific method.

---

[*] Email: arconsig@ufrgs.br; Phone: + 55 51 3308 7615; Fax: + 55 51 3308 7003.

There are different ways to do that. Behavioral commitment or rituals found in different religious denominations may be a first measurable approach. They may include frequency of praying, going to church, etc. There is an inconvenience, though, where an unhealthy and negative side of religion may present as an obsession. Another possibility is taking brain images from persons who are representative of their religion. It has already been done with some Buddhist monks who meditate. Moreover, we could still compare some religious principles which guide their followers to some behavioral neuroscience findings.

Some principles, such as love and peace, are shared among different religious denominations, whereas some others are not. The Holy Bible is followed by Jews (the Old Testament) and Christians (the New Testament) of different denominations.

As an effort to investigate the origin of good mental health found in some religious people, it will be shown that some versicles from the Holy Bible are in agreement with some behavioral neuroscience findings.

The omission of the principles of other religions from this study does not mean or imply their lack of importance. These issues should be raised by other neuroscientists who are more familiar with them. This step is a trial to integrate neuroscience and religion, aiming at good mental health and well-being for our society.

1. OVERVIEW: PROMOTING MENTAL HEALTH

Prevention of mental disorders is a public health issue and it requires a bio-psycho-social approach. According to the WHO (2004), protective factors for prevention of mental disorders include positive attachment and early bonding, positive parent-child interaction, social support of family and friends, ability to cope with stress, and ability to face with adversity, among others.

Some studies indicate a positive correlation between religion and/or spirituality and well-being, satisfaction with life and mental health. Most of these results are applicable to mentally healthy individuals as well as to ill people, where the outcome looks better for the religious/spiritual people. It is worthy to investigate the reasons why this works in this way.

It is possible that the relationship between religion and spirituality and mental health varies depending on the specific dimension of religion and spirituality one is measuring. Optimism and social support are dimensions of religion and spirituality linked with mental health. In terms of optimism, higher levels of intrinsic religiousness and higher levels of prayer fulfillment are associated with higher levels of optimism, which in turn is associated with satisfaction with life. The mechanisms and pathways that connect religion/spirituality with health are still not clear (Salsman et al., 2005). The positive psychology movement, the recognition of the role of spirituality and religion in health and well-being, and the stress-related growth have been raised as important issues in mental health research, with important implications for those who suffered from trauma and violence (Ai and Park, 2005). Family and social support, hope and meaning in life contribute to the positive psycho-spiritual well-being in patients with advanced cancer. Whereas emotional distress, anxiety, helplessness, hopelessness and fear of death all detract from the psycho-spiritual well-being (Lin and Bauer-Wu, 2003), spiritual well-being of terminally-ill individuals keeps psychological distress of patients who are facing death to a minimum (McClain et al., 2003). Helping others is associated with higher levels of mental health, above and beyond the benefits of receiving help and other known psychospiritual, stress and demographic factors. People who are more likely to help others are older and female, and tend to be church elders; they also practice more prayer activities, report more satisfaction with prayer life, and engage in positive religious coping. On the other hand, giving beyond one's own resource is associated with worse mental health (Schwartz et al., 2003).

Sherman et al., (2005) reinforce the importance of assessing the spiritual needs of patients with advanced illness and their family caregivers. Spiritual interventions that enhance religious well-being may include prayer, scripture readings, and religious rituals and practices. Interventions to enhance existencial well-being may involve true presence, active listening, unconditional love, life review, positive affirmations, forgiveness, hopefulness or experiencing nature.

The present chapter will mainly deal with a possible link between mental health, the oxytocinergic system studied in animals and humans, and some readings of the Holy Bible.

2. STRATEGY

A temptative connection between mental health, basic neuroscience and the Holy Bible can be established once a meaningful and elementary vocabulary is known in each area and then crossed.

Some protective factors raised by the WHO (2004) for good mental health include attachment and early bonding, positive parental-child interaction, social support of family and friends, and ability to cope with stress. For those researchers who have been working with maternal behavior in basic neuroscience, an immediate connection with the oxytocinergic system can be established. Besides, the above relationships could be looked at further as an integration of partial emotional components such as love, fear and anger. These variables can be quantitatively expressed in adequate experimental protocols in animal research. Correlations among them are also found in the Holy Bible. A common thought seems to be apparently visible through a word web shared between applied and basic neuroscience, spirituality/religiosity, and the Holy Bible.

3. MENTAL HEALTH, NEUROSCIENCE AND THE HOLY BIBLE

Positive bondings throughout life favor good mental health. Whereas love underlies and emphasizes the bonding, other emotions, such as fear and anger expressed under a variety of social encounters may keep people distant. An ideal bonding should guide one to a peaceful unity and self transcendence, without impairment to the elementary components.

Under a neurobiological approach, some peptide systems have been implicated in positive affective states, both in animal and human studies. Several lines of evidence have implicated oxytocin in the central neurohormonal modulation of behaviors, such as attachment (love: romantic or friendship), sexual behavior, social recognition, memory, aggression, anxiety, stress, immunity, trustability in social interactions, and in the ability of inferring the internal state of another person (Leengoed et al., 1987; Insel, 1992; Consiglio and Lucion, 1996; Pedersen, 1997; Nelson and Panksepp, 1998; Giovenardi et al., 1998; Francis et al., 2000; Kendrick, 2000; Gimpl and Fahrenholz, 2001; Kosfeld, 2005; Domes et al. 2007). Oxytocin has been previously known by its peripheral effects on uterine contraction and milk ejection. While magnocellular neurons in the paraventricular nucleus of the hypothalamus are engaged in the milk ejection reflex during lactation, parvocellular neurons may exert modulatory effects on maternal behaviors (Giovenardi et al., 1998).

Oxytocin can be released by sensory stimuli perceived as positive, including touch, warmth and odors. Positive social interactions release oxytocin, reduce sympathoadrenal activity and increase parasympathetic vagal activity. The antistress effect of oxytocin becomes more pronounced after repeated exposures. Thus, individuals living within a social bond or supportive social group would be likely to be exposed to repetitive oxytocin release (Uvnäs-Moberg, 1998a,b). Oxytocin is anxiolytic and attenuates the stress response to psychogenic provocation in female mice (Amico et al., 2004).

So, the oxytocinergic system is very relevant when dealing with attachment.

In another perspective, different aspects of love are highlighted within the Holy Bible: the holism (Coloss 3:14), altruism (1 Cor 13:5), optimism and hope (1 Cor 13:7), higher level of priority (1 Cor 13:1-3; 1 Cor 13:13) and endurance (1 Cor 13:7-8). Directions toward love are suggested regarding attitudes (1 Cor 16:4) and it includes the idea that it must go beyond the speech and turn into action and truth (1 John 3:18) with an intensity aimed to a point that enables loving the enemies (Mt 5:43-44). It awares that this fearless behavior (1 John 4:18) is risky in a possible potential dangerous encounter and advices to be wise (Mt 10:16). A clear inverse correlation is expressed between love and fear (1 John 4:18) and a positive relationship between fear and punishment (1 John 4:18).

A possible link between love and anger can be established within the Scriptures. Since love is referred as being patient, kind, never envious, rude, resentful or never get annoyed (1 Cor 13:4-5) as well as able to love the enemies (Mt 5:43-44), it seems to show an inverse relationship between love and anger. Other advices reinforces a complementary idea of avoiding anger: through soft speech (Prov 15:1), avoiding the company of angry individuals (Prov 21:19, Prov 22:24-25), slowing down anger and expressing the advantages or reasons of doing so (Prov 16:32, Eccles 7:9).

Animal and human studies indicate the major role of the amygdala in controlling fear and anxiety. The amygdala is involved in detecting threat stimuli and linking them to defensive behaviors (Zald, 2003). The expression and endogenous activation of vasopressin and oxytocin receptors may regulate the autonomic expression of fear, through the excitement of distinct neuronal population in the central amygdala (Huber et al., 2005). Whereas low levels of oxytocin in the amygdala are related to high levels of aggression (Johns et al., 1998), exogenous oxytocin into the amygdala decreases maternal aggression (Consiglio and Lucion, 2005).

Love is present in affective (romantic, parental, friendship), social and sexual contexts. It is well recognized in a parental-child relationship, between father/mother, father/child, mother/child, as well as in a more social way among friends and the human being in general. Behaviors about parents are cited (Luke 11:11-12) and attitudes with future consequences are suggested within a family: toward parents (Prov 29:17) and sons (Prov 1:8-9). Friendship is another raised issue and worthed like a family member (Prov 17:17; Prov 18:24).

The mother-infant relationship has short and long term consequences. A behavioral change toward calmness and increased social interaction is seen in response to suckling in lactating animals and women, a pattern that is the opposite of a defensive reaction. On the other hand, the mother-infant interaction may interfere in later affective, social, sexual contexts. This relationship may not be apparent under basal circumstances, but may become apparent under stressful events in adulthood. Since mental health is dependent upon the way an adult cope with stress, attachment is clearly an important issue, either as part of the personal history or as a present and future individual perspective. Early life events (e.g. brief handling) attenuate the behavioral and neuroendocrine responses to stressors encountered in adulthood. In contrast, if neonates are subjected to a more severe stressor, such as protracted separation from the dam, then the adult response to a stressor is exaggerated (Anisman et al., 1998). The amount of maternal licking and arched-back nursing received in infancy is positively related to and appears to influence central oxytocin receptor expression in adult female (although not males) rats. The relevant brain areas to this oxytocin receptor concentration are the medial preoptic area, paraventricular nucleus of the hypothalamus, bed nucleus of the stria terminalis, lateral septum, and the central nucleus of the amygdala (Francis et al., 2000; Francis et al., 2002; Champagne et al., 2001), some of them relevant to the symptoms expressed in depression, that probably could be preserved by a highly maternal mother. Proximal separation of experienced rat mothers from pups for 6 days markedly depletes OT immunostaining in many forebrain regions (proximal separation refers to isolating pups in small cages so dams can hear, smell, and see pups, but have very limited physical contact with them). Also, the rate of reemergent maternal behavior occurring during the first several hours after unobstructed access to pups is restablished and is significantly greater in rat dams that had been proximately separated from pups for 4-6 days than in rat dams that had been totally separated from pups for the same period of time (Pedersen et al., 1995).

Helping others is associated with higher levels of mental health. On the other hand, giving beyond one's own resource is associated with worse mental health (Schwartz et al., 2003). Helping others may be seen as love in action, sharing in a fair way (2 Cor 8:13-15); at the same time it benefits who is being

A Possible Neuroscience Approach to Some Health Benefits ... 149

helped, and it does too for the one who is helping, whenever it does not go beyond someone's own limit (Act 20:35, 2 Cor 8:13-15). Besides, an ability of inferring the internal state of another person may be useful to help others and it has been shown to be improved by oxytocin. Moreover, being able to help others necessarily implies in a non-impaired action and possibly keeps active the prefrontal cortex which is responsible for executive functions. An opposite situation of hypoactivation of the prefrontal lobe is seen in depression.

The concept of forgiveness is both spiritual and social-psychological in nature, and possibly linked to some measures of human health and well-being. It has been proposed a three crucial fundamental basis of forgiveness. First, interpersonal forgiveness occurs in the context of an individual's perception that the action or actions of another person were noxious, harmful, immoral, or unjust. Second, these perceptions typically elicit emotional responses (e.g. anger or fear), motivational responses (e.g. desires to avoid the transgressor or harm the transgressor in kind), cognitive responses (e.g. hostility toward or loss of respect or esteem for the transgressor), or behavioral responses (e.g. avoidance or aggression) that would promote the deterioration of good will toward the offender and social harmony. Third, by forgiving, these negative emotional motivational, cognitive, or behavioral responses are modulated, so that more prosocial and harmonious interpersonal relations can possibly be resumed (McCullough and Worthington, 1999).

Alternatively, forgiveness is defined by some church members not as a capacity of forgetting, but actually the attitude of not taking into account a harmful action taken by others against oneself when this could be relevant to make a decision, letting it go.

So, an approach for studying forgiveness could include emotional components such as love, anger and fear, motivation, memory and behavior. A way to optimize forgiveness could include intense love and low levels of anger and fear. The emotional component that underlies the perception of a threat includes the amygdala. In terms of memory study, it should be said that the aversive memory was consolidated, but not evocated. It had been shown that oxytocin administered into the (rat) brain had no role on consolidation of aversive memory, although it did have an impairment effect on the evocation of the aversive memory (de Oliveira et al., 2007). Moreover, as already mentioned, oxytocin is also implicated in attachment and low levels of aggression. Within the Holy Bible, forgiveness is stimulated (Mt 18:21) and it is related to the intensity of love of the person who forgives or is forgiven (Luke 7:40-47) and the consequences of not forgiving are indicated (John 20: 23).

A mental health attitude may include either stimulation of positive actions and inhibition of negative ones. In Biblic terms, it should be recognized as a possible interpretation for the good or bad treasure of someone's heart (Luke 6:45).

Stressful life events may alter the oxytocinergic system and possibly trigger a depressive disorder. Under a strong stress reaction, oxytocin and other hypothalamic neuropeptides would act as antioxidants and be deviated from acting on the neural substrates that underlie some affective behaviors (Consiglio, 2006). An overall disruptive process is then seen regarding relationships, engagements with work and future plans, leading to social and economical impairments, besides a spreading suffering wave.

According to the Bible, in times of difficulties, oppression is identified as risk factor for mental health (Eccles 7:7); however, a resilient behavior is apparent (2 Co 4:8-9), persistence is incentivated (Luke 11:8), emphasis to the final action is given (Eccles 7:8) and the viewpoint that love takes death away may be all relevant to restore positive attitudes in those who are hopeless, have impaired planning and decision-making and have a suicide ideation as it is seen in depression (1 John 3:14).

Anger and depression have long been associated and causally linked. The severity of depression in depressive disorder may be related more to anger expression than to anger suppression (Koh et al. 2005). A conceptual link between aggression (in general) and social withdrawal has been already proposed, based on the same biological structures and events (Lopez et al. 2004). Depression may be characterized as a state of low positive affect. An individual becomes increasingly vulnerable to a depressive disorder when he/she perceives the imminence of a social defeat (Sloman et al., 2006). Patients with major depressive disorder and anger attacks have higher levels of perceived stress, indicating a potential reactive component to their depression (Farabaugh et al., 2004).

So far, the oxytocinergic system has been linked to attachment among mother-infant as well as to bonding and support among friends and lovers; it has an anti-stress (Uvnäs-Moberg, 1998a,b) and anti-aggressive role (Consiglio and Lucion, 2005). An impaired mother-infant relationship promotes an altered oxytocinergic neural system as adults that will be underlying altered stressful reactions (Francis et al., 2000; Francis et al., 2002; Champagne et al., 2001). In other words, an oxytocinergic neurobiological basis may help prevent some mental disorders.

It looks like different speeches used in neuroscience and in the Scriptures may be used to describe a same image of a healthy or sick society.

4. Schematic Summary

Taken together, the ideas raised here highlight different approaches centered to an axial idea of a mentally healthy society, and could be summarized as follows:

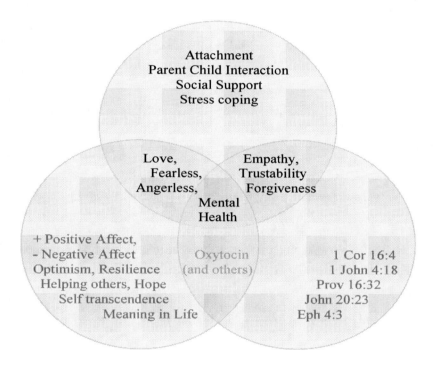

Figure 1.

5. Final Comments

Attachment is relevant either in a strict context such as in family, as well as in a more general social way. The same (ideal) picture that love may underly a peaceful and healthy social unity seems to be at least partially describable in terms of the behavioral neuroscience or the Holy Scripture. Further studies are necessary to deepen these insights.

* * * * * * * * * * * * * * *

Excerpts from the Holy Bible

Old Testament

Eccles 7

[7]Surely oppression maketh a wise man mad; and a gift destroyeth the heart. [8]Better *is* the end of a thing than the beginning thereof: *and* the patient in spirit *is* better than the proud in spirit. [9]Be not hasty in thy spirit to be angry: for anger resteth in the bosom of fools.

Prov 1

[8]My son, hear the instruction of thy father, and forsake not the law of thy mother: [9]For they *shall be* an ornament of grace unto thy head, and chains about thy neck.

Prov 15

[1]A soft answer turneth away wrath: but grievous words stir up anger.

Prov 16

[32]*He that is* slow to anger *is* better than the mighty; and he that ruleth his spirit than he that taketh a city.

Prov 17

[17]A friend loveth at all times, and a brother is born for adversity.

Prov 18

[24]A man *that hath* friends must shew himself friendly: and there is a friend *that* sticketh closer than a brother.

Prov 21

[19]*It is* better to dwell in the wilderness, than with a contentious and an angry woman.

Prov 22

[24]Make no friendship with an angry man; and with a furious man thou shalt not go: [25]Lest thou learn his ways, and get a snare to thy soul.

Prov 29

[17]Correct thy son, and he shall give thee rest; yea, he shall give delight unto thy soul.

New Testament

Act 20

[35]In every way I showed you that by working hard like this we should help the weak and remember the words that the Lord Jesus himself said, 'It is more blessed to give than to receive.'

1 Cor 13

The Supremacy of Love

[1]If I speak in the tongues of humans and angels but don't have love, I have become a reverberating gong or a clashing cymbal. [2]If I have the gift of prophecy and can understand all secrets and every form of knowledge, and if I have absolute faith so as to move mountains but don't have love, I am nothing. [3]Even if I give away all that I have and surrender my body so that I may boast but don't have love, I get nothing out of it.

[4]Love is always patient,
Love is always kind,
Love is never envious
Or vaunted up with pride.

Nor is she conceited,
[5]And never is she rude,
Never does she think of self
Or ever get annoyed.

She never is resentful,
[6]Is never glad with sin,
But always glad to side with truth,
Whene'er the truth should win.

[7]She bears up under everything,
Believes the best in all,
There is no limit to her hope,
And never will she fall.

^{8}Love never breaks down. If there are prophecies, they will be done away with. If there are tongues, they will cease. If there is knowledge, it will be done away with. ^{9}For what we know is incomplete and what we prophesy is incomplete.^{10}But when what is complete comes, then what is incomplete will be done away with.^{11}When I was a child, I spoke like a child, thought like a child, and reasoned like a child. When I became a man, I gave up my childish ways. ^{12}Now we see only a blurred reflection in a mirror, but then we will see face to face. Now what I know is incomplete, but then I will know fully, even as I have been fully known. ^{13}Right now three things remain: faith, hope, and love. But the greatest of these is love.

1 Cor 16
^{4}Everything you do should be done in love.

2 Cor 4
^{8}In every way we're troubled but not crushed, frustrated but not in despair, ^{9}persecuted but not abandoned, struck down but not destroyed.

2 Cor 8
^{13}Not that others should have relief while you have hardship. Rather, it's a question of fairness. ^{14}At the present time, your surplus fills their need, so that their surplus may fill your need. In this way things are fair. ^{15}As it is written,

> "The person who had much didn't have too much,
> and the person who had little didn't have too little.

Coloss 3
^{14}Above all, clothe yourselves with love, which ties everything together in unity.

Eph 4
^{3}Do your best to maintain the unity of the Spirit by means of the bond of peace.

1 John 3
^{14}We know that we have passed from death to life, because we love one another. The person who doesn't love remains in death.

1 John 3

[18]Little children, we must stop loving in word and in tongue, but instead love in action and in truth.

1 John 4

[18]There is no fear where love exists. Rather, perfect love banishes fear. For fear involves punishment, and the person who lives in fear has not been perfected in love.

John 20

[23]If you forgive people's sins, they are forgiven. If you retain people's sins, they are retained."

Luke 6

[45]A good person produces good from the good treasure of his heart, and an evil person produces evil from an evil treasure. For it is out of the abundance of the heart that the mouth speaks.

Luke 7

[40]Jesus said to him, "Simon, I have something to say to you." "Teacher," he replied, "say it." [41]"Two men were in debt to a moneylender. One owed him 500 denarii, and the other 50. [42]When they couldn't pay it back, he generously canceled the debts for both of them. Now which of them will love him the most?" [43]Simon answered, "I suppose the one who had the larger debt canceled." Jesus said to him, "You have answered correctly."

[44]Then, turning to the woman, he said to Simon, "Do you see this woman? I came into your house. You didn't give me any water for my feet, but this woman has washed my feet with her tears and dried them with her hair. [45]You didn't give me a kiss, but this woman, from the moment I came in, has not stopped kissing my feet. [46]You didn't anoint my head with oil, but this woman has anointed my feet with perfume. [47]So I'm telling you that her sins, as many as they are, have been forgiven, and that's why she has shown great love. But the one to whom little is forgiven loves little."

Luke 11

[5]Then he said to them, "Suppose one of you has a friend, and you go to him at midnight and say to him, 'Friend, let me borrow three loaves of bread.

[6]A friend of mine on a trip has dropped in on me, and I don't have anything to serve him.' [7]Suppose he answers from inside, 'Stop bothering me! The door is already locked, and my children are with me in bed. I can't get up and give you anything!' [8]I tell you, even though he doesn't want to get up and give him anything because he is his friend, he will get up and give him whatever he needs because of his persistence. [9]So I say to you: Keep asking, and it will be given you. Keep searching, and you will find. Keep knocking, and the door will be opened for you. [10]For everyone who keeps asking will receive, and the person who keeps searching will find, and the person who keeps knocking will have the door opened.[11]What father among you, if his son asks for bread, would give him a stone, or if he asks for a fish, would give him a snake instead of the fish? [12]Or if he asks for an egg, would he give him a scorpion?

Mt 5

[43]"You've heard that it was said, 'You must love your neighbor' and hate your enemy. [44]But I say to you, love your enemies, and pray for those who persecute you.

Mt 10

[16]Behold, I send you forth as sheep in the midst of wolves: be ye therefore wise as serpents, and harmless as doves.

Mt 18:21

[21]Then Peter came up and asked him, "Lord, how many times may my brother sin against me and I have to forgive him? Seven times?" [22]Jesus said to him, "I tell you, not just seven times, but seventy-seven times!

REFERENCES

Ai, AL; Park, CL. Possibilities of the positive following violence and trauma: informing the coming decade of research. *J. Interpers. Violence* 2005, 20, 242-250.

Amico, JA; Mantella, RC; Vollmer, RR; Li, X. Anxiety and stress response in female oxytocin deficient mice. *J. Neuroendocrinol.* 2004, *16*, 319-324.

Anisman, H; Zaharia, MD; Meaney, MJ; Merali, Z. Do early-life events permanently alter behavioral and hormonal responses to stressors? *Int. J. Devel. Neurosci.* 1998, 16(3-4), 149-164.

A Possible Neuroscience Approach to Some Health Benefits ... 157

Champagne, FC; Diorio, J; Sharma, S; Meaney, MJ. Naturally occurring variations in maternal behavior in the rat are associated with differences in estrogen-inducible central oxytocin receptors. *Proc. Natl. Acad. Sci. USA* 2001, 98, 12736-12741.

Consiglio, AR; Lucion, AB. Lesion of hypothalamic paraventricular nucleus and maternal aggressive behavior. *Physiol. Behav.* 1996, 59(4-5), 591-596.

Consiglio, AR; Borsoi, A; Pereira, GA; Lucion, AB. Effects of oxytocin microinjected into the central amygdaloid nucleus and bed nucleus of stria terminalis on maternal aggressive behavior in rats. *Physiol. Behav.* 2005, 85(3), 354-362.

Consiglio, AR. Depression under the perspective of oxytocin. *Central Nervous System Agents in Medicinal Chemistry* 2006, 6, 293-310.

De Oliveira, LF; Camboim, C; Diehl, F; Consiglio, AR; Quillfeldt, JA. Glucocorticoid-mediated effects of systemic oxytocin upon memory retrieval. *Neurobiol. Learn Mem.* 2007, 87(1), 67-71.

Domes, G; Heinrichs, M; Michel, A; Berger, C; Herpertz, SC. Oxytocin improves "mind-reading" in humans. *Biol. Psychiatry* 2007, 61(6), 731-733.

Farabaugh, AH, Mischoulon, D; Fava, M; Green, C; Guyker, W; Alpert, J. The potential relationship between levels of perceived stress and subtypes of major depressive disorder (MDD). *Acta Psychiatr. Scand.* 2004, 110(6), 465-70.

Francis, DD; Champagne, FC; Meaney, MJ; Variations in maternal behaviour are associated with differences in oxytocin receptor levels in the rat. *J. Neuroendocrinol.* 2000, 12(12), 1145-1148.

Francis, DD; Young, LJ; Meaney, MJ; Insel, TR. Naturally occurring differences in maternal care are associated with the expression of oxytocin and vasopressin (V1a) receptors: genders differences. *J. Neuroendocrinol.* 2002, 14, 349-353.

Gimpl, G; Fahrenholz, F. The oxytocin receptor system: structure, function, and regulation. *Physiol. Rev.* 2001, 81(2), 629-683.

Giovenardi, M; Padoin, MJ; Cadore, LP; Lucion, AB. Hypothalamic paraventricular nucleus modulates maternal aggression in rats: effects of ibotenic acid lesion and oxytocin antisense. *Physiol. Behav.* 1998, 63(3), 351-359.

Holy Bible:
-*The King James Version*, (Cambridge: Cambridge) 1769.

-International Standard Version, New Testament, (Yorba Linda, CA: Davidson Press) 1999.

Huber, D; Veinante, P; Stoop, R. Vasopressin and oxytocin excite distinct neuronal populations in the central amygdala. *Science* 2005, 308, 245-248.

Insel, TR. Oxytocin - a neuropeptide for affiliation: evidence from behavioral, receptor autoradiographic, and comparative studies. *Psychoneuroendocrinology* 1992, 17(1), 3-35.

Johns, JM; Nelson, CJ; Meter, KE; Lubin, DA; Couch, CD; Ayers, A; Walker, CH. Dose-dependent effects of multiple acute cocaine injections on maternal behavior and aggression in Sprague-Dawley rats. *Dev. Neurosci.* 1998, 6, 525–532.

Kendrick, KM. Oxytocin, motherhood and bonding. *Exp. Physiol.* 2000, 85, 111S-124S.

Koh, KB; Kim, DK; Kim, SY; Park, JK. The relation between anger expression, depression, and somatic symptoms in depressive disorders and somatoform disorders. *J. Clin. Psychiatry* 2005, 66(4), 485-491.

Kosfeld, M; Heinrichs, M; Zak, PJ; Fishbacher, U; Fehr, E. Oxytocin increases trust in humans. *Nature* 2005, 435, 673-676.

Leengoed, E; Kerker, E; Swanson, HH. Inhibition of post-partum maternal behavior in the rat by injecting an oxytocin antagonist into the cerebral ventricles. *J. Endocrinol.* 1987, 112, 275-282.

Lin, H-R; Bauer-Wu, SM. Psycho-spiritual well-being in patients with advanced cancer: an integrative review of the literature. *J. Adv. Nurs.* 2003, 44(1), 69-80.

Lopez, NL; Vazquez, DM; Olson, SL. An integrative approach to the neurophysiological substrates of social withdrawal and aggression. *Dev. Psychopathol.* 2004, 16(1), 69-93.

McClain, CS; Rosenfeld, B; Breitbart, W. Effect of spiritual well-being on end-of-life despair in terminally-ill cancer patients. *The Lancet* 2003, 361, 1603-1607.

McCullough ME; Worthington, EL. Religion and the forgiving personality. *J. Personality* 1999, 67(6), 1141-1164.

Nelson, EE; Panksepp, J. Brain substrates of infant-mother attachment: contributions of opioids, oxytocin, and norepinephrine. *Neurosci. Biobehav. Rev.* 1998, 22(3), 437-452.

Pedersen, CA. Oxytocin control of maternal behavior. Regulation by sex steroids and offspring stimuli. *Ann. N. Y. Acad. Sci.* 1997, 807, 126-145.

Pedersen, CA; Johns, JM; Musiol, I; Perez-Delgado, M; Ayers, G; Faggin, B; Caldwell, JD. Interfering with somatosensory stimulation from pups sensitizes experienced, postpartum rat mothers to oxytocin antagonist inhibition of maternal behavior. *Behav. Neurosci.* 1995, 109(5), 980-990.

Salsman JM; Brown, TL; Bechting, EH; Carlson, CR. The link between religion and spirituality and psychological adjustment: the meaning role of optimism and social support. *Pers. Soc. Psychol. Bull.* 2005, 31, 522-535.

Schwartz, C; Meisenhelder, JB; Ma, Y; Reed, G. Altruistic social interest behaviors are associated with better mental health. *Psychosomatic Medicine* 2003, 65, 778-785.

Sherman, DW; Ye, XY; McSherry, C; Calabrese, M; Parkas, V; Gatto, M. Spiritual well-being as a dimension of quality of life for patients with advanced cancer and AIDS and their family caregivers: results of a longitudinal study. *Am. J. Hosp. Palliat. Care* 2005, 22, 349-362.

Sloman, L; Farvolden, P; Gilbert, P; Price, J. The interactive functioning of anxiety and depression in agonistic encounters and reconciliation. *J. Affect Disord.* 2006, 90(2-3),93-99.

Uvnäs-Moberg, K. Antistress pattern induced by oxytocin. *News Physiol. Sci.* 1998a, 13, 22-26.

Uvnäs-Moberg, K. Oxytocin may mediate the benefits of positive social interaction and emotions. *Psychoneuroendocrinology.* 1998b, 23(8), 819-835.

WHO: Prevention of mental disorders – effective interventions and policy options: Summary Report. World Health Organization: Geneva, 2004.

Zald, DH. The human amygdala and the emotional evaluation of sensory stimuli. *Brain Res. Brain Res. Rev.* 2003, 41(1), 88-123.

In: Religion
Editors: P. Bellamy and G. Montpetit

ISBN 978-1-61470-382-2
©2012 Nova Science Publishers, Inc.

Chapter 8

DOES RELIGION CAUSE VIOLENCE?

Joseph Chuman
Columbia University, New York, NY

THE INTERNATIONAL RELIGIOUS RESURGENCE

Among the most dramatic and unpredicted phenomena of the past thirty years has been the resurgence of religion on the world scene. Defying secularization theorists who predicted that religion would increasingly retreat to the margins of society in the wake of industrialization, modernization and scientific development, religion has returned with energy born of four centuries of relative privatization and rejection from the political sphere. Not only has religion challenged the presumptions of the liberal secular state, it has forced itself on the world with paroxysms of violence which have dashed the hopes that the close of humankind's bloodiest century would usher in a new epoch of peace.

Clearly not all violence is fomented by religion, nor is religion a salient factor in much of the world's recent conflicts. The wars raging in Congo, in which up to four million people have perished, are waged along primarily tribal lines and reflect brute power struggles, in which religious difference plays no significant role. The Shining Path guerillas of Peru engaged in terror, as do Basque separatists and narco-terrorists in Colombia, but religion is not a factor in this violence.

Nevertheless, the fusion of religion and politics has found expression in each of the world's historical religions. In India, Hindu nationalists seek to replace the official secular ideology of the state with the doctrine of "Hindutva" and a new explicitly Hindu constitution. The result has been an invigorated outbreak of mass violence targeting the Muslim minority, and to a lesser extent directed at Christians. In Sri Lanka, the government dominated by Sinhalese Buddhists has been embroiled in an egregiously terroristic struggle with the Tamil Hindu minority, a conflict sanctioned by sectors of the Buddhist priesthood. In the West Bank, religious Messianists comprise the trenchant hard core of the settler movement as suicide bombings and Israeli retaliation remain continual occurrences of that tragic conflict. While power sharing has diminished Catholic-Protestant strife in Ulster, the peace is fragile and sporadic violence remains a looming possibility. In the United States, the rise of politicized evangelical and fundamentalist Christianity has moved the political landscape far to the right. Though the Christian right has not been violent on the domestic scene, it has provided the context within which members of extremist fringe groups have been empowered to murder doctors providing abortions and has given sanction to violence-prone militia groups touting racist and anti-Semitic propaganda. On the American foreign relations front, Christian evangelicals comprise the largest constituency for the invasion of Iraq, in part legitimating that support via theological rationales linked to Armageddon End Times scenarios.

It is the awakening of politicized Islam, especially since the Iranian revolution of 1979, that has evoked new challenges and has spurred thinking about role of religion in the international political theater. The list of violent acts against American targets, or perceived surrogates of Western hegemonic interests, committed in the name of Islam is long - from the assassination of Anwar Sadat by the Egyptian Islamic Group in 1981, though the killing of foreign tourists at Luxor in the 1990s to the state sponsored terrorism of Iran, to the Islamic Jihad groups in the Occupied Territories. With Hizbollah in Lebanon and the brutal and terroristic civil war sustained by fundamentalists in Algeria, the list grows to include post 9/11 assaults in Bali, Tunisia and Morocco. Inclusive of attacks on American identified targets both at home and abroad have been the first assault on the World Trade Center in 1993, bombings in Riyadh, Saudi Arabia in 1995, the Khobar Towers attack in 1996, the destruction of United States embassies in Tanzania and Kenya in 1998, the USS Cole in Yemen in October 2000, culminating in the destruction of the World Trade Center and assault on the Pentagon.

The latter unprecedented attack on America launched the "war against terrorism", the pursuit of the Al Qaeda network worldwide, and the routing of their Taliban hosts in Afghanistan while providing justification for the invasion and occupation of Iraq.

In great measure the return of religion reflects a crisis of modernity and dissatisfaction in broad sectors of the developing world with the failure of the liberal secular state to sustain adequate standards of living and provide a framework of hope for more bountiful futures. It's a condition severely aggravated by the disparities wrought by rapid globalization. In the Arab world, in particular, the promise of Western secular governments has transmogrified into oppressive military dictatorships in many cases sustained by American support. Secularism, touted as a vehicle toward development in the early phases of the post-colonial era, is now perceived as a looming vestige of imperialism. Despair with secular government, both liberal and Marxist, originating in the West, has inspired the call for cultural liberation rooted in religion and movements to replace secular nationalism with various agendas propounding religion-based nationalism.

THE QUESTION OF RELIGION AND VIOLENCE

With the demise of hostilities following the collapse of the Soviet Union in 1991 and the end of the Cold War, theorists see the alliance to religion and its resurgence as filling the vacuum of political loyalties, thus establishing a new framework governing international relations. According to political theorists such as Samuel Huntington and Mark Jurgensmeyer, we are confronting "a clash of civilizations" and a "new Cold War" replacing the paradigms of bi-lateralism and the policy of containment that dominated relations between the West and the Soviet bloc for the past half-century.[1] Religion is the anchor of this new framework, for as Huntington alleges, "religion is the central characteristic of civilizations..."[2] suggesting that religion is a dominant engine of violence.

The religious resurgence and the growth of violence and terror committed in religion's name bring into relief the issue of religion's dynamic relationship to violence. The specific question of whether religion causes violence is the

---

[1] Samuel P. Huntington, The Clash of Civilizations (Cambridge: Cambridge University Press, 1999) Mark Juergensmeyer, The New Cold War? (Berkeley and Los Angeles, 1993).

[2] Huntington, p. 47.

164   Joseph Chuman

focal inquiry of this essay, recognizing that in these times we cannot avoid placing the religious factor in the forefront of analysis if obstacles to peace are to be overcome.

We are confronted straightaway with the knotty problem of teasing out the religious factor from other dynamics – economic, political, ethnic, psychological and ideological – which comprise the matrix from which violence is spawned. Human motivation is never mono-causal, but is a product of a complex of dynamics and contexts. Is religion a root cause of violence? Does it function primarily as a legitimator of violence, the causes of which are rooted in other dynamics? Or in violence between different religious groups, does religion serve merely as marker identifying the boundaries between groups? In short, is religion an effective cause of violence, or is its role epiphenomenal?.

In this regard, the typology presented by political theorists, Andreas Hasenclever and Volker Rittberger is instructive. They sketch three possible roles in assessing religion's place in violent conflict. *Primordialists* see religion as an important independent variable in spurring violence. "Collectives at the national as well as international level tend to form alliances around common cosmologies and tensions arise and escalate primarily between alliances with different cosmologies."[3] The primordial view, so described, coheres with "the clash of civilizations" hypothesis. For *instrumentalists*, religious differences can aggravate arenas of conflict, but conflict is "rarely if ever caused by them." Violence would have been caused in any event, driven by economic and other factors. For *moderate constructivists,* religion is a motive force in engendering violence – or forestalling it. Religion provides legitimation when other factors are present in violence prone situations, and religious leaders can either provide that legitimation or withhold it. Instrumentalists and moderate constructivists both agree that political and economic forces are primary in the fostering of inter-group violence. And both concur that wars cannot be initiated without leadership elites. Yet for the latter, appeals to religious rhetoric and motivations are not unlimited. According to Hasenclever and Rittberger, while instrumentalists "...suggest that, ultimately, determined leaders can manipulate religious traditions at will and that the justification of violence is at best rhetorical but not a substantial problem, moderate constructivists insist

---

[3] Andreas Hasenclever and Volker Rittberger ,"Does Religion Make a Difference? Theoretical Approaches to the Impact of Faith on Political Conflict"in Fbio Petito and Pavlos Hatzopoulos, eds. Religion in International Relations (New York: Palgrave MacMillan, 2003), p. 108.

Does Religion Cause Violence? 165

that religious traditions are intersubjective structures that have a life of their own."[4] In other words, religion is an "intervening variable" whose influence can lead to violence or to peaceful accommodation.

This cluster of issues raises a second core problem: In order to assess the power of religion to motivate violence, we must ask how religion operates in the lives of its adherents. I have found that in many contemporary discussions of religion, there is often neglect of the functional nuances of religion. Many commentators impose upon the category of religion an implied monlithicism that neglects the reality that religion is highly differentiated force from religion to religion, from adherent to adherent and within the hearts and minds of individual believers. The nuanced and differentiated nature of religion, I contend, is a prerequisite for understanding its relationship to violence.

RELIGION, THICK AND THIN

Religious and secular dispositions and actions comprise a dynamic mix in both individuals and collectives. There is a descending slope from the pervasively religious to the secular with innumerable intervening gradations, though no human behavior can be construed as purely religious or wholly secular. Within highly religious traditional cultures the intrusion of practical concerns, inclusive of strategies for survival, mercantile activity, and the pursuit of prevailingly pragmatic interests etc., ensure the infusion of non-religious modes of thought and behavioral motivators. Contrawise, even the most secular of individuals and cultures harbor values that transcend empirical verification and rational analysis, and so in the wider sense can be understood as religious, though not so named. Consequently, the determination of religion as a root cause of violence, or its prevailing cause, requires an analysis of the pervasiveness of the religious factor amid a range of intersecting motivators within individuals and groups.

The ability of religion to serve as a substantial resource of human behavior is a theme richly explored in the social sciences. Freud's polemical assault on religion as the leading competitor with the scientific weltanschauung, and its role in providing consolation in the face of existential hardships, bespeaks its inspirational power.[5] For Clifford Geertz religion is "a system of symbols

---

[4] ibid., p.104.

[5] See especially Sigmund Freud, *The Future of an Illusion* (Garden City: Anchor, 164) ch. 7and *New* Introdu*ctory Lectures on Psychoanalysis,* lecture xxxv.

166   Joseph Chuman

which acts to establish powerful, pervasive, and long lasting moods and motivations in men by formulating conceptions of a general order of existence and clothing these conceptions with such an aura of factuality that the moods and motivations seem uniquely realistic."[6] The motivational factor of religion and its realism is such that "It alters, often radically, the whole landscape presented to common sense, alters it in such a way that the moods and motivations induced by religious practice seem themselves supremely practical, the only sensible ones to adopt given the way things 'really' are."[7] For Mircea Eliade, the human being is a *homo religiosus* who strives to live primordially in a sacralized cosmos. Within the consciousness of the religious person of archaic societies the religious sphere is the "really real", the realm of power which he is propelled to seek.[8] And for Emile Durkheim, religion is a dynamic concept fueled by the collective power of the group on which the individual depends.[9]

It is significant to note that the definitions and descriptions of religion of these classical thinkers are drawn from traditional societies, and not from the advanced industrialized world which has experienced pervasive secularization. Under the force of modernization, the religious element will be diluted by other motivators, and its role significantly pushed to the background. Yet, as these thinkers have clearly established, religion, as expressed prevailingly through myth and ritual, can serve as a powerful root cause motivating behavior. This power results, moreover, from religion's ability to banish chaos and its resultant anxiety, while locating the individual within the framework of an ordered universe. The question I now turn to is whether religion is inherently violent or contains combustible elements which readily burst into violence with requisite stimulus.

For many theorists, there are elements distinctive to religion that make it especially dangerous. Borrowing from the theologian, Paul Tillich, Lloyd Steffen identifies religion with that which is ultimately transcendent. Because religion incorporates ultimacy at its core it "opens up a realm of power like no

---

[6] Clifford Geertz, "Religion as a Cultural Symbol" *The Interpretation of Cultures* (Basic Books: 1973) p. 90.

[7] ibid., p.122.

[8] The dichotomization of reality into sacred and profane space and time is foundational to Eliade's theory of religion. See Mircea Eliade, *The Sacred and Profane* (San Diego, New York, London: Harcourt Brace and Company, 1987.

[9] Emile Durkheim, *The Elementary Forms of the Religious Life* (New York: Collier Books, 1961).

Does Religion Cause Violence? 167

other."[10] "Religion can motivate and sanction violence, having the power sufficient to legitimate harmful acts in a realm of ultimate meaning and through ultimate authority."[11] While ultimacy can point humans beings toward the good, and be a potent source of human flourishing, for Steffen, religion turns malignant when ultimacy is identified with absolutism. The Absolute, which is all encompassing, envelops both the good and all that opposes the good. When absolute evil becomes ultimate, hatred, destruction and violence take on religious meaning. A discrete religion which appeals to the Absolute also becomes the locus for the assertion of its own positive identity to the exclusion of those deemed to be "outsiders." Hence religion becomes the venue *par excellence* for dividing good from evil, those blessed by God from the accursed, the saved from the damned, the believer from the heretic. This capacity to create divisions between communities renders religion a powerful agent in fomenting xenophobia and xenophobic violence. When religious minorities reside within a dominant culture their juxtaposition, coupled with differences in worldviews, can grow fractious as a result of cognitive dissonance that emerges between the groups. Moreover, absolute justice is divine justice, and no power commands with the authority and power of one's commanding God. The divine mandate to slay the infidel is poised to resist compromise and subordination to any earthbound requirement.

For Sigmund Freud, religion is essentially violent. Freud made use of the leading social science of his day, borrowing from the thought of Charles Darwin, James Frazier and Emile Durkheim, among others. Though his theory of religious origins is dated, it finds a place in the canon of the sociology of religion.

Freud envisions a primal horde living under the rule of an authoritarian father, who appropriates the females of the tribe.[12] The brothers arise to slay the primal father whom they subsequently cannibalize. Motivated by guilt, the brothers establish a totem, which they both venerate and fear, while creating a taboo against incest. For Freud religion is an edgy affair. Religious devotion is aligned with the repressive moral functions vested in the superego that heighten intra-psychic tension and seek release. Behind religion, and masked from the contemporary believer in metaphor and symbol, is the act of the primal parricide. At its core, religion is driven by aggression and violence.

---

[10] Llloyd Steffen, *The Demonic Turn* (Cleveland: The Pilgrim Press, 2003) p.39.

[11] ibid., p. 37.

[12] Freud's most elaborate rendering of his theory of religious origins is found in *Totem and Taboo* (W.W. Norton and Company. Inc: New York, 1950).

168   Joseph Chuman

Rene Girard carries forward the Freudian approach to religion. For Girard the dynamics of aggression and sex are replaced by mimetic desire. As he notes, "Two desires converging on the same object are bound to clash. Thus, mimesis coupled with desire leads automatically to conflict."[13] Whenever the disciple borrows from his model what he believes to be the 'true' object he tries to possess that truth by desiring precisely what the model desires. Whenever he sees himself closest to the supreme goal, he comes into violent conflict with his rival."[14] The purpose of religion is to divert this violence-laden desire and render it harmless. Speaking of religious practice, Girard concludes, "The idea of ritual purification is far more than mere shadow play or illusion. The function of ritual is to 'purify' violence, that is to 'trick' violence into spending itself on victims whose death will provoke no reprisals."[15] Again, we observe that religion is played out in symbolic form cloaking its fundamentally violent character.

Moving beyond essentialist theories to the manifest content of religious myth, it is noted that the scriptures of world religions are replete with values that are life and peace affirming, while in other places they invoke martial metaphors, military conflict, and divinely sanctioned killing. The Ten Commandments prohibit murder. (Exodus 20:13). The Book of Psalms enjoins believers to "Depart from evil, and do good; seek peace, and pursue it." (Psalms 34:15). The Hebrew prophets Micah and Isaiah describe Messianic times as period wherein "they shall beat their swords into pruning hooks: nation shall not lift up a sword against nation, neither shall they learn war anymore." (Micah 4:3, Isaiah 2:4).

In The New Testament, Jesus is a messenger of peace. "Blessed are the peacemakers, for they shall be called sons of God." (Matthew 5:9). "...if anyone hits you on the right cheek, offer him the other as well." (Matthew 5:19). "For he is our peace, who has made us both one, and has broken down the dividing wall of hostility..." (Ephesians 2:14).

But we find in both the Jewish and Christian scriptures passages that can be employed to justify violence and war making. In the Hebrew bible, it is written, "the Lord is a warrior." (Exodus 15:3). After the Israelites enter the Promised Land under the leadership of Joshua, God commands the extermination of the resident population inclusive of "men and women, young

---

[13] Rene Girard, *Violence and the Sacred* (Baltimore and London: Johns Hopkins University Press, 1977) p. 146.

[14] ibid., p. 148.

[15] ibid., p. 36.

and old, oxen, sheep and donkeys" thus giving license to divinely sanctioned genocide (Josh. 6:21). In Exodus and Deuteronomy, the children of Amalek are defined as Israel's perpetually enemy, "The Lord's war against Amalek is from generation to generation" (Ex 17.14,16; Deut. 25.17-19). Despite later interpretation, the Gospel is not wholly pacifistic. Jesus proclaims that he had "not come to bring peace to the world, but a sword" (Matt 10:34). The final text of the Christian canon, the Book of Revelation, is a kaleidoscope of phantasmagoric images centered on apocalyptic war between the legions of the blessed and the legions of Satan culminating in final judgment and the establishment of a new heaven and earth.

In Islam, *jihad* or striving, is a central aspirational concept of Muslim life. Those who portray Islam as a religion of peace will underscore a spiritual interpretation of *jihad* as striving for a moral and virtuous life in submission to the will of God. Such spokespersons will invoke Muhammad's proclamation on returning from battle. "We return from the lesser *jihad* to the greater *jihad*." Or when referring to martial conflict, will invoke the Koran's commitment to defensive war. "And fight in the way of God with those who fight you, but aggress not: God loves not the aggressors." (2:190) But Mohammed is not solely an administrator and prophet. He is also a military leader who vanquishes neighboring tribes. (e.g 8:6). Citations drawn from the Koran have also been used to justify *jihad* for expansionist and aggressive purposes, including terrorist assault on the stated enemies of the Islamic *ummah*. "When the sacred months have passed, slay the idolators wherever you find them, and take them, and confine them, and lie in wait for them in every place of ambush." (9:5) In Islam, as with all the traditions, text and mythos can be employed for multiple purposes and are endowed with multiple meanings that elude definite interpretation from which there can be no dissent. Words, in the final analysis, are sanctioned by their use.

The Vedas, the most sacred scripture of Hinduism, has warriors calling on the gods to engage in their own violent conflicts. Perhaps the most beloved of Hindu epics, the *Bhagavad Gita* is a military saga that validates *dharmic* responsibility for killing. Buddhism is arguably the most pacifistic of all the great religions, yet, violence is permitted under certain limited circumstances. The Pali Chronicles of Sri Lanka, which have assumed scriptural significance, tell of the battles waged by early Buddhist kings.[16]

In times of relative tranquility, when religious cultures are not pressed by economic austerity or political challenges, military myths can be read

---

[16] Juergensmeyer, *The New Cold War?* p. 158.

170 Joseph Chuman

metaphorically as inspirational sources by which to engage in spiritual struggle. In times of stress, by contrast, material otherwise interpreted metaphorically can be transmogrified into a call for literal violence against external enemies. As Mark Juergensmeyer reminds us, religious war is cosmic war. [17] It is violence tied to divine command, and what would otherwise be interpreted as a merely political cause, becomes a sacred cause, an eternal cause to which all other interests are subordinated. The cosmic character of religious warfare also accounts for its often-expressed dramatic and symbolic manifestation.

The discussion until this point has been of "thick" religion, implying that religion is a root motivator of human behavior, inclusive of violent behavior. Yet, central to my thesis is the assumption that religion is never of this unalloyed character. It is always intermixed with practical and secular concerns that dilute its strength. This political fact suggests that heterogeneous cultures require and are based upon the infusion of secular values to remain viable, orderly and cooperative. In a globalized world, experiencing the "universalization of particularisms",[18] this interpenetration of non-religious values into religious life at virtually all levels has become inescapable. Religious cultures are today increasingly, and in many instances, pervasively, exposed to forms of economic organization, bureaucratic management, high technology, and political discourse inclusive of the secular and universal values of human rights which emerge, in great measure, from outside those cultures and carry a prevailing instrumental and non-religious valance. The contemporary religious resurgence is, therefore, in great measure, reactive to the imposition of globalized values, with which it is inextricably interdependent. This ensures, that however ostensibly parochial the religious reaction, and however intense, resurgent forms of religion and the communities inspired by them lack the organic character of traditional religion. They are ineliminably infused with secular values, diminishing the univocal power of religion in motivating behavior.

Political scientist, Benjamin Barber, has speculated on the dialectics of globalization and the reactions it has spawned in the form of communal and religious resurgence. In Barber's analysis, the forces of modernization, Westernization and globalization, the forces of "McWorld", are inseparably

---

[17] ibid., pp. 156-163.

[18] See Robert McCorquodale and Richard Fairbrother, "Globalization and Human Rights" in *Human Rights Quarterly* 21.3 (1999) p. 724.

Does Religion Cause Violence? 171

yoked to the emergent parochial backlash, termed "Jihad." Yet, the phenomenon of contemporary reactive religion is not pre-modern, for it is ineluctably apiece with the dynamics of modernization.

> Jihad stands not so much in stark opposition as in subtle counterpoint to McWorld and is itself a dialectical response to modernity whose features both reflect and reinforce the modern world's virtues and vices – Jihad *via* McWorld rather than Jihad *versus* McWorld.[19]

The interpenetration of the new communalism with the dynamics of modernity ensures that religion is more accessible to transformation, more unstable, more of an elective and contractual phenomenon than organic. This mitigating factor opens the possibility for evolving accommodation with the values that make for cooperation and peace, which I explore at the conclusion of this essay.

The role of religion within the psychological framework of the individual roughly parallels the situation involving collectives. Human personalities as well as groups harbor sentiments that are differentiated in their structure.[20] Religious thoughts and emotions can be complex and held by the believer in ways that encompass reflection, criticism and reworked interpretation. While religion claims to be the most comprehensive of interest systems, it is not the only interest system that drives and inspires behavior. Human beings, as noted, are motivated by physical needs and employ pragmatic strategies necessary to ensure survival, as well as modes of ratiocination that have little to do with religion. While the culture in which an individual lives out his or her life may be deeply influenced by religion, the processes and dynamics of mercantile activity, domestic maintenance and the manipulation of the accessories of the workplace may bear little relevance to religious values per se. They are primarily secular in content, and serve, no less, to inform the personalities of individuals. Moreover, we may speculate that if the religious impulse is rooted in human temperament, no less is the impulse toward skepticism, all of which tends to mitigate the power of religion as a motivator.[21]

---

[19] Benjamin Barber, *Jihad vs. McWorld* (Balantine Books: New York, 1996) p. 157.

[20] See Gordon W. Allport The *Individual and His Religion*, ((MacMillan Publishing Co., Inc.: New York, 1974) pp. 65-71.

[21] Speculation on the innateness of skepticism has been discussed by the contemporary science writer and atheist, Natalie Angier. See "Confessions of a Lonely Atheist", *New York Times Magazine*, Janaury 14, 2001.

172 Joseph Chuman

Beyond the operation of religious dynamics within the personalities of individual believers, a point that needs greater attention is that the appropriation of a religious identity differs in intensity from person to person. The affirmation of a religious identity can imply deep commitment to a religious life, inclusive of belief, ritualized behaviors and deference to religious authority, reinforced by immersion in a thick religious culture. On the opposite end of the belief spectrum, a religious identity may signify little more than a formality that is passively held. In such cases, religious motivation for behavior may be small or not appreciably existent.

The assessment of whether religion "causes" violence, rests, therefore in great measure on whether the subject is religious in the "thick" or "thin" sense. Without positing that religious is epiphenomenal in motivating action, including violence, I conclude that in most cases we need to look for ulterior dynamics – economic, political, ethnic, historical and especially the pursuit of power-- as the primary sources for violence between peoples, including war. The causal role of religion in conflict is, as suggested, dependent upon the pervasiveness of religion in the culture and the actors involved. My conclusion is that religion can be a contributing cause of violence, but more often serves as a legitmator of violence, which springs from other sources. Religious differences, can, moreover, be manipulated by elites to further justify violence. Whereas religion can identify the differences between groups, by demarking their respective shared cosmologies, religion requires the "spark" of underlying, more materially based causes in order to burst into violence.

This analysis moves me away from the primordialist camp, and closer to the position of moderate constructivists. Here the observations of Hasenclever and Rittberger are again useful.

> Moderate constructivists…propose to view religion as an intervening variable, i.e., as a causal factor intervening between a given conflict and the choice of conflict behavior. In this way, the impact of religious traditions on conflict behavior is deeply ambiguous: They can make violence more likely, insofar as a reading of holy texts prevails that justifies armed combat; on the other hands, they can make violence less likely, insofar as a reading of holy texts prevails that delegitimizes the use of violence in a given situation or generally.[22]

---

[22] Hasenclever and Rittberger, p. 115.

RELIGION -- UNIVERSAL, PAROCHIAL AND ROMANTIC

The salience of the religious factor in current politics, and its fretful role as a legitimator of violence, raises the crucial question of the relative potentials for religion as an agent for inter-group cooperation, and as a force for peace. My analysis to this point suggests that religion can be a substantive dynamic in bending political conflicts in the direction of active violence or its avoidance - and we would hope, optimally, toward brotherhood and cooperation. Yet, to the extent that religion can be teased out as an independent variable, we may appropriately ask whether the religious factor is weighted more toward one end of the spectrum than the other. Even if we allow for the secularizing dynamics, both individual and collective, underscored by the "thinning" tendencies wrought by the influences of modernization and globalization, my own assessment of the role of religion is that it more readily allies itself with the forces of violence than with those of cooperation and peacemaking.

Religious apologists ubiquitously put forward the socially and ethically salutary values of the historical traditions –the affirmation of human dignity, their commitment to brotherhood, their prophetic commitments to the poor, marginalized and disenfranchised. In these times of vehement polemical assault on secularism, religion is positioned as providing salvific and necessary structures of meaning. The rise of religion out of the despair of secular culture allows for the wielding of great rhetorical and effective power in both the developed and developing world. In the American context this has resulted in a progressive dismantling of the "wall of separation" between church and state, and attendant disenchantment with secular government.

I do not gainsay the universal values of religion and their propensity to foster respect and brotherhood necessary for a peaceful world order. Nor do I underestimate the central importance of religious values and teachings in shaping culture, often toward beneficent social ends. The inspiration of the *"philosophia perennis"* has notably served to motivate the activism of stewards of the prophetic tradition yielding for humankind its most noble exemplars.[23] It is often -- and correctly -- noted that it is a mistake to identify religion with extremism and fundamentalism.

---

[23] One cannot understand the political activism of Mohandas Gandhi apart from his commitments as a devout but reforming Hindu. Likewise, Martin Luther King's political mission can only be adequately grasped through an understanding of his rootedness in the

174 Joseph Chuman

At the same time, I maintain the resurgence of religion on the contemporary scene has caused many, both religious apologists and secular critics outside the traditions, to romanticize religion while claiming for it a benevolence that it does not frequently merit in practice. The promotion of religion in our times suffers from intellectual essentialism. Too often religious teachings (frequently cherry picked from scriptures for apologetic purposes) are upheld at the expense of more penetrating critiques of how these teachings function when deployed through the necessary media of social practice. In short, religious teaching, if it is to find expression in the real world, cannot avoid being molded by political concerns and psychological processes, dynamics beholden to the vagaries of the quests for security and power.

As a broad generalization, religious belief, and practices related to it, are strewn between two opposing poles: The universal pole, reflected in the noble teachings of the traditions, constitutive of brotherhood, respect for the sacredness of all human beings, commitment to tolerance and regard for the stranger; the opposing pole, which conduces toward the communal and the parochial, toward the longing to feel at home with others who share common histories, values and ways of life.

For Durkheim, communal bondedness is constitutive of religion, and it is defined by the function of uniting people of common belief into a group. Religion is revelatory of humankind's social nature to which it seeks to give expression. As Durkheim observed,

> The really religious beliefs are always common to a determined group, which makes profession of adhering to them and of practising the rites connected with them. They are not merely received individually by all members of this group; they are something belonging to the group, and they make it a unity. The individuals which compose it feel themselves united to each other by the simple fact that they have a common faith. [24]

For contemporary theorists, such as Robert Bellah, religion serves as a source of social solidarity strengthened through an evocation of common memories. [25] In Juergensmeyer's view, those sharing religious belief are bound

---

African-American Baptist Church. For a treatment of the religious sources of Gandhi's political philosophy, see Dennis Dalton, *Mahatma Gandhi* (Columbia University Press: New York, 1993). For a brief sketch of King's intellectual and religious sources see James Cone, "The Theology of Martin Luther King, Jr." *Union Theological Quarterly Review* volume xl, number 4, 1980.

[24] Durkheim, p. 59.

[25] Robert Bellah et al., *Habits of the Heart* (Perennial Library: New York, 1985) p. 114.

through a common "ideology of order" reinforced by the appeal to a transcendent, absolute and unchanging realm. As he notes, "Members of these communities...share a tradition, a particular world-view, in which the essential conflict between appearance and deeper reality is described in specific and characteristically cultural terms. This deeper reality has a degree of permanence and order quite unobtainable by ordinary means."[26] For Juergensmeyer, secular nationalism can play this role, and so in the modern context competes with religious loyalties. Yet, one can legitimately argue that when it does so, secular nationalism, to that extent, functions religiously.

The unifying and identity building power of religion cannot be underestimated. For the Christian devotee, engaging in the rite of the Eucharist binds the believer together with all of his co-religions in space and time. Vertically she is united with all Christians everywhere; and with all fellow believers extending from the Last Supper to the Second Coming. The resonance of such ritual with the mythopoeic propensities of mind and imagination serve to strengthen the power of communalism all the more. Human beings are narrative beings who dwell in their narratives. The ability of religion to satisfy the existential needs for meaning, identity, rootedness in an absolute and unchanging reality and for social solidarity are explicative of its appeal and power in creating communal cohesion.

These centripetal vectors of religion are directly proportional to its ability to separate insiders from outsiders, and intensify the divisions between those blessed by God and those who are damned. The stage is set, as noted, for xenophobia, and when ignited by the political and economic tensions, violence. In threatening environments, even small differences can be magnified to serve as causes for inter-group strife.

In contrast to these dynamics, the positive resources found in religious teachings, which work to engender respect across parochial lines, I argue, are relatively weak. It should be noted, moreover, that there is no "religion-in-general." There are only specific religions with their distinctive ways of life, and concrete values rooted in their specific cultures. [27] Hence, all commitments to universal values, by necessity, are perceived from *within* religious communities and are winnowed, and often diverted by values and concerns that are themselves parochial. In this sense, it is perhaps not

---

[26] Juergensmeyer, *The New Cold War?* (University of California Press: Berkeley and Los Angeles, 1993) p. 26.

[27] For a discussion of the misplaced value of "religion-in-general" within the debate over foundations for human rights, see the international legal theorist Louis Henkin, "Religion, Religions and Human Rights" *Journal of Religious Ethics* volume 26.2 fall, 1998.

176 Joseph Chuman

surprising that when religious groups have agitated for religious freedom, it is most often for sake of the group itself; the freedom of other religious communities have mattered far less. Despite the fact that it is undertaken with universalistic rhetoric, the ecumenical project initiated by many faiths in the past three decades is often tentative and fragile. And the religions, for the most part, have been slow to adopt the international human rights agenda, premised, as it is, on universal values. In the final analysis, the religions, for the most part, are interest groups, which, more often than not, are governed by the impulse to protect their respective turfs.

THE TRANSFORMATION OF RELIGION INTO A FORCE FOR PEACE: DIALOGUE, DEVELOPMENT AND DEMOCRACY

Globalization, as its critics note, has further widened the disparities between the wealthy and the desperately poor. It has favored neo-capitalist accumulation and broadened the hegemonic presence of Western values. But despite backlashes that have revived religious cultures, it has ensured that all cultures have been brought closer together and have been increasing permeated with modernizing elements. The Princeton scholar of religion, Cornel West, has noted that all cultures are a product of "radical hybridity" and this is especially true under the forces of globalization currently operative.[28] The purity of "culture", in my view, is itself another romantic fallacy very much in evidence among contemporary critics and activists. If globalization is defined by the spread of economic markets, it is no less defined by the pervasiveness of new communication technologies and the salience of the human rights culture together with its attendant universal norms. These elements can work to assuage the insular forces that set the stage for the transmogrification of religion into a catalyst for violence.

My argument to this point has been that as a discrete social and psychological phenomenon, the power of religion to bind people into an "in" group is a more powerful motivator than the universalizing values found in the traditions. But, as noted, these respective religious potentials can become

---

[28] For a discussion of the hybridization of culture within the dialectics of multiculturalism, see Cornel West *Prophetic Thought in Postmodern Times* (Monroe, Maine: Common Courage Press, 1993) p. 2ff.

resources for war or peace dependent on the political and economic environments in which the religious culture is played out.

This analysis, therefore, opens the door to strategies that will help ensure that the religions can be harnessed as peacemakers, as opposed to the divisive markers and influences that have enabled inter-group violence, war and genocide. Among these strategies are the pursuit of dialogue among the religions, the fostering of economic development, especially as it benefits the poor and marginalized sectors of society, and the strengthening of democracy, on both national and local levels.

By invoking these secular strategies, I am not asserting a secular ideology as hegemonic. My thesis recognizes the continuously coextensive and mutually interactive relationship of religion and secular values. What I do maintain is that in a pluralistic world in which religious communities are drawn closer together, and religious distinctiveness is highlighted, such communities need to be girded with zones of liberality My conclusion is that only secular values can to that job.

The proximity of cultures in our time makes inter-religious dialogue both possible and necessary. If we avoid economic reductionism and accept that religious teaching can serve as an independent resource for human action, as my analysis allows, then dialogue within a respectful framework can serve a positive purpose. While such dialogue is most often carried forward by intellectual elites, the proliferation of NGO's on the international scene has ensured that much productive dialogue can and, does go on the grass roots level. The economist, Amartya Sen, reminds us that tolerance, for example, is by no means an exclusively Western value.[29] Values inherent in one culture, on further investigation, can be understood to have parallels in other cultures, and at times even origins outside one's culture. Values and cultural possessions, through processes of natural accretion, are and can be grafted from one culture to another without condescension or debasement of the receiving culture. Culture, inclusive of religion, is not a static, but a dynamic phenomenon, and religions change owes as much to external influences as it does to deliberate adjustment within traditions. Dialogue can assuredly be one of these salutary external influences. In the domain of inter-religious dialogue, if we wish to ensure that practices emerge which are consonant with human rights, we are best situated, as Daniel Bell suggests, if we can build on those

---

[29] Amartya Sen, *Development As Freedom* (Anchor Books: New York, 1999) p.235.

178   Joseph Chuman

local resources that promote those values. [30]I would argue that constructive dialogue cannot go on in many instances unless Western interlocutors are willing and able to understand and accept that the values which make for peace within the local religious tradition. All of this presupposes a stance of openness, understanding and empathy, an environment that can work to nurture, both procedurally and substantively, a sensibility of respect and appreciation across religious lines.

Related to the call for inter-religious dialogue is the need for education within the denominations themselves. Here religious leadership needs to evoke the positive resources for peace making in order to move the traditions away from parochial preoccupations and toward an orientation adaptive to a global pluralistic environment. The teachings of all the historical religions manifest the conceptual and moral frameworks of universalism and holism with regard to the creation and the unity of humankind. Hinduism espouses a common human origin, and has been especially pluriform in its acceptance of paths, including atheism, which can lead to liberation. Compassion lies at the center of Buddhist virtues, and like Hinduism, sees its specific doctrine as a vehicle amongst others which conduce to spiritual ends. Clearly, the monotheistic faiths have thicker boundaries that define insiders and exclude others. Yet, all, as noted, have a universal pole which can serve as a basis for tolerance and inter-group harmony. In Judaism, man is made "in the divine image" (Genesis 1:27) and the Talmud teaches that "the righteous of all nations shall have a share in the world to come." (Tosefta Sanhedrn 13:2) In Christianity, the parable of Good Samaritan (Luke 10:29-37) and the Golden Rule (Matthew 7:12) speak to regard for the stranger. In the Koran, sura 2:256 teaches "Let there be no compulsion in religion."

Contemporary religions bear the task within our globalized world, which have brought the diverse faiths closer together, to raise the profile of their positive resources that affirm peacemaking. A reverence for life needs to supersede preoccupation with doctrinal issues which work to strengthen divisions among the faiths. All religions have leaders and reformers who speak to the more universalizing elements in their traditions. Often these representatives have been the minor voice. Whether the press of the dangers humankind confronts in the contemporary world will move these representatives into dominant positions within their faith communities remains an open question. Much depends on leadership within the religions and

---

[30] Daniel A. Bell, "The East Asian Challenge to Human Rights: Reflections on an East West Dialogue" *Human Rights* Quarterly, volume 18.3 1996.

dynamics outside of them. My thesis entails that changes in the underlying economic and political ground and the infusion of liberalizing forces which come from outside of the religious realm are necessary to enable the salutary forces in the religions to gain more traction. But how religion is interpreted and transmitted by religious elites, especially in critical moments, is also deterinative.

Endemic poverty and economic injustice are breeding grounds for political instability and the emergence of autocratic regimes. When the capabilities of people who yearn for economic advancement are thwarted, the seeds are sown for religious extremism and demagoguery, which can ripen into violence. Though the Marxist critique of religion has proven to be too reductionist, it remains nevertheless true that the quashing of dignity, and of hope in an a more bountiful and equitable future, can lead people to turn toward the parochial realms of religious tradition and transcendental realities as alternative sources of meaning. Such conditions, as noted, can be exploited by religious elites and bent in violent directions.

A direct correlation between poverty and inequality and religious violation is admittedly not self-evident. It has been pointed out that Africa and Latin America also suffer broad reaching economic dislocations, yet religious violence on those continents is relatively rare. It has also been noted that Osama bin Laden is a millionaire, and that the perpetrators, of the September 11, 2001 terrorist assault on the World Trade Center and the Pentagon, with few exceptions, were from middle class families for whom economic opportunity was not foreclosed. But the economic status of these individual actors does not nullify the importance of poverty and equality as the fertile ground from which violence is spawned, in combination with religious sanctions interpreted by religious elites. My thesis is that religious violence is a product of a combination of elements of which grievances resulting from economic disparity and depravation are active agents.

Juergensmeyer in his cross cultural study of religious violence has noted the correlation between social marginality rooted in conditions which lead to economic dead ends, and the vulnerability of young men, in particular, to be lured into acts of religious violence. He notes:

> In the cultures of violence that have led to religious terrorism, the anxieties of all young men – concerns over careers, social location and sexual relationships – have been exacerbated. Experiences of humiliation in these matters have made them vulnerable to the voices of powerful leaders and images of glory in a cosmic war. In Palestine, for example, where the

180   Joseph Chuman

unemployment rate among young men in their late teens and early twenties has hovered around 50%, economic frustration has led to sexual frustration. Without jobs, which is usually a prerequisite to searching for a wife in traditional societies, they cannot marry. Without marriage, in strict religious cultures such as that of of Palestinians Arabs, they cannot have sex. The Hamas movement has provided a way of venting the resulting frustrations in a community that supplies a family and an ideology that explains the source of their problems and gives them hope. [31]

Juergensmeyer has documented analogous situations among fighters in the Islamic Resistance Movement in Algeria and movements for Sikh empowerment in India.

While poverty and economic disparity of themselves do not cause violence in religious communities, it is difficult to conclude that without these factors serving as contextual dynamics, religious teaching conducing to violence could be sustained. My views concur with Oliver McTernen in his following observation:

> Inequality does matter and needs, therefore to be addressed to avoid the danger of communal strife in multifaith/multicultural societies as well as to lessen the risk of global terrorism. Extreme poverty, social injustice, unemployment, illiteracy all contribute to the milieu that can provide both a trigger and a fertile recruiting ground for high-minded and idealistic young religious entrepreneurs who believe that it is their sacred or religious duty to act on behalf of the downtrodden and to spearhead social and economic change. [32]

Amartya Sen, and the philosopher, Martha Nussbaum, have argued, economic development is itself a good, while it broadens the scope within which human capabilities and freedoms can flourish. If we wish to offset the potential of religion to become violent then we need to work to ensure that the future remains open to the possibility of economic advancement. This requires that the widening disparities of wealth wrought by globalization be hemmed by more equitable distribution of opportunities for development on local levels, that environmental despoliation be halted through a rational commitment to conservation and sustainability, and a world-wide ethos of

---

[31] Mark Juergensmeyer, *Terror in the Mind of God* (University of California Press: Berkeley and Los Angeles, 2000) p. 191.

[32] Oliver McTernan, *Violence in God's Name* (Orbis Books: New York, 2003) p. 125.

human rights and dignity work to leaven the killing dynamics of the unfettered market. In these visionary endeavors the religions themselves can play a salutary role.

Related to the values issuing from economic development is the need to artfully promote the values of democracy. Democracy, in this regard, needs to be understood as not merely access to the formal rituals of the electoral process, though it must ineluctably include these. Rather, in the spirit of John Dewey, it is a commitment to a way of life that suffuses personality, as it gives shape to society. At the heart of the democratic character style as well as to democratic political structures is what the human rights theorist, Michael Ignatieff and others refer to as "agency." [33] At a minimum, agency presupposes a modicum of freedom, what Isaiah Berlin called "negative liberty"; the freedom to make choices, and the power to work to mold society and nature by the lights of one's personality. The ability to express one's agency, to actively participate in the world around oneself, like the promises of development, keeps before people the promise of a better future. Democratic participation is a wellspring of personal investment of the energies and hope that ward off the frustrations commensurate with political repression and autocracy. The liberating air sustained by freedom and democracy propels development, and it is of itself the best political environment serving to countermand religious extremism and violence.

CONCLUSION

Religion cannot merely be identified with its intellectual and scriptural traditions; neither solely with its teachings and doctrines. The religions function, to a greater of lesser extent, as the matrices in which people live out their lives, frame their consciousness, anchor their identities and solidify their communion with all fellow believers. While the cognitive elements of religion can be effective resources in motivating believers toward tolerance and peaceful acceptance of those who differ, the role of religion remains powerfully conditioned by the underlying economic and political environments in which all human life remains deeply rooted.

---

[33] Michael Ignatieff, *Human Rights* (Princeton University Press: Princeton and Oxford, 2001) p.57.

The dangerous moment we are in, a moment in which we witness the fusion of religion and violence, provides the most ominous challenge to world peace for the foreseeable future. If it is true that human beings require frameworks of meaning which religion (and non-religious world views) provides, then it is no less true in these times, and especially in these times, that we need a resurgence of secular values manifested in the structures and content of civic society projected onto the international stage. Religious communalism, unassuaged by exposure to cultural diversity, devoid of the promises of economic justice and equality and drained of democratic resources is fated to take a dark, inward turn. If the great religious traditions are to fulfill their venerable hopes as beacons of peace and mutual co-existence, we need to forge a new blueprint providing a nuanced understanding of how religion dialectically responds to the realities in which it finds itself. It is out of such an understanding that state actors, non-government organizations and concerned citizens can frame enlightened policies in pursuance of a more peaceful world order.

INDEX

#

20th century, 2, 19
9/11, 162

A

abuse, 40, 83
access, 6, 14, 105, 121, 148, 181
accommodation, 22, 130, 165, 171
accounting, 4
acid, 157
activation, 147
activism, 173
actuality, 95, 97, 98
adaptation, 69, 85
adjustment, 40, 51, 82, 86, 87, 88, 159, 177
adolescents, 38, 74
adult, 38, 51, 74, 75, 77, 80, 81, 85, 88, 148, 150
adulthood, 85, 148
advancement, 14, 179, 180
advocacy, 81
affective disorder, 83
affective states, 146
affirming, 168
affluence, 124
Afghanistan, 163
Africa, 76, 179
African American, 79, 174

age, 9, 10, 11, 23, 24, 27, 43, 75, 77, 87, 88, 119
aggression, vii, 33, 50, 146, 147, 149, 150, 157, 158, 167, 168
aggressive behavior, 38, 157
agriculture, 8, 12, 111
AIDS, 159
Al Qaeda, 163
Algeria, 162, 180
alters, 67, 166
altruism, 64, 65, 67, 147
amygdala, 147, 148, 149, 158, 159
ancestors, 66
anger, 45, 84, 146, 147, 149, 150, 152, 158
animals, 145, 148
antagonism, 7
antagonist, 158, 159
anthropologists, 70
antioxidants, 150
antisense, 157
anxiety, 44, 49, 51, 145, 146, 147, 156, 159, 166
anxiolytic, 147
apathy, 34
appointments, 42
Arab world, 163
architect, 116, 119, 120, 121, 125, 129, 133, 134, 142
Aristotle, 92, 93
Art Nouveau, 139, 140
Asia, 29

184 Index

assassination, 162
assault, 85, 162, 165, 169, 173, 179
assessment, 47, 66, 84, 94, 172, 173
atheists, ix, 73, 75, 76, 77, 78, 79, 80, 81, 82, 83, 84, 85, 88
atomism, 96
atoms, 96
attachment, 6, 37, 78, 81, 144, 145, 146, 147, 148, 149, 150, 158
attacks, 150
attitudes, 147, 148, 150
attribution, 14
authority, 2, 5, 10, 19, 107, 119, 120, 167, 172
autonomic, 147
autonomy, 7, 14, 78
avoidance, 149, 173
awareness, 14, 41

B

backlash, 171
base, 10
behavior, 39, 40, 48, 49, 52, 57, 60, 61, 62, 63, 66, 67, 146, 147, 148, 149, 150, 157, 158, 159, 172
Belgium, 6, 30
bending, 173
benefits, vii, x, 5, 33, 37, 45, 46, 50, 88, 126, 143, 145, 148, 159, 177
beverages, 4
Bible, 82, 110, 111, 141, 144, 145, 146, 147, 149, 150, 152, 157, 168
Big Bang, 96
biological, x, 143, 150
birth control, 13
birth rate, 16, 76
births, 8, 11, 15, 16, 17, 21
bonding, 144, 145, 146, 150, 158
brain, 60, 144, 148, 149
Brazil, 143
breastfeeding, 12, 17, 19, 20, 21, 26, 27
breeding, 104, 179
Britain, 77, 104, 113, 114, 115, 117, 119, 125, 126, 129, 130, 142

brothers, 25, 27, 167
Buddhism, 169

C

calculus, 94
cancer, 42, 74, 78, 87, 88, 145, 158, 159
candidates, 79, 87
capacity, 149
caregivers, viii, 34, 35, 45, 46, 47, 48, 49, 51, 145, 159
case examples, viii, 34, 35, 41
case study, 130
catalyst, 176
category a, 12
Catholic Church, ix, 6, 7, 10, 13, 19, 103, 113, 118, 125, 132
Catholics, 3, 7, 29, 113, 114, 116, 119
cattle, 104
causal relationship, 78
causality, 2, 66, 74, 92
Census, 142
challenges, 43, 88, 100, 162, 169
chaos, 166
chemical, 60, 99
child mortality, 4, 11, 13, 30, 31
childcare, 18, 20, 28
children, 1, 4, 5, 10, 13, 14, 16, 17, 21, 22, 23, 25, 26, 27, 28, 42, 43, 76, 110, 113, 136, 155, 156, 169
China, 37, 74
Christian religious building, ix, 103
Christian worship, ix, 103
Christianity, 39, 104, 162, 178
Christians, 79, 107, 144, 162, 175
citizens, 104, 182
city, 16, 115, 117, 118, 165
civil servants, 18
civil war, 104, 105, 162
civilization, 40
clarity, 67
classes, 7
classicism, 121
classification, 16
cleaning, 19

Index 185

climate, 20, 21, 23
clothing, 22, 26, 166
coal, 136
cocaine, 158
cognition, 60
cognitive, 60, 61, 79, 149, 167
Cold War, 163, 169, 175
Colombia, 37, 161
common sense, 166
communalism, 171, 175, 182
communication, viii, 7, 55, 58, 63, 176
community, 3, 4, 6, 8, 67, 82, 107, 109, 110, 120, 167, 170, 175, 177, 178, 180
comparative analysis, 14, 28, 88
compassion, 108
complexity, 3, 35
components, 146, 149
composition, 27, 98, 136
compulsion, 178
conference, 19, 107, 108
conflict, 44, 78, 84, 162, 164, 168, 169, 172, 175
conformity, 5, 6, 140
Congo, 161
Congress, 29
consciousness, 166, 181
conservation, 17, 95, 180
construction, 50, 106, 115, 116, 121, 133, 137, 138
consumption, 4
contamination, 8, 12
controversial, x, 6, 74, 143
convergence, 7, 37
conversations, 42
cooperation, viii, 55, 58, 64, 66, 67, 70, 171, 173
coping strategies, 51, 88
copper, 109, 110
copyright, 104, 106, 108, 110, 112, 117, 138
correlation, 2, 5, 21, 29, 46, 52, 60, 63, 74, 144, 147, 179
corruption, 97
cortex, 149
cosmos, 96, 166
cost, 6, 14, 115, 117

Cox regression, 2, 3, 9, 23, 24
critical period, 23
criticism, 60, 63, 171
cultural norms, 7
culture, vii, 1, 2, 6, 10, 11, 12, 14, 17, 18, 19, 28, 29, 50, 69, 80, 167, 171, 172, 173, 176, 177

D

danger, 19, 180
dark matter, 59
Darwinism, 68
database, 141, 142
death, 11, 15, 16, 17, 22, 23, 145, 150, 154
debt, 155
Decade of the Brain, x, 143
democracy, 7, 177, 181
demographic, 4, 6, 10, 15, 16, 30, 145
demography, 2, 3, 7, 16
depression, 46, 49, 51, 82, 83, 89, 148, 149, 150, 158, 159
depth, 41, 84
despair, 44, 154, 158, 173
destruction, 95, 162, 167
determinism, 36, 38, 52
developed countries, 76
diffusion, 18, 19, 26, 28
dignity, 34, 36, 47, 49, 173, 179, 181
discrimination, 11, 79, 82
disease progression, 86
diseases, 12, 20, 21, 22, 23, 25, 26, 28
disorder, 35, 40, 44, 150, 157
distress, 44, 46, 47, 50, 51, 52, 53, 82, 145
distribution, 18, 141, 180
diversity, 132, 182
dominance, 132, 138

E

East Asia, 178
economic development, 177, 180, 181
economic status, 4, 23, 179

186   Index

education, 4, 6, 10, 19, 28, 77, 78, 79, 83, 89, 113, 178
elaboration, ix, 103, 116, 119, 124, 130, 140
elders, 145
emotion, 45, 50, 53
emotional, 39, 46, 51, 53, 145, 146, 149, 159
emotions, 146, 159
empathy, 178
empirical methods, 37
empirical studies, viii, 34
employment, 23
empowerment, 180
endogenous, 147
endurance, 147
enemies, 147, 156, 169, 170
energy, x, 43, 95, 161
England, 30, 70, 104, 107, 108, 109, 111, 113, 114, 115, 129, 130, 131, 132, 138, 140, 141
entrepreneurs, 112, 180
environment, 3, 5, 20, 23, 26, 38, 51, 60, 82, 84, 138, 178, 181
equality, 83, 179, 182
ethics, 14
Euclidean space, 94
Europe, 2, 29, 30, 76, 80, 119, 125, 142
everyday life, 4, 40
evidence, viii, 3, 36, 40, 45, 55, 56, 57, 61, 66, 68, 70, 78, 82, 83, 93, 146, 158, 176
evil, 49, 155, 167, 168
evolution, 29, 61, 70, 71, 100
exclusion, 6, 167
executive function, 149
exercise, 39, 47
exogenous, 147
exposure, 4, 182
external influences, 41, 177
external locus of control, 38
extremists, 64

F

factories, 12, 22, 23, 27

faith, 45, 80, 113, 120, 143, 153, 154, 174, 178
family, vii, 4, 6, 13, 20, 21, 22, 23, 25, 33, 44, 45, 47, 48, 53, 82, 105, 144, 145, 146, 148, 151, 159, 179
fear, 5, 145, 146, 147, 149, 155, 167
federalism, 7
feelings, 41, 43, 44, 80
fertility, 2, 3, 4, 5, 6, 8, 9, 10, 11, 13, 16, 21, 22, 28, 29, 30
fever, 17, 22
financial, 44, 119, 123
financial capital, 119
fish, 26, 156
fishing, 8, 21
fitness, 66, 67
food, 4, 12, 22
force, 28, 36, 96, 164, 165, 166, 173
forgiveness, 145, 149
France, 6
free will, vii, 33, 35, 36, 37, 38, 39, 40, 41, 44, 45, 47, 48, 49, 50, 51, 52
freedom, 34, 35, 36, 39, 47, 104, 176, 181
Freud, 165, 167
Fribourg, vii, 1, 7, 11, 12, 13, 14, 15, 16, 18, 19, 20, 21, 22, 24, 25, 26, 27, 30
friendship, 146, 147, 152
fusion, 162, 182

G

gastroenteritis, 2, 12, 14, 17, 20, 21, 22, 23, 25, 26
Geneva, 159
genocide, 169, 177
geography, 141
Germany, 30, 82, 83
gift, 152, 153
gifted, 107, 119
globalization, 163, 170, 173, 176, 180
God, 5, 13, 14, 18, 39, 46, 47, 51, 52, 57, 60, 61, 62, 63, 70, 76, 77, 78, 80, 86, 88, 92, 93, 100, 101, 102, 119, 129, 167, 168, 169, 175, 180
governments, 15, 28, 163

Index

Great Britain, 104, 130
group cooperation, 64, 173
group therapy, 44
grouping, ix, 103
groups, 143
growth, 17, 69, 145, 163
guardian, 42, 69
guilt, 43, 167

H

hair, 155
Hamas, 180
handling, 148
happiness, 41, 42
harassment, 82
harm, 149
harmony, 149, 178
hate, 156
head, 152, 155
health, viii, ix, x, 2, 4, 5, 6, 7, 12, 13, 14, 16,
    17, 18, 20, 27, 28, 34, 37, 38, 40, 41, 46,
    47, 50, 51, 52, 73, 74, 75, 81, 82, 83, 84,
    85, 86, 88, 143, 144, 145, 146, 148, 149,
    150, 159
heart, 150, 152, 155
high school, 77, 82
higher education, 89
Hispanics, 81
history, 5, 8, 88, 142, 148
HIV, 74, 86, 88
holism, 147, 178
homes, 77, 114
hopelessness, 145
host, 18
hostility, 149, 163, 168
housing, 26, 104, 127
human agency, 50
human behavior, 165, 170
human capital, 13, 17, 28
human dignity, 36, 173
human experience, 75
human health, 149
human nature, 50
human rights, 170, 175, 176, 177, 181

husband, 10, 21, 42
hybridity, 176
hybridization, 176
hygiene, 14, 20
hypothalamus, 146, 148
hypothesis, 3, 4, 5, 6, 8, 10, 21, 22, 25, 26,
    58, 64, 65, 66, 69, 86, 96, 164

I

ideal, 19, 106, 121, 146, 151
identification, 63
identity, x, 41, 83, 84, 103, 109, 140, 167,
    172, 175
ideology, 4, 5, 8, 17, 18, 83, 140, 162, 175,
    177, 180
image, 59, 78, 144, 150, 169, 178, 179
immigrants, 110, 136
imperialism, 163
improvements, 115
income, 3, 22, 23, 26, 79
independence, ix, 103, 108
independent variable, 22, 23, 164, 173
India, 37, 162, 180
individuals, viii, ix, 5, 29, 34, 35, 37, 40, 45,
    47, 50, 58, 62, 65, 66, 67, 73, 75, 76, 77,
    80, 82, 83, 84, 85, 87, 143, 144, 145,
    147, 165, 171, 174
industrialisation, x, 8, 22, 26, 161
industry, 8, 111
inequality, 179
infant mortality, vii, 1, 2, 3, 4, 5, 6, 11, 12,
    13, 14, 15, 16, 17, 18, 20, 21, 22, 24, 25,
    26, 27, 28, 29
infarction, 85
inhibition, 150, 159
injections, 158
injury, 74, 83, 87
insanity, 48, 49
institutions, vii, 1, 2, 3, 5, 6, 7, 14, 28, 30,
    82, 101
intelligence, 14, 17, 44
intensity, 147, 149
interaction, 144, 145, 146, 148, 159
interest groups, 176

188 Index

international relations, 163
interpersonal relations, 149
investment, 13, 28, 181
Iran, 162
Iraq, 162, 163
iron, 110, 131, 140
Islam, 39, 65, 162, 169
Islamic world, vii
isolation, 4, 8, 20
Israel, 50, 169
issues, viii, ix, 6, 14, 16, 36, 56, 61, 69, 73, 85, 91, 100, 144, 145, 165, 178

J

Japan, 76
Jews, 4, 29, 34, 144
jihad, 169
justification, 2, 163, 164

K

Kenya, 162
King, 157
kinship, 58, 67

L

landscape, 109, 162, 166
Latin America, 179
law, 7, 93, 152
lead, 14, 44, 61, 82, 83, 116, 165, 178, 179
leadership, 164, 168, 178
Lebanon, 162
Lesion, 157
liberation, 163, 178
light, 3, 26, 59, 101, 105, 134
locus, vii, 33, 35, 38, 39, 52, 167
longitudinal study, 51, 159
love, 69, 144, 145, 146, 147, 148, 149, 150, 151, 153, 154, 155, 156

M

magnitude, 94
major depressive disorder, 150, 157
major issues, ix, 73
majority, vii, 33, 37, 42, 74, 77, 79, 82, 92, 99, 109, 111
man, 36, 44, 59, 69, 152, 154, 178
manipulation, 67, 70, 171
marriage, 3, 5, 13, 16, 19, 23, 42, 43, 88, 180
mass, 10, 28, 95, 107, 114, 119, 162
materials, 130, 137
mathematics, 92, 93, 99, 100
matter, 59, 94, 98, 101, 112, 180
measurement, 50, 96
media, 14, 19, 75, 174
medical, vii, ix, 4, 7, 12, 14, 16, 17, 19, 27, 73, 83, 84
medicine, 13, 17, 28, 86, 87, 88
membership, 79, 83, 86, 109
memory, 146, 149, 157
memory retrieval, 157
mental disorder, 35, 144, 150, 159
mental health, viii, x, 34, 37, 46, 47, 50, 51, 74, 75, 82, 84, 85, 88, 143, 144, 145, 146, 148, 150, 159
mental illness, 40, 42, 44, 46, 47, 51, 52, 58
meta-analysis, 40, 46, 50
methodology, 5, 74
Miami, 33
mice, 147, 156
Middle East, 76
military, 163, 168, 169
militia, 162
mimesis, 168
minorities, 52, 79, 82, 83, 84, 86, 167
mission, 44, , 132, 173
Missouri, 55
modernism, 13
modernity, 14, 163, 171
modernization, x, 7, 161, 166, 170, 171, 173
modulation, 146
mold, 181
monks, 144

Index

189

morality, 16, 85
Morocco, 162
mortality, vii, 1, 2, 3, 4, 5, 6, 11, 12, 13, 14, 15, 16, 17, 18, 19, 20, 21, 22, 23, 24, 25, 26, 27, 28, 29, 30, 31, 51, 87
motherhood, 158
mothers, 148, 159
motivation, vii, 33, 35, 36, 38, 39, 149, 164, 172
mountains, 153
multiculturalism, 176
murder, 162, 168
music, 43, 45
Muslims, 64, 81

N

nationalism, 163, 175
nationalists, 162
natural science, 93, 95, 99, 100
natural selection, 59, 66, 70, 71
negative consequences, 63
negative reinforcement, 38
neglect, ix, 23, 27, 73, 165
neonates, 148
Netherlands, 29, 30, 31, 125, 141
neuropeptide, 150, 158
neuroscience, x, 50, 143, 144, 145, 146, 150, 151
neutral, 80
New England, 70
North America, 109
nucleus, 146, 148, 157
nuns, 120
nursing, 88, 148

O

openness, 14, 78, 178
openness to experience, 78
opioids, 158
opportunities, 28, 82, 180
opportunity costs, 10
oppression, 150, 152

optimism, 144, 147, 159
organ, 113, 115
ownership, 41
oxytocin, 146, 147, 148, 149, 150, 156, 157, 158, 159

P

parasympathetic, 146
paraventricular, 146, 148, 157
parents, 2, 5, 10, 13, 18, 76, 78, 136, 147
parity, 27
Parliament, 15
participants, 1, 37, 41, 63, 65, 84
pathways, 29, 145
patients, 145, 158, 159
peace, x, 144, 154, 161, 162, 164, 168, 169, 171, 173, 177, 178, 182
Pentagon, 162, 179
peptide, 146
perceived control, 39
perception, 149
permit, 2, 12, 14, 20, 23, 28
personal history, 148
personal identity, 41
personality, 78, 158, 181
Peru, 161
Philadelphia, 31
physical health, 38, 40, 85, 88
physicians, 8, 14, 17, 18, 19
physics, 93, 94, 95, 97, 99, 100
Plato, 56
pleasure, 13, 45
policy, 7, 18, 28, 159, 163
political instability, 179
political opposition, 7
politics, 18, 162, 173
popular support, 65
population, ix, 2, 6, 7, 8, 15, 16, 17, 19, 73, 74, 75, 76, 77, 78, 79, 82, 84, 87, 109, 110, 111, 113, 114, 130, 140, 147, 168
positive attitudes, 150
positive correlation, 144
positive mental health, 46
positive relationship, 147

poverty, 106, 179, 180
power sharing, 162
prayer, ix, 64, 65, 82, 88, 103, 144, 145
prefrontal cortex, 149
prejudice, 79, 82, 84
president, 79, 80
prevention, 12, 144
principles, 20, 92, 99, 144
privatization, x, 161
probability, 27, 57
problem solving, 38, 51
profanity, 80
professionals, 14, 87
project, 45, 123, 141, 142, 176
proliferation, 177
promote, 149
propaganda, 162
proposition, viii, 56, 93, 94, 95, 96, 97, 98, 99
prosocial behavior, 40, 67, 68, 69, 70
protection, 12
protective factors, 144, 145
Protestants, 7
protocols, 146
provocation, 147
proximal, 148
pruning, 168
psychiatrist, 49
psychoeducational program, 52
psychogenic, 147
psychological distress, 47, 52, 82, 145
psychological problems, 78
psychological processes, 174
psychological well-being, viii, 34, 74, 84
psychology, 36, 37, 38, 50, 60, 69, 85, 87, 88, 145
psychopathy, 50
psychosis, 44
psycho-social, 51, 144
Psychosomatic, 159
psychotherapy, 41
public health, 14, 16, 17, 83, 144
public life, 79
publishing, 16, 17
punishment, 5, 46, 51, 52, 147, 155

purification, 168
purity, 176

Q

quality of life, viii, ix, 34, 49, 73, 74, 83, 86, 87, 159
quantification, 93, 95
questioning, 3, 100
questionnaire, 17

R

racial minorities, 82
radicalism, 104, 109
radio, 41
rat, 148, 149, 157, 158, 159
reactions, 39, 48, 53, 78, 150, 170
reading, 19, 157, 172
realism, 166
reality, 60, 165, 166, 175
receptors, 147, 157
recognition, 19, 140, 145, 146
reconciliation, 159
recovery, 41, 74
recruiting, 84, 180
reductionism, 177
reflection, 154
reformers, 178
regression, 2, 3, 9, 23, 24
regulation, 4, 157
rehabilitation, 87
reinforcement, 52
rejection, x, 78, 94, 161
relationship, 144, 146, 147, 148, 150, 157
relatives, viii, 34, 45, 47, 48, 49, 50, 52, 53, 67
relativity, 95, 96, 99
relevance, 13, 23, 81, 171
relief, 154, 163
religiosity, 5, 7, 19, 46, 47, 53, 74, 81, 83, 86, 87, 88, 89, 146
religious, 143, 144, 145

Index

religious beliefs, vii, viii, 5, 33, 55, 56, 57, 58, 59, 60, 61, 62, 64, 65, 66, 67, 68, 82, 174
religious traditions, 164, 172, 182
religiousness, 46, 85, 86, 144
replication, 81
repression, 10, 114, 181
requirements, 2, 12
research, x, 143, 145, 146, 156
researchers, 3, 11, 46, 60, 66, 68, 79, 84, 146
resistance, 22, 88
resources, 124, 140, 175, 177, 178, 181, 182
response, 49, 67, 92, 147, 148, 156, 171
retaliation, 162
rewards, 2, 5
rhetoric, 164, 176
rights, 7, 44, 170, 175, 176, 177, 181
risk, 3, 9, 10, 12, 20, 21, 22, 23, 24, 25, 26, 27, 28, 150, 180
Roman Catholics, 113
root, 97, 102, 164, 165, 166, 170, 177
rules, 5, 8, 20, 63, 93
rural areas, 105

S

sadness, 43
safety, 42
sanctions, 2, 5, 179
satisfaction, 144, 145
Saudi Arabia, 162
scarcity, 38
schizophrenia, vii, 33, 35, 41, 42, 44, 45, 46, 47, 48, 49, 50, 51, 52, 53
school, 7, 10, 18, 20, 77, 82, 110
science, 17, 28, 59, 61, 69, 88, 89, 93, 100, 101, 167, 171
scientific, 28, 68, 143
scientists, 143
scope, 180
searching, 156
seasonality, 23, 25, 26
secularism, 173
security, 174

self-awareness, 41
self-control, 37, 39, 44
self-efficacy, vii, 33, 35, 38, 39
self-esteem, vii, 33, 38, 40, 44, 46
self-interest, 35
senses, 58, 59, 60
separation, 148
septum, 148
services, 5, 6, 7, 14, 45, 76, 113
set theory, 94
settlements, 133
severe stress, 148
severity, 150
sewage, 12, 20
sex, 23, 24, 27, 80, 158, 168, 180
sexual behavior, 86, 146
sexuality, 4
shape, 29, 181
sharing, 148
sheep, 156, 169
shock, 44, 116
shortage, 19, 108
showing, 16, 63, 104
sibling, 23, 27, 42
social, 144, 146, 147, 148, 149, 150, 151, 158, 159
social activities, 43, 44
social behavior, 68
social class, 26
social consequences, 36
social context, 67
social environment, 5, 82, 84
social group, 147
social influence, 6
social institutions, 82
social interactions, 146
social life, 50
social norms, 10
social sciences, 165
social situations, 82
social support, 144, 146, 159
social withdrawal, 150, 158
socialization, 82, 86

society, vii, x, 28, 33, 40, 79, 81, 85, 86, 111, 140, 144, 150, 151, 161, 177, 181, 182
socioeconomic status, 10
sociology, 167
solidarity, 36, 79, 82, 174, 175
solution, 125
somatic symptoms, 158
somatosensory, 158
South America, 76
Soviet Union, 163
spacetime, 97
Spain, 119, 139, 140
special relativity, 96
species, 59
speculation, 66, 68
speech, 147
spending, 168
spinal cord, 74, 83, 87
spiritual, 144, 145, 149, 158
spirituality, vii, ix, x, 52, 73, 74, 81, 83, 84, 85, 86, 87, 88, 92, 100, 143, 144, 146, 159
Sprague-Dawley rats, 158
Sri Lanka, 162, 169
stained glass, 115
standard of living, 26
standardization, 15
state control, 7
states, 5, 51, 58, 59, 80, 94, 95, 97, 99, 101, 129, 132, 146
statistics, 2, 5, 10, 15, 16, 17, 21, 28
stereotypes, 84, 89
sterile, 12
stigma, 44, 51, 82, 84, 85
stigmatized, 19, 80, 82
stress, 35, 51, 82, 87, 144, 145, 146, 147, 148, 150, 156, 157, 170
stressful events, 46, 148
stressors, 148, 156
structure, ix, 3, 8, 14, 51, 61, 103, 105, 113, 120, 124, 125, 127, 129, 137, 140, 157, 171

style, 39, 105, 108, 110, 117, 119, 120, 121, 123, 125, 126, 127, 129, 130, 131, 133, 136, 138, 140, 181
substance abuse, 83
substrates, 150, 158
suffering, 150
suicide, viii, 16, 40, 56, 64, 65, 66, 68, 69, 83, 107, 150, 162
superego, 167
supernatural, viii, 55, 56, 57, 58, 60, 62, 63, 66, 70, 71
suppression, 150
surplus, 154
surrogates, 162
survival, 1, 3, 14, 18, 23, 24, 28, 165, 171
sustainability, 180
Switzerland, vii, 1, 6, 7, 11, 13, 15, 17, 28, 30
symptoms, viii, 34, 35, 41, 43, 44, 45, 46, 48, 49, 148, 158
synthesis, 92
systems, 146

T

Taliban, 163
Tanzania, 162
target, 79, 82
taxonomy, 76
teachers, 114
techniques, 28
technology, 170, 176
telephone, 77, 79
tension, 45, 164, 167, 175
terraces, 125, 129
terrorism, 64, 65, 66, 68, 69, 162, 163, 179, 180
terrorists, 161
testing, 20, 62, 65
therapy, 43, 44
thoughts, 39, 40, 41, 171
threat, 147, 149
time, 148, 154
time periods, 100
tin, 109, 132

Index

trade, 9, 24, 28
traditions, 14, 64, 66, 165, 169, 172, 173, 174, 176, 177, 178, 181, 182
training, 17, 19, 27, 87, 120
transactions, 63
transcendence, 75, 146
transformation, 8, 97, 111, 171
transgression, 5, 6
translation, 111
transplant, 74, 86
trauma, 145, 156
treatment, 45, 52, 74, 174
trial, 144

U

unemployment rate, 180
unification, 15, 16, 17
uniform, 95
United Kingdom (UK), 1, 52, 80, 89, 103, 110
United States (USA), 37, 48, 73, 77, 79, 85, 88, 107, 157, 162
universe, 93, 166
urban, 105, 106, 113, 116, 123, 129
USS Cole, 162

V

variables, 2, 3, 4, 8, 10, 23, 24, 25, 26, 63, 146
variations, 2, 76, 129, 157
varieties, 51, 87
vasopressin, 147, 157
victims, 168
violence, vii, x, 67, 145, 156, 161, 162, 163, 164, 165, 166, 167, 168, 169, 170, 172, 173, 175, 176, 177, 179, 180, 181, 182
vision, 59, 74, 81, 85
vote, 7, 79, 81, 87
voters, 81
vulnerability, 75, 179

W

Wales, x, 30, 103, 104, 105, 106, 107, 109, 110, 111, 113, 114, 117, 118, 119, 125, 126, 129, 130, 132, 136, 137, 138, 140, 141, 142
war, 104, 162, 163, 168, 169, 170, 172, 177, 179
Washington, 68, 69
water, 12, 19, 20, 26, 155
wealth, 17, 130, 138, 180
welfare, 6, 7, 14
well-being, viii, 34, 46, 52, 74, 81, 83, 84, 86, 89, 144, 145, 149, 158, 159
Welsh diaspora, x, 103
West Bank, 64, 162
Western Europe, 80
windows, 105, 113, 115, 120, 121, 123, 126, 129, 131, 138
withdrawal, 78, 150, 158
workers, 26, 27, 34, 105, 106, 109, 110, 111, 113
World Health Organization (WHO), 144, 145, 159
world order, 173, 182
World Trade Center, 162, 179
worldview, 41, 84
worldwide, 76, 163
worms, 4

X

xenophobia, 167, 175

Y

Yale University, 142
Yemen, 162
young adults, 51
young women, 23